Sunrise over Half-Built Houses

Dagger Editions (an imprint of Caitlin Press Inc.)
3375 Ponderosa Way
Qualicum Beach, BC V9K 2J8
www.caitlinpress.com

Text and cover design by Vici Johnstone
Cover image by Marina Crawford

Printed in Canada
Caitlin Press Inc. acknowledges financial support from the Government of Canada and the Canada Council for the Arts, and the Province of British Columbia through the British Columbia Arts Council and the Book Publisher's Tax Credit.
Library and Archives Canada Cataloguing in Publication

Sunrise over half-built houses : love, longing and addiction in suburbia / by Erin Steele.
Steele, Erin, author.
Canadiana 20240360109 | ISBN 9781773861500 (softcover)
LCSH: Steele, Erin. | LCSH: Recovering addicts—British Columbia—Vancouver—Biography. | LCSH: Self-actualization (Psychology) in women. | LCGFT: Autobiographies.
LCC HV5805.S64 A3 2024 | DDC 362.29092—dc23

SUNRISE OVER
HALF-BUILT HOUSES

ERIN STEELE

Dagger Editions, 2024

You're every age you've ever been and ever will be.
—Unknown

Soul gave me this box of emptiness. What I say is one truth I know.
—Rumi

For David

Contents

Note from the Author

Try as it might, a book cannot reflect the infinitely whole and complex nature of people and experience. There are a million ways to look back and categorize the trajectory of a life, and this book represents one particular trajectory, from one mind, with one particular thematic undercurrent. And while I've remained anchored to my truth, it's just that—my truth. Which means, many infinitely whole and complex humans are now chiselled into characters. With respect and acknowledgement of the subjective nature of both truth and perception, most names have been changed, as well as many descriptions and identifying details.

Prologue

Some turn to Jesus and some turn to heroin.
—Joni Mitchell

I've changed completely and hardly at all. But this isn't a story about change; not really. More like what moves us through that change—the pulling hunger, the vehicle.

There are places, things I've done, I'd like to keep hidden in corners. But a story needs shape, doesn't it? And the things we work so hard to hide do shape us, whether or not we admit them. So I'll start in the suburbs, in Fraser Heights, where everything is beautiful on the outside. Manicured and kempt. The kind of place that holds you by the wrists, gently, but with an ever-tightening grip. I'll start on a warm night—the darkness of the past inconsequential, the darkness of the future unimaginable. The summer of 2002, eighteen years old. The Smashing Pumpkins. David, my boyfriend.

⌒

I'm obsessed with the song "Mayonaise." *Fool enough to almost be it. Cool enough to not quite see it. Doomed.* I'd etched the word onto the inside cover of my journal, outlining it over and over in black ballpoint pen. Doomed.

My parents are out of town so I park my old blue VW Golf, SuperBeast, diagonally across the cobblestone driveway, as close to the front door as possible, hatchback open, speakers blaring the warbled tune. There's a broken guitar in it, the recording of "Mayonaise," but the Smashing Pumpkins left it in and it fits. Like it's not broken at all.

Every time the song ends I jump up and rewind the tape, start it over. I do that when a song gets in me like that—listen to it over and over. Twyla and David don't complain. We have everything we think we need, so we're happy: cigarettes and pot and alcohol, people on their way. Twyla's new boyfriend shows up in his Mustang with the racing stripes; it's what she likes most about him. A girl gets out of the passenger seat. Blossom, she tells me with an easy laugh, four-pack of Mike's Hard Lemonade in hand, sweater hanging off her forearm, flashing blue eyes. Flashing blue eyes that linger on mine.

"Mayonaise": *Can anybody hear me? I just want to be… me.*

We all head into the backyard, the last bits of the day, of summer, glinting around us. Golden grass. The trellis, an elongated shadow on the ground. In the air, no hint of cool. David's across from me, his easy giggle lassoing mine effortlessly. He doesn't notice or doesn't mind that I keep looking at her—Blossom—through the smoke, through the banter, and she's looking at me too, those flashing eyes. Things start to blur and somehow we end up in the downstairs bathroom, just the two of us. We sit beside each other, knees bent in the narrow space between the two walls, our bodies pressed together like a question mark. I'm fluttering, high and—something else. We share hash in a pipe, taking turns blowing the smoke toward the ceiling fan, something between us palpable, but I don't know what it is, don't know what it means. And I feel it—like I feel my eyelids blink, the warmth in my palms, my breath catch in my throat. Her body, my body, shoulders to elbows, hips to knees, knees to ankles, feet. We finish the bowl and neither of us moves until nothing else makes sense but to get up and rejoin the party.

The night ends. David tries to stay over but I refuse, pushing him out the door as usual. I've never slept beside him and I'm not sure I want to. I never do see Blossom again, but the feeling of her, of that night, stays with me. The warm humming in my gut, her eyes, that song, the taste of cigarette smoke when I thought smoking was so damn cool—it's sweet nostalgia with the slightest edge of pain. Like a butter knife pressing against me. I could shift to alleviate it, but I don't.

Last Resort

longing
/ˈlôNGiNG/
noun
a yearning desire.

1

One summer vacation when I'm about twelve, my family pulls into a camp-ground late at night, all four of us needing the outhouse. I remember exactly where it is and navigate, our feet crunching on gravel through the dark maze, me confidently rounding this corner, then that, until our flashlights illuminate a wooden structure carved with a crescent moon. "You were only ever here when I was pregnant with you," my mom insists, confused, pushing open the door, its squeaky hinge loud in the silence of the night. Yet I remember being here—I do. The womb is a place. One we've all been.

☾

Something happens, suddenly, when I start grade eleven at the brand new high school up the street, though I only admit it in chicken scratch in a journal I'll eventually trash in shame. Soela. *I love her. I'm in love with her.* Like half the student body she's a stranger and these feelings rush me, hard, nearly from the moment I first see her, my stomach somersaulting in anticipation of math class, which we share. When I see her tall bun shifting from side to side at the far-thest end of the hallway from me, this pang overtakes my body. I have her shape memorized from every distance. She'll sometimes wear sweatpants to school and she'll sometimes wear makeup. And she's always laughing and friendly with everyone, whichever high school stereotype you fall into. My feelings for her are like a cup overflowing with sparkles from the sun—but it doesn't fit into the construct of my life. It doesn't make sense or have a place, although in a lot of ways it feels more real than anything. So I go dark. Quiet. I observe her when-ever I can, but forming words is like trying to wring water out of a dry cloth. In math, I pass a blank worksheet along to her and she looks me in the eyes and says, "Thanks, hon." I play it over and over in my mind.

☾

We don't understand need in the womb. It's warm, we're comfortable, we get what we need without knowing we need it. It's only when we're born that we crave and want, we cry and we suck our thumbs.

⌒

I'd spent the last two years at my previous school tensing through the muggy heat of bullies. Of too-close plastic choker necks, plaid shoulders, Lip Smacker lips, cold eyes. Maybe it was the undercut my mom's hairdresser gave me, to my silent horror. Or the black-and-white printout of Tommy Lee Jones from *Men in Black* who I thought was so cool, who I so wanted to be, in my locker. The vitriol—*loser, little freak, lesbian, Little Boy*—came from everywhere and I lived on high alert, doing my best to keep my head down, looking not at faces but at spots on hallway floors where fluorescent lights reflected on glossy laminate. Their words became my thoughts. Or, perhaps, their words confirmed my thoughts: *I'm a freak.* Now, I'm turtled in. Now, I'm encased in silence.

In my journal: *My life is screwed. I hate the way I look, the way I feel, the way I think. I wish I were thin and beautiful and could please everybody. Most of all, I don't want to think. I hate everybody and I wish I was alone in this ugly world. Just me and my room. And no music or people.*

I don't mean it, though. Not really.

At my previous high school, I ducked under the central staircase one lunch hour and found Twyla, a friendly face who lived on a dead-end street near our elementary school. She looked at my teary face and reminded me about the soccer camp we both attended as kids. How she broke her arm but nobody believed her until she disappeared and came back with a cast.

"That showed them," she told me, her smile lopsided.

I wiped my tears and laughed and we've stuck together ever since. Twyla has a marred Cabbage Patch doll look to her—wavy, bright orange locks and a melon face, skinny legs and dark, darting eyes. When she says things like "My dad is a heavyweight champion" or, much later, "No, Kevin and I didn't steal your dad's tools," you're never sure where on the scale of truth it actually falls.

⌒

"I'm from the nice part of Surrey" is what I tell people about Fraser Heights, holding my pretty neighbourhood up against the crime-laden pockets that surround it and make the suburb of Vancouver, Canada, infamous. Here, blond, blue-eyed realtors gleam fake smiles from bus stop benches. Here, the houses are huge and occupied by mid-to-well-off professionals—the business owners, the lawyers. To the north of the neighbourhood, far below and through kilometres of forest, the massive Fraser River nears last call before the Pacific Ocean.

I overhear that Soela from math class is trying out for the basketball team, so I try out too. When the results get posted, I round the corner between the change rooms and the gym, my palms sweaty. I can see the list before I read it and want nothing more than to be on it. I run my finger down the names, hope whooshing out of me at warp speed, until I see it, my name, the last line on the printout.

She cheers for me when I catch a pass, sneakers squeaking, bright court, loud whistles. I sit beside her on the bench tensely aware of her presence, concrete poured atop my already set silence. After those games I pull on my Fraser Heights Falcons sweatsuit and walk home down the sidewalk in the cool 5:00 p.m. dark, replaying everything in my mind. Her smiling eyes looking into mine. Her scratchy voice cheering *me* on. The replays are as comforting as holding a heating pad on a stomach ache, at first. But I want more. Nothing lesbian, just *more*. I never think about anything like kissing her—I just need to be enveloped. I love her, but it's not physical, I tell myself. But that *more*, whatever it is, I crave. I crave it with an intensity that's nearly frightening. So I do the normal thing. I date boys. Start drinking.

I grew up in the neighbourhood's smallest house with the biggest yard near the freeway off-ramp—a forest that would later be bulldozed muting the traffic noise. On snow days, the slope adjacent to the freeway transformed into the perfect sledding hill. My brother and I would spend hours sliding down and climbing up, cheeks pink, giggles mingling with semi trucks whooshing by. There are at least a dozen houses there now, where we used to live. Where we used to scratch our arms and stain our hands blackberry purple late into the golden edge of summer.

Our house, which my parents rented, was beside the dried flower warehouse my dad worked at for thirty-five years, also long gone now. Once, the warehouse had a rat infestation and they instructed my dad to spend the day killing rats, but not with poison—"Just get rid of them." My dad. My dad, who would hold the camcorder in front of a flower, a waterfall, a natural arch, for minutes at a time. Could this explain the champagne-cork anger that could, after long days, pop and bubble?

I wonder if the space inside some people is bigger. Like how my dad is six feet two and my mom is five seven and I'm five ten. But we all do it—yearn. Turn to things outside ourselves in search of some feeling.

In grade six, we moved into a bigger house on 108th Avenue with enough counter space in the kitchen for my mom to pour herself into cooking, her slight frame curled above the counter. Cookbooks with frayed Post-its sticking out of pages, scrawled with grades (A+++) and notes on how to make each recipe better next time. My mom avoids feelings—mine, hers, all of ours—like they're a pushy credit card salesperson at the mall. But the cooking, the perfecting of recipes, the love and attention—that's for us.

They don't know how to talk to me, my parents. I adopt their grit and their love for music but also their reactions—my dad's big emotions, my mom's shutting down.

That first year at Fraser Heights Secondary School, I'm acquiring boyfriends like earrings, or pants. I have four at once, mainly because I can't bear to lead awkward breakup conversations. Once, I take the alley home because I told one of them "Sure" to coming by after school. It's pouring rain and the back gate to my house is locked. I try to get over the seven-foot fence, reaching and jumping, thumping against the fence's wet surface, sliding down to the ground. Reach, jump, thump. Reach, jump, thump. I soak my thin jacket and it sticks, wet, against my skin. Still, preferring all this to seeing a boyfriend I'm not interested in, I stay in the alley, freezing, stomach growling, until I'm sure he's given up and gone home.

I separate what I feel for boys—a fleeting sexual curiosity—with what I feel for Soela: everything. I want to stack up my boyfriends and put them away, and I want to write Soela love poems. And I keep this all to myself.

⌒

David has the personality of a morning person on a tropical vacation—jovial and in love with every moment. We find each other wedged into a tiny practice room in Mr. Gong's ten/eleven-split band class. The room is tiny with him and me and my trumpet and his trombone. I have to make a concerted effort to keep our knees from touching. David's different; I can tell right away. And not just because of his hair, which is a collection of gel-caked stalagmites.

"Can I try it?" I nod at the trombone.

"Yeah, of course!" He springs up and twirls, adeptly avoiding me and the music stands between us to bestow the trombone like a gift.

"Why, thank you, good sir," I say, and we both laugh.

"Do you think it's weird that Mr. Gong has the perfect name for a band teacher but he's actually a horrible teacher?"

I feel a tinge of sadness imagining Mr. Gong, with his comb-over and pants pulled too high at the front of a class of kids who just won't shut up, grasping his pin of a conductor wand.

"I kind of feel bad for him," I say. David's eyes get wistful for a moment and I can tell he does too. "But yeah. It's super weird."

I'm dating a guy whose house I go over to and drink powdered iced tea, me scooping spoonful after spoonful of the sickly sweet mixture into my glass, turning it into near sludge, the silver of the spoon clinking as I stir. We make bets, playing *Mario Kart 64*. If I win, we walk to the corner store and he buys me a Slurpee and a pack of Nerds. If he wins, we head downstairs and onto the bed in the unfinished basement and he lies on top of me and kisses me with smooshy wet lips and grinds up against me. When David and I grow insepara-ble, I bear the awkward breakup conversation.

David's house is huge, usually vacant and fully stocked, so we spend much of our time there listening to Slipknot, Deftones, Limp Bizkit, Korn and Mari-lyn Manson. My parents bottle their own wine, so before they get wise, I survey the rack and, like Jenga, pull out bottle after bottle. We get drunk and lie on David's waterbed and rip around the house, or hang out at nearby J.R. Park. At school he waits for me outside my classes and we interlock fingers and giggle about Ms. LeBlanc drinking three Diet Cokes in an hour.

Meanwhile, I'm living this whole other life. My yearning for Soela is eroding into something dark and confusing, out of desperation, passion, desire like I've never felt before. I watch her all the time. Watch for her in the hallways, know when she'll be at her locker, what classes she has when and where, and every time I see her, my body pangs this beautiful melancholy. It's visceral and feels more real than anything else.

At basketball games, I sit on the bench with shoulders curled inward. I'm worried that I stink from running around or that I have bad breath, so I curl into a ball as best I can and keep my hand over my mouth, my legs crossed tightly together. Every time Soela claps or cheers or calls "Nice try" to someone on the court, I turn to her, smile into her gemstone eyes, my brain a black hole sucking up half thoughts while blaring, *Say something, say anything, something funny, be supportive, clap, cheer, anything. Anything!* But I'm trapped.

See, I've already turned into Little Me. I'm in here, but tiny. I'm stuck at the bottom of a dark well, unable to speak when I want to or think I should. Little Me is colourful and rich, blood and guts, but shrunken. The alcohol helps, at first. Eventually, I'll try the drug ecstasy and it'll help me use my mouth, be who I am. But what I'll really have acquired is a collection of fake limbs, fake organs, fake vocal cords, fake thoughts, fake blood. And I won't recognize that for a long time.

Walking home in the autumn dark after basketball, I blast Korn on my Discman, bagpipes and rhythmic whisperings about happiness, Soela's eyes, em-blazoned in my mind, eclipsing everything else. I turn up the music so loud my eardrums recoil, then I turn it up more.

2

At night, when I'm frustratingly awake and my thoughts roll through complex mazes, I strip the covers off my body and, in my mind, lie on a muddy hill in the pouring rain. My body shivers. I'm freezing and incapacitated in the waning light of day, tears flowing out of me, sheet rain pounding. I lie like this for a while, freezing and alone. Then I imagine the sound of footsteps sticky in the mud, growing louder, and then someone is there, not speaking but covering me with the softest, warmest blanket; with gentle hands, pushing the hair slicked to my face behind my ear, arms wrapped around me. In bed, I pull my covers back on, alleviating the chill. My mind, my bed, reality, fantasy blurred, held, whispers, "It's okay, it's okay," and I cocoon into fetal position and fall asleep.

I have compartments, many of them sealed.

⌒

I'm dissecting my pink Bic razor in my bedroom, Papa Roach playing low enough for me to hear someone coming. Using scissors, I yank off the ends of the razor, and two paper-thin strips of metal clink onto my desk. I look at them, not sure how this is going to go. What do I want? What am I doing?

I thought that if I ever cut myself, it would be for a feeling of control where I otherwise feel helpless, to manage deep inner pain, as a relief valve on a water cooler helping everything else flow smoothly. I want to be one of those people in so much pain that cutting feels like the only choice. I want it to medicate me. But the truth is, I just want Soela to look at me with concerned eyes. The anticipation of a kind and worried "Erin?" tugs me on this otherwise nondescript night. I push the thin blades off the desk and carefully into my palm and exit my room for the bathroom across the hallway, quietly shutting both doors.

I'm calm and oddly disconnected. School was fine—nothing particularly bad or good happened. Soela smiled at me. David was away. Social studies was boring.

I pull my face close to the mirror, stare into my green eyes, at Little Me looking out, desperate me looking in, and nod a few times, in permission of what's going to happen next.

I pull the sleeve of my black hoodie up my arm a few inches. Pick up one of the pieces of metal with my thumb and forefinger. I look down at my skin, my intact skin, and bring the razor to its surface. Tentatively, lightly, I scrape it across. The razor breaks the skin easily and I watch with curiosity as a red line appears, and little beads of blood. A surge of power, slight apprehension. I do it again, this time pressing harder. I look up at myself in the mirror, my face more present, understanding.

"This is okay," I whisper at my reflection, although I'm already convinced. I'm light and tingly and claiming myself. Taking steps toward the future I want. It's not conventional, that's for sure, but I know what I want and I'm going after it. "This is okay."

And it works. In math class, one loose fist curled against my forehead, trying to work out the numerical chaos with my other hand, I recognize her voice without having to look up.

It's the moment I'd painted brilliantly in my mind, here. Sunbeams, like ecstatically outstretched arms across landscapes. A symphony of vibrant colours, of newness, of everything.

"Erin, what happened?"

Her use of my name is an automatic body high. I turn my head and our eyes meet, spark, for a nanosecond before I cast them back toward my desk.

"Nothing," I mumble, not raising my head again, knowing exactly what she's talking about.

"Did your cat do that to you?"

I glance at her again; her brow is slightly furrowed.

"I don't have a cat."

I haven't seen that look on her before, but soon I'll see a lot of it. I'll instigate a lot of it.

3

Sometimes David plays the piano for me. He composes music—beautiful, elaborate songs, and I wonder if his family ever hears them. A lot of the time, it's just David alone in that big empty house. His parents, both heads of local colleges, are busy—soon we'll find out with exactly what.

The house is so big it has its own piano room—barely wide enough to stretch out our arms, the room is the tallest in the house and is mostly windows. David sits there on the piano bench, his neck craned down like an injured bird. The edges of his sleeves are frayed because he bites and chews on them. His head, a dyed black collection of spikes, leads the music, and his hands and fingers follow—so delicate and graceful, like they, he, are home.

ᵔ

David's walking me home in the dark, our gloved hands clasped together. It's freezing—the tip of my nose is numb and my legs are prickles against my jeans. We're talking about the weekend, our words carried from our mouths on white clouds.

"We could drink at my place," he says, his green eyes bright, peering into mine.

Before I can respond, the sky, the telltale orange of the sky, almost bloated, gently gives way and white flakes begin their fall to the ground. I swear we see it start from high above us; and then it's all around. He stops, reaches out his other hand and grabs my wrist, like we can't move forward without giving nod to the moment.

"Snow!" he exclaims with that childlike demeanour he sometimes has, his green eyes shining so bright. I feel it too. It's secret, special, reserved for just the two of us. All I muster is "Aah." I look up at the sky with its orange hue, a city of flecks moseying toward my face where I let them land and transform to water. One lands on my eyelid and I rub it away, look at David. He's smiling too, his chin aimed toward the sky.

"I love you," I say, without apprehension.

Our eyes meet and there's no awkwardness; there's even no hiding, though we both have unacknowledged storms raging in us.

"I love you too."

He puts his arms around my waist, I put mine around his shoulders, and we hold each other on the sidewalk, where no cars or pedestrians have gone by, and it feels like we live in a private snow globe.

"We should make a deal," he says, pulling back a bit. The street light above his spikes, which curl from length and being wet, casts diagonal shadows on his face. His eyes, still bright. Now he's talking about the future. "No matter where we are, if we aren't together or can't be together or whatever, let's always call each other on the first snowfall."

I smile in that shy, life-is-simple teenager-girl-in-reciprocated-love kind of way. "Deal."

The world can seem so vast sometimes—so loud. Like a white piece of paper a kid scribbles all over with a Sharpie. Snow softens everything into a manageable size, like there's nothing much further than where we are now. Kind of like a womb.

The trouble with snowfall—or I guess what makes it so special—is that it always disappears.

⌒

Replaying brief encounters with Soela isn't giving me the same rush of feelings as before. My mind hitches on a memory—her calling me "hon," her looking at me wistfully, or at least that's how I colour it in. I bounce these glimpses over and over in my mind, but like a basketball deflating, I have to beat my hand lower, harder, more frantically, and my wrist hurts and I'm just left with a dull thunk.

So I tiptoe into this new world. I tiptoe in, incognito, and a door locks behind me.

After supper on a Thursday night, I'm sitting at my desk in my room, a blank sheet of paper in front of me, pen in hand. My body's light with anticipation, nervousness, excitement, apprehension. Rain beats against my window, against the tiles on the roof. It's raining hard, but I hear it only in the moments between songs on the Goo Goo Dolls CD *Dizzy Up the Girl*. Its case is on my desk—on the cover, a girl all dressed up, belly down on her bed. It feels like I'm her.

I write in all caps, how I think I've seen it done in the movies—untraceable. Finding her address was easy, in the white pages. I'd found it weeks before and recorded it in my journal. For what? At the time, I didn't know. They were the only Criptons in Fraser Heights.

I start writing:

SOELA CRIPTON,

It's how I imagine skydiving feels—counterintuitive, wrong on so many levels, but if you just do it, you *will* feel an entirely new feeling. Just waiting there for you through the whooshing chaos.

THERE ARE LONELY PEOPLE ALL AROUND YOU. I HAVE BEEN QUIETLY WATCHING AND I KNOW YOU COULD HELP THEM. ON THIS LIST IS ONE PERSON WHO HAS TRIED TO END THEIR OWN LIFE.

I open the yearbook and pick out half a dozen people looking back at me with half smiles and sad eyes. Place myself in an inconspicuous third to last.

YOU HAVE THE POWER TO HELP THESE PEOPLE. SMILE AT THEM. TALK TO THEM. AND THEY WILL BE OKAY.
TRENCH COAT GODFATHER

I derive the name from the Columbine High School shooters, how they called themselves the Trench Coat Mafia. I do this mainly to deflect suspicion. Nowhere in me is an instinct to hurt anyone. Nowhere in me is any anger. I crease the sheet of paper and fold it into a third of itself and slip it inside the envelope I've already stamped and addressed. "Acoustic #3" is playing, its lilting strings and minor guitar progression and John Rzeznik's slowed voice singing about screaming and people not listening. The song ends and I listen to the rain. I then get up from my desk and quietly exit my house, careful not to rouse my parents' attention from *Survivor*, and walk the block and a half to the mailbox. After nervous hesitation, I push the letter through the slot, kicking off something I have neither the strength nor the power to stop on my own, because despite all its flaws—it's mostly made of flaws—it gives me exactly what I want. What I think I need.

Now, where Soela once glanced at me, her gaze lingers.

4

I want to stop, but I can't.

It's like I'm walking along train tracks—tracks that stretch to the horizon, as unswerving as a ruler—living two completely different lives on either side. I hop off to the left and there are the letters, the cutting, the daydreams, Soela. I hop off to the right and there are David and Twyla, goofy teenagers, cruising the Lower Mainland in my parents' car, at "the gym," at "the library." Mixtapes blasting too loud on sensitive speakers, we cruise to all the places we can't bus to. White Rock, 1001 Steps. We talk about other kids and laugh and sing. We're uninhibited—which is all I ever really want, when I think about it.

But I always want more.

No matter how much I laugh, no matter how fulfilled my friends make me feel, no matter how much fun I have, the space inside me persists. It's like a rock cavern, just above the shoreline of the ocean. Hard and permanent, it's not going anywhere; it's not growing bigger per se—at least no faster than at a glacial pace—yet it's close enough to the depths of the ocean that it gets a taste of salt water, which it craves. At high tide it's filled, and this always stings because, inevitably, the waves that settle into its spaces and grooves get sucked back out, leaving an empty cavern once again, and the wanting that comes with it.

This is how I'm built, I figure: to want, to crave. It's my blueprint. Isn't it all of ours, to some extent? The space inside? Or is it really just a reflection of the world we're born into that shakes us by the shoulders and shouts, "More! More! More!"?

I feel like the Phantom of the Opera. Even in grade six, sitting in a Vancouver theatre, peering down at the stage through cheap, plastic binoculars, the play's braid of love and of silence courses through me. Of longing, of a deep-rooted inability to express love conventionally, of selfishness, of regret, of ultimate redemption through sacrifice—I could feel it all, even then. The Phantom—a tragic, wistful man—falls in love with Christine after hearing her beautiful voice. But he lives in a lair lit only by candlelight and hides, always, behind a mask. He writes threatening letters to the theatre company, demanding Christine be cast in the lead role, and it works. They sing together, and he's coaxed out of hiding, and out of shame. Christine is taken by the Phantom's mysterious allure, but she has unwavering plans to marry Raoul. So the Phantom makes a plan. He eventually tries to lure her away from her life, her love, but Raoul follows and in a frantic moment, the Phantom forces an ultimatum: Raoul can live, but Christine must stay with the Phantom in darkness forever. Christine, who admits she once loved the Phantom, is now disgusted, singing that it's not his face but his soul that's truly distorted. In the end, the Phantom screams at them both to leave and he is, once again, alone. Among the last lines of the musical, the Phantom sings, softly, his love for Christine far from earshot of anybody else.

⌒

I'd just slipped the fourth letter through the mailbox slot when my family packs us up into our camper. It's the first day of Christmas break. The truck rumbles on and the four of us shiver until the heat kicks in. The falling sleet turns the asphalt a shiny black and the sun has yet to blip over the horizon. We're the only car on the road when we head out of Fraser Heights, out of Surrey, out of Canada. By the end of a full day of driving, the seats are sticky and our legs, now in shorts, are stiff from being so long on the road. The Canadian cold and Trench Coat Godfather and a dozen albums on tape—Paul Simon's *Graceland* and Barenaked Ladies' *Gordon*—and stories of the Southwest, of the Windigo monster, are all behind us.

We make it to Death Valley for Christmas, and the part of me that's carefree gets to dance. My brother Bobby and I surf down sand dunes and pretend we're Star Trek characters at Artists Palette, where the rocks are a mind-boggling multicoloured pastel. It pulls my guard down, and later, sitting in the pool near Furnace Creek Campground, our home for the holidays, I'm watching European tourists lounge in the pool like it's a bathtub and laughing with my mom at the idea they got some killer deal to visit the United States. Like they failed to take "hottest place in North America" literally.

Out of the corner of my eye, I see my mom glance at me several times, both of us lounging in the pool, facing the collection of tourists. I'm sitting on the wrong side of her—had forgotten to always sit on people's left, so they don't see what I'm doing to my arm with my right hand. She turns full onto me, her voice sharp. "What is that?"

I know what she's asking. I meet her where it's terse. "Nothing," I say with an edge that mirrors hers. From then on we both pretend she didn't see what she saw, that what is, isn't.

I'm cranked back to thinking about the letter. Would Soela think about me on Christmas? How cold is it back in Surrey? Did she get it? What was she thinking? What would she do? It was the most threatening yet:

> YOU HAVE NO IDEA WHAT ERIN STEELE HAS GONE THROUGH.
> SHE THINKS I'M SOMEBODY I'M NOT. SHE IS VERY HURT AND
> VERY LONELY AND I DID SOMETHING BAD TO HER. AND IT WAS
> SO GOOD.

My thoughts make me shiver, and my eyes well up with tears.

⌒

In grade one, my parents let me bring the sharpest knife in the house to school to carve a pumpkin. My dad creates a cardboard sheath and shows me how to carefully pull it out and put it back in. How to angle it. How to absolutely not cut myself. No matter what, do not cut myself.

Then I'm at my desk at the back of the classroom and then there's blood— lots of it. I squeeze my other hand around my thumb and sit there quietly until I go pale and Carl, beside me, says, "You cut yourself."

I still have the scar.

⌒

January's dark, back in Surrey, and freeze-you-from-the-inside cold. The rain, unrelenting, pummels the ground, never moseying like it sometimes does in the spring. It'll get you right away if you step out in it. I'm sitting at the computer, on ICQ instant messenger, feet away from my parents who can't see the screen. My dad's tense on the edge of the couch, yelling at the TV, at the Vancouver Canucks; my mom's cross-stitching and furrowing her brow at his brashness. It's like I'm not here, to them, yet I'm more here than ever, more blood and guts, my stomach twisting in knots of positive anticipation—Kristie Gunn, Soela's best friend, just popped online.

"How are you doing sweetie?"

My smile floods my insides and I wring my hands before placing them on the keyboard.

"I'm okay. Things with David are going really good, but I just feel like there's something missing. I don't know," I type back, not sure what else to say.

I put my elbows on the computer desk and chew the edge of the nail off my thumb. The spaghetti my parents are cooking fogs up the glass door behind me, and I'm a loose representation of myself.

"Oh hon, it's okay." Kristie writes back. "You know sometimes I feel that way with Shane. I know he really loves me but I sometimes wonder if I feel the same way about him. It's like his family loves me and all."

I consider her message. They seem like a fairy-tale couple—his long arms are always draped around her in the hallways like there's nothing in the world he loves more.

"Hmm… maybe that's just the way relationships are." I'm not sure what else to say.

"Yeah. Maybe. Well hon, take care of yourself. If you feel like David isn't right, you don't have to be with him. I have to go eat dinner."

"Okay sounds good. Thanks for talking with me."

I truly mean it.

"Bye sweetie," she says.

I smile, copy and paste the conversation into a Word document and print it.

"What's that?" my dad asks as the ribbon moves loudly back and forth.

"Nothing," I tell him.

○

The night before Valentine's Day, I walk the thirty-plus minutes across the overpass to Guildford Mall. It's raining out, hard, and I shiver looking at balloons at the flower kiosk beside the liquor store. I settle on one with two toddlers, a sepia boy and girl, holding hands. A boy and a girl in love. Simple and commonplace. Is it me? Maybe. It's what's normal—romance and cuteness, popping hearts, sweet treats. The effort does make my stomach do a half-hearted sock-footed slide. Though that's nothing beside the ecstatic jig it performs for Soela, deep under my skin and tissue and muscle in the privacy of my depths. I wonder if she'll wear red to school tomorrow.

I pay for my balloon, fresh flowers tinged with the smell of bottle returns yanking my senses in opposite directions. I pick up icing sugar, a heart cookie cutter and food colouring from London Drugs and push back out into the downpour. At home, rain drums against the roof and the windows and I mix ingredients and cut out two dozen hearts to bake in the oven. My parents are in the adjoining living room engrossed in one of those new celebrity dance reality shows. Once the cookies are out of the oven I draw "Erin Loves David" carefully on every one, decorating the lettering with crunchy red sprinkles. I package them neatly into a Tupperware container and tie a ribbon around it and declare my love in a Hallmark card.

At school the next morning, I'm by our lockers—our usual meet-up spot. The tall balloon draws attention to me like a highway tourist trap, I know. I'm blooming inside with excitement. My locker neighbour shows up friendly.

"Nice balloon! Lucky David! Where is he?"

"I don't know." I look around, my chest holding the pressure of a squeezed football.

My friendly locker neighbour drums his fingers on his textbook. Jackets are off all around us, and the pace picks up in the hallway as the clock moves toward the first bell. Some days, David doesn't come to school. But I couldn't imagine he wouldn't show up on Valentine's Day.

"I'm going to class," he tells me and takes off. The first bell sounds and I wait and hope until the murmur of surrounding students dies off and it's just me and my tall balloon alone in the hallway.

5

I'm in grade one and my parents are sitting side by side in front of my teacher's giant desk, on plastic grade one chairs.

"Did something happen to her? She's very, very quiet." She looks at my parents, her bright blue eyeshadow-wrapped eyes flooded with concern. "It's just not normal."

My parents, then in their thirties, look at each other, then back to the teacher with her bellowing voice and sympathetic eyes. It's dark outside and dim in the classroom filled with grade one art, cursive and arithmetic scrawled on green chalkboards.

"No, nothing. She's just shy. She's always been like that," my mom tells her.

The teacher looks back and forth between them, pausing longer than comfortable for either of them.

⌒

It's still winter when Soela or more likely her parents call the police.

A few days before that, she approaches me at my locker. I see her coming from the other end of the hallway; even my peripheral vision has her gait memorized. I touch the damaged corner of my yellow math textbook and slip a loose paper out of a folder, cock my head and look at it and slip it back in. The anticipation feels like no time at all and an eternity. Then she's right beside me; I pretend to be absorbed with something.

"Hi, Erin."

Streamers through my body. I turn to her. Her voice is upbeat, but she looks uneasy—exasperated almost. I return her greeting with a half smile. She comes up to about my chin. I look down at her, then back to my locker and back to her again. My body rings on high alert, but I keep that contained—I'm like a nondescript stone with the most beautiful and rare shimmering fossil inside, but you'd never know it; you'd have to take a hammer to me.

"How's it goin', hon?"

I shrug. "Pretty good."

I know she sees the fresh cuts on my arms. I also have two small inter-secting slices underneath my left eye. Her exasperation bubbles up. "So, do you know this guy?"

I glance at her again, then hang my head toward the floor. I can't mess this up. "Yeah." I mutter it and wrinkle up my face, soaking up and memorizing the care and concern in hers before returning my eyes to the glossy, scuffed floor. She looks like she's about to say something but doesn't.

And then, "Erin." She speaks slowly. "Did something happen?"

Her voice is so soft and gentle, and when I raise my eyes again, her face is exactly the same. In a way, this moment has everything I want. To be seen, to be cared about—to be gently placed in a cocoon of warmth with the whispered promise "I'll watch the door; you just rest." It feels like her hands softly caress my face: "It's okay, it's okay."

"I…" I start, and exhale quickly in frustration that I can't find the words. It's so real, yet so fake. I can't speak, but even if I could, it would be a lie. So then why are the emotions brewing inside me so intense? Why do they feel more real than anything else in my life? I rub my hand hard over my forehead. Soela looks at me.

"Erin. If you can't say it, you should write it. Just write me a note!"

Her exasperation overflows—I feel it—but she smiles and makes the sug-gestion with vigour. I look at her again. With hope and with apprehension.

"Yeah, just write me a note," she repeats. This is the longest conversation we've ever had.

"Okay. Okay, I will."

And I do. I fabricate an account of "what happened" and how it made me feel. I write that I met a guy named Trent who's older than me and who seemed really nice at first, but things got really messed up. I write that I can't go into too much detail about that part because I'm embarrassed and feel really weird about it. I write that I only know his first name and that he just started randomly talking to me one day at Taste of Heaven, the restaurant across from the school. I write that he was really easy to talk to at first, so I opened up to him about how I felt. I write that he changed really quickly. Once I folded up the note and passed it to her in the hallway, I had a pretty good idea of what she'd believe when she read it.

She writes me back. Leaves the note tucked just barely out of my locker, and I press it into my palm like a long-anticipated salve and hold it in my hand, in my pocket, all day. Finally I open it, slowly, when I'm home, in the privacy of my room, on my bed, where I can take in her lettering and what she's saying with it.

I love how she writes her *g*'s and *y*'s, with their hanging tails curling in the opposite direction—it's so unique. I practise it myself, on a blank piece of paper. I can hardly believe what she's saying—finally, this is it. I'm getting exactly what I want. In her beautiful letter to me—her letter that ends "Luv Soela"—is an invitation to her house. The police want to talk to me about "what happened," but that feels secondary. I'm going to her house. This is what I want, I think. This is the whole reason, isn't it? I wanted her attention and now I have it.

All the letters, all the nervousness, all the risk: I'm standing outside my parents' house under light drizzle, waiting for Soela's family's beige Saturn to pull up, to illuminate the raindrops with its headlights, and it all feels worth it. This is what I want. This is finally it. I'm not thinking about what Soela and her family are actually going through because of me. The nagging in my stomach tells me what I'm doing is wrong, but the payoff eclipses that: how she looks at me, how her voice softens when she speaks to me, how she calls me "hon," how Kristie Gunn calls me "sweetie." I'm silent at school, but now I'm suddenly cared about—suddenly seen and cared about by the person I think is the most amazing, beautiful, caring person in the school. But it's not "like that." I love her, but not "like that."

Kristie knows about the visit.

"Hey sweetie," she writes on ICQ, an hour before I'm standing outside. "I hear you're going to talk to the police tonight."

"Yeahhhhh," I write back. "Pretty nervous."

"Aww sweetie, it's going to be okay. Just tell them the truth."

"I know, it's hard though. I mean, he's not a bad person," I write.

"You can do it. Soela's family is amazing and they're all going to be there. You don't have to hide anything."

"I just don't want my parents to know," I write, suddenly twigging to the severity of the situation.

"Oh hon, I can't help you with that. That's up to the police."

"I have to go get ready," I write.

Colourful swirls push through my body—behind keyboards and holding pens is where I take risks.

"Thanks for being there for me Kristie," I write—a small but loaded collection of words that I'd never be able to speak.

"Aww hon, of course! Luv ya!"

The colourful swirls push out my chest and my whole body beams.

I turn to my mom, who's sitting on the couch. "I'm going to my friend Soela's house. She's going to pick me up with her mom."

"Okay, sure," she says and has no idea who Soela is to me, what's really going on. I take the stairs two at a time.

And then I'm at her house. Kristie's right—her family is great. Her brother and sister and parents are all there, and they all treat me similarly to how Soela does—kindly. Her dad nudges a twenty-pack of Timbits toward me on the counter and I say "No," then like a giddy schoolgirl I take one anyway and flash him a faux-guilty smile. Soela shows me her room. It's small and crammed, and we sit on the floor. I don't look around much because I'm magnetized to her.

"I'm going to show you something." She smiles, lighthearted. "Do you want me to show you something?" From under her bed she pulls out a colourfully decorated box. "It's my Chris box," she tells me, and I smile deep into her eyes, not particularly understanding, not needing to understand. She's in love with a boy with slicked-back hair who'd written her love notes and given her a rose, now dried and curled up in the box. I think it's the sweetest, most sentimental thing in the world, and the thought of her decorating the box with glue and sparkles makes me smile inside, bigger than I'd ever let on.

The police officer arrives—Constable Rob Kekoa, it says on the RCMP card he hands me—and Soela and I are called into the dining room. The cop is big and bulky and kind of looks like someone who, when not in uniform, might wear a tan grass skirt and play God songs on ukulele. He has the note I'd written Soela laid out in front of him. The seven of us sit around the large table comfortably, he and I on adjacent edges. I think back to what Kristie told me—"Soela's whole family will be there and they're great"—and when I look around the table, I see that's true. All their eyes are on me, but they're concerned and encouraging. Not judgmental.

"Erin, can you tell me what happened?"

Kekoa's voice is warm, but his face stoic; I can't read him. I stumble over my words, recounting nothing more and nothing less than what I'd written in the letter, empty words I'd memorized by reading it over and over before folding it up for delivery. He writes down everything I say in a small spiral TV-cliché notebook. It's easy, really—he doesn't ask me any direct questions, nor does he press me on anything.

"I really don't want my parents to know," I say.

He tells me he'll see what he can do, but he'll likely have to talk to them at some point. Later he'll tell me he knew I was hiding something, but that evening he lets on in no way.

6

Soela's room, her family, her eyes peering into mine, the letters, overwhelmingly ping-pong in my head as I try to keep up my normal life. Unless I'm drinking—drunk—I'm a half human, existing in one moment, living in several others at the same time. David notices my arm one day, gently brings it up.

"What happened there?" His voice can get so soft—welcoming like an off-white, plush studio where you can't help but enter and curl up in, where it's easy to reveal yourself honestly. I couldn't stay mad at him long after Valentine's Day.

"Uh, I don't know. I just cut myself."

"Why?"

"I don't know. It just feels good in some weird way."

He rubs the back of his neck and furrows his eyebrows for a moment, staring at the ground, like he might be able to figure this one out, but then just looks up at me. His eyes are wistful, undeniably, then his face morphs into a teasing smile. He nods and pokes me gently in the ribs with his thumb.

"Just don't kill yourself. Couldn't live without ya."

Still, keeping things in their respective kennels is getting increasingly hard. My parents are at a concert for the evening. It's pouring rain and David, Twyla and I are lounging in my room, bored, listening to Papa Roach's "Last Resort," its staccato yell-singing, its intensity. It's like Little Me inside is surrounded no longer by blank space, neutral air, but by a lightning cloud saturated with pulsing electricity. I've felt like this for weeks. I'm also drunk. We stole bottles of port from my parents and, unable to find a corkscrew, pushed the corks inside. We're each drinking out of a bottle. I'm sitting behind my desk like an executive, swivelling in my office chair, and David's cross-legged on the floor. Twyla's on the bed. I feel the storm beating against my inner outline—I want to talk about it all. I want to gush about Soela like a schoolyard crush, but it isn't like that. It's not that. I want to tell them I went to her house, but I can't because it'll risk pulling the veil off everything. So the electricity rages and the pressure builds and I feel like I'm going to explode inside, and then I see the knife. By this time I've graduated from those tiny razors I yanked out of the Bic to kitchen knives I took from the kitchen drawer. This one, the size of my outstretched hand from pinky to thumb, is still stained red from last time. It's tucked under the picture frame with the photo of me, Twyla and David at Deception Pass State Park. Before everything.

Twyla, to either of us, neither of us: "So do you think Maggie and JJ are having sex?"

Twyla and David are in a place of palm trees and calm seas. David presses his pointer to his chin and looks up into the corners of his eyes. Takes a swig before responding. "Hmm." His lips are stained purple, his green eyes lively. "Well, yeah. That's what kids do, right?"

He looks at me with that teasing smile and I nearly explode into tears.

"It's not fair."

I stand suddenly, responding not to their conversation but to everything brewing under the surface. It sounds more like "It'ssat fai," though, followed by a shut-mouth scream. My eyes sting red and a tsunami overtakes my shore— destroys palm trees and buildings and concrete walls and everything in its path.

Four sober round eyes stare at me. I grab the knife, holding it like a threat against my arm.

"No," Twyla says worriedly, firmly.

I slice hard and heavily across my forearm, creating the first of a series of white scars that will never go away. Blood flows from the wound; Twyla cries out and looks at David; I slice again. And again. Then buckle into a fit of tears, which are the only thing left of the storm. I drop the knife and my shoulders and sob. Twyla springs into action, runs to the bathroom, pulls all the toilet paper she can off the roll. David has tears in his eyes and hugs me. My arm suddenly hurts. I wrap my own arms with the toilet paper and tell them sorry, I'm so sorry, but I don't—can't—explain anything.

Secrets are like a pressure cooker and a pressure cooker needs its valve.

I breathe.

The wind settles.

Everything's quieter in the aftermath.

They go home and we never talk about what happened.

ᄋ

David's came as a shock, not long after. His secret.

"I found a picture of my dad kissing another man," he blurts out. "In the scanner."

We're celebrating our six-month anniversary alone at his parents' house, stuffed on the baked pasta dish he made for us. I look around the six red roses and the tall white candles at our table's centre to get a read of his face. It's solemn.

He blurts, "I think my dad's gay and my mom's a lesbian."

I laugh, instinctively, but the look on his face stops me.

"I'll show you," he says.

Sure enough, upstairs, still in the scanner is his dad, with dark body hair spilling out the edges of a white tank top and short shorts. His body's pressed upward to kiss a taller, slimmer, greyer man on the mouth.

"It's got to be a joke," I tell David, my thoughts somersaulting. It doesn't look like a joke, but it doesn't make sense. "Come here." He leads me out of the computer room, on this bizarre treasure hunt, to his mom's walk-in closet—the back of it. There's a line of books on a shelf, ordinary and expected titles: *She's Come Undone* by Wally Lamb, a handful of Tom Clancy and Jonathan Kellerman thrillers, nursing textbooks.

"What," I say, my mind flashing to the brief lesbian sex scene in *She's Come Undone*, after which Dolores Price kills all her lover's fish. But David pulls all those books off the shelf, and the horizontal ones above them, dropping them to the floor. Each thud makes me cringe. His face is determined, glowing with sweat. Then, a box the size of my palm, which he pulls out and opens—looks at me with those big green eyes—and closes again.

"They're letters," he says, never looking more serious, more sure of his conclusion. "From a woman."

I look down at the box, wanting twisting in me to open it, to open it all up. His face says it all, though, and it's undeniable.

I'd known David's parents longer than I'd known him. His dad was a long-time Scouts leader to my brother; his mom was my Guides leader.

"So they have lovers?"

"I think they do. You know, my mom goes out overnight with her friend, says she doesn't want to drive late, but I bet this is what it is. And my dad's always with this guy. Like, never home."

I shake my head. "This is so fucked up. Do they know you know?"

"No." He's sure of that.

"Do they know about each other? They must, right? Like—it can't be a coincidence?"

David's eyes soften for a minute and he looks at me, defeated. "I don't know." He looks and sounds tired.

Is everybody living a double life? Behind those boxes with their clearly stencilled outlines that society expects us to exist within? Behind them, have we created a colourful free-for-all, because we don't *actually* fit in them?

I rub David's shoulder and reach in for a hug. If he's sad and confused about the whole thing, about his discoveries, he either quashed those feelings or is hiding them well. Our feet soft on the carpet in front of the California king that dominates like a painfully obvious lie, we know everything we thought we knew about his family is a fabrication, at least to an extent. We know they must be only "staying together for the kids" and sooner or later they'll sit David down and share some level of the truth with him, and he'll have to sit there and look surprised and shocked and sad and ask questions like he hasn't already figured out all the answers himself.

My eyes are no longer weary and my brain's a hub of activity. We're still upstairs, lingering in the hallway. I push my body hard against his. Kiss him. He reacts as he always does, pressing back, inviting me in, pushing his tongue into my mouth. The idea's always more exciting than the act. As always, we take it to his bedroom, and as always he lies on top of me, pushing himself hard against me, panting in my ear. Quickly, we fall into what I secretly call "the routine." The series of moves with no surprise twists. He kisses my neck, then touches my breasts, pulls off my shirt, puts his hand down my pants. Sometimes he whispers "I want to be inside of you" like it excites me as much as it seems to excite him, and I ignore it, turn my cheek, avoid it, always.

Today, my mind wanders from him pressing on top of me to the box in the back of the closet. Then it wanders to letters. Then love.

7

Spring pokes its head out of winter with sporadically warm days and delicate new leaves, and I get sloppy with the letters. It's been months, and I'm stuck in a loop of writing, pushing them through the mail slot, waiting for Soela's gaze to connect with mine, for her to talk to me, to feel seen and felt and euphoric. Then I expect it to fizzle, and it does, and I'm left with only an uncomfortable tug that pulls and pulls until I can't resist and I write another letter and push it through the mail slot and wait for Soela's gaze to connect with mine.

The next letter I write, I don't even bother with capital letters. I know, just under its surface, there's a dark phoniness. That it sometimes feels real, like a dream, but it's not. And the more Soela seems exasperated with me, the greater the tug to write more letters. Like I can control how she feels about me through Trench Coat Godfather. I hate it and I need it. It's the next letter, I think, that's my undoing.

> SOELA CRIPTON,
> YOU HAVE NOT REACTED IN A CARING WAY TOWARD ERIN
> STEELE, SO I HAVE DONE THE ULTIMATE DIRTY DEED.
> I LEFT HER CRYING AND LYING IN A FIELD UNDER THE RAIN,
> SHIVERING AND COLD AND ALONE.
> YOU DID THIS TO HER AND IT CAN NEVER BE TAKEN BACK.
> GOOD LUCK TRYING TO GET HER TO TALK ABOUT IT, SHE HAS
> COMPLETELY SHUT DOWN.
> TRENCH COAT GODFATHER

It's a Friday evening, dark and raining, and from my bedroom I hear a car pull up. I get up and spread the blinds on my window, bending them to look down to the driveway. It's an RCMP vehicle pulled in behind my parents' BMW, obstructing the sidewalk by a couple of feet. A second later, the car's hum turns off and its driver-side door opens. Constable Rob Kekoa gets out. *Shit.* I look around my room in a panic, not sure what to do, then quietly start downstairs to get him before his finger reaches the doorbell, undoing everything I've worked so long to avoid. It's like a shot to the stomach, the sound of the doorbell, and it stops me midway down the staircase. *Fuck.* Frozen, I hear my parents' movement in the living room; it's unusual for the doorbell to ring, particularly in the evenings. I go to the door anyway, getting there first.

"Hi, Erin, are your parents around?"

Kekoa's face is slack. His voice sounds colder than it did before, I think. My brain scrambles to come up with a way to get him out of there, then my mom's barefoot pat-pat is on the cold tile behind me. I turn my neck to look at her and she's looking past me, at Kekoa. *Fuck.* There's nothing left to do. My parents are going to hear that I was assaulted in some way, that somebody is writing letters to a girl I go to school with on behalf of me. They're going to know it's me. My mom's eyes are cautious, their blue-grey asking, *What's this about?* Her forehead's a flower of creases.

"Can I help you?" my mom asks politely.

"Mrs. Steele?" He's warmer addressing her. "Can I come in and speak with you and Mr. Steele?"

It occurs to me that she's worried something happened to Bobby. Maybe something did happen to Bobby; I feel a slight panic. Maybe this is just a coincidence—maybe Kekoa is our neighbourhood constable. He comes in and takes off his black RCMP boots. By this time, my dad has exited the living room and he and Kekoa shake hands. My dad's face looks older, greyer, expectant like a senior at the hospital. Now I'm really worried about Bobby. I've been so wrapped up in my little world, I've been ignoring the fact Bobby has been coming home in the middle of the night, reeking of pot. That he's constantly skipping out on school. It occurs to me I actually have no idea what he's been up to. My mom invites Kekoa to sit at the dining room table. Not quite sure what to do with myself, I linger, but as Kekoa pulls a chair back from the table to sit on, he turns to me, solemn once again.

"I think I should talk to your parents alone, Erin."

His use of my name makes both my parents look at me, their faces now solemn too. They don't speak. This isn't about Bobby, I know. They know it too, now, I think.

My room feels like a holding cell where I'm awaiting a court appearance I know I'll lose at. I lie down, put my ear to the bottom crack of the door, but hear only a murmur of voices, not words. My heart's pounding, my ears ringing. I'm trying to pace, to work it out, but my room's walls suffocate me. I can't link my mind to a solution. I need a solution. I think, *I'll tell my parents I met him through Adam from Victoria*—the boy I met on the internet who came over on the ferry for the day a couple of years earlier. He was cute and played guitar and we made out and shared a basket of fries with too much vinegar at Taste of Heaven before he left and we never spoke again. I could associate this "mysterious guy" with him and the cops would never find him. I'd tell my parents that when I tell them I'm going to the gym or to the library with Twyla, I'm actually meeting up with him. It feels believable. My body calms down enough for me to sit on my bed. In the twenty-five minutes Kekoa talks to my parents, I become a train station at rush hour, each train wildly different. Fear. Calm. Anger. Sadness. Frustration. They flood me, each wildly different feeling, then they zoom away. By the time I hear someone coming up the stairs, I'm a wreck of sweat and guilt and nervousness so gnarled it feels permanent.

My mom knocks twice and opens the door in a single movement. She doesn't meet my eyes but simply states, "I think you'd better come downstairs." *Fuck.* I have no idea what I'm walking into. I follow her downstairs. In front of Kekoa, who's sitting across from both my parents, is a file folder with an impressive amount of paperwork sticking out its edges. My mom sits down and I linger standing. My dad has his hand on his forehead and he's looking down at the table, glaringly not at me. My stomach's a turntable playing the most despised record of the century.

"Have a seat, Erin," Kekoa says. The first set of eyes to look into mine are his. "I know who Trench Coat Godfather is," he says, his gaze not breaking from mine. This is unexpected.

"Really?" I try to look surprised, to maintain eye contact, but I drop my gaze.

"It's you."

The oxygen ejects itself from every one of my cells simultaneously and I slump into nothingness. This is it; it's over. I fix my gaze on the Aztec-style table runner, its frayed edges. Instantly, this becomes the most awkward, horrible moment of my life. And it's inevitable.

It was a handwriting sample. Kekoa opens his folder and presents two sheets of paper side by side—his findings. One was the note I'd written Soela about "what happened," and the other, the latest, most menacing message from Trench Coat Godfather. Somebody had highlighted specific letters from each one—the *r*'s matched; the *s*'s were a possible match, Kekoa explains. I neither deny nor explain anything, but it doesn't feel up for debate. He's already spoken to the Criptons, he says. They know.

"What did they say?" I can't help myself.

"They're not pressing charges. But you will have to get help. Part of that means seeing a psychologist."

I glance at my parents, and my mom, her head down, face strained, nods.

"You know, you had a lot of people fooled for a long time, Erin," Kekoa says. "We had to get the division involved."

I say nothing but think, *You could have figured this out before things got so intense.*

"You need to stay away from the Criptons, Erin, but you need to write them an apology letter."

It strikes me as odd that he's handing me the tool that he's simultaneously revoking with a slap. But I know I have a way with words, and though it's wrapped in police tape, this feels like a gift. If I play it just right, maybe I'll get some understanding. Maybe everything can be okay.

Kekoa collected a victim impact statement from the family, which he relays. It expresses the fear they lived in—how they drove Soela to her friend's house half a block away because they were terrified somebody was out to harm her. How they felt helpless and stayed up countless nights worrying. It feels strange and uncomfortable that they felt real fear. I didn't mean for that to happen.

"You're a good writer, Erin," Kekoa says. His voice regains its warmth, which gives me hope. "Use that. Everything will be okay; just stay out of trouble. The family expressed that they felt very sad for you."

His words feel like a hug, abridged. My parents are still both looking down at the table. We're all silent.

"I just want to talk to your parents one more time," he says, this time gently.

I get up and head up the stairs to my room, shutting the door behind me quietly, like this is all just a bad middle-of-the-night dream.

It's faint, but somewhere, deep inside of me, I feel it: relief. It really is over.

⌒

The comedown—the thing we must endure to make it out the other side. But what is the other side? Maybe the other side is where we come face to face with whatever pushed us to the feel-good thing in the first place.

Can it really just be the loudness of the world itself? Or could it be something so gutting we refuse to remember? Is it brave to try to find out? Or is it stupid? And what if it's something we can't pinpoint, or something we can't remember, or something we won't face? Are we then doomed to hopscotch from one thing to the next, until the end?

⌒

I don't come downstairs until late the next day, and nobody tries to make me do otherwise.

I'm in grade two and have created what feels like a master replica of the skeletal human body. I label each part—*fihbya, tihbya, ribbs, nee*—and draw a wide and goofy smile on his face. Puffed with pride, I hang him in the hallway outside the classroom and stand nearby, ready for the evening's open house.

First, a loud laugh muffled by pursed lips. Another parent points at my skeleton. I'm trying to understand the joke while more parents crowd my project, laughing. A woman with a big pink purse throws her head back. A dad steadies himself on his wife's arm. I furrow my brow and shift my weight.

"'Ribbs'!" A tall woman points and doubles forward, and the whole group laughs.

"The spelling's horrible! Who's teaching these kids?"

My face warms and I quickly turn from the crowd and the other kids and projects and beeline for the bathroom, where I shut myself into a stall and sit on the toilet and let the tears flow out of my eyes, my body absorbing the sounds I suppress.

The weekend after Kekoa's visit, when my parents are on their typical Costco run, I have one more conversation with Kristie on ICQ. It's Saturday afternoon, less than twenty-four hours after Kekoa delivered the news. My face is puffy from crying and red and raw from wiping tears. This new fear has sprouted at the base of my spine; branches of it grow up my back, along my arms, down my legs, into my lungs, and slice through the centre of my heart. Yet still, I live.

From the same place I saw Kekoa's cruiser pull up the night before, I watch my parents pull out of the driveway and signal left toward Guildford. My body relaxes.

They haven't talked to me about what happened and I don't want them to, and they'd probably rather not—rather stuff it like a sleeping bag into a dry sack and cinch it up tight and toss it into the crawl space and forget about it. And me, it's like my skin is suddenly gone and loud investigators are shining flashlights at me and I need to hide and get out of there but I can't move, even a tiny bit, so I just hold my breath and count seconds and will them to stop looking.

Like watching *E.T.*, no older than eight. It has a happy ending, technically, but E.T. has to go and Elliott has to stay and it guts me. I'd learned to hide my sadness already but these tears are a-comin'. So I pretend. I pretend I'm a whiny kid having a tantrum and I sob, "I want to watch it again, I want to watch it again." But I don't, not really. It's a front. I don't know whether or not my parents catch on to this.

When their car disappeared up the street toward Costco, my feeling of impending doom softened, slightly. My senses are still on high alert—I just can't shake it—but I know Bobby's out, so I leave my bedroom and head downstairs to the computer. The tree inside me is sprouting leaves, cramming every space in my body with its foliage, and I'm uncomfortable and I *should* feel uncomfortable. I sit down at the computer, anxious. I don't know what Kristie will say to me; I don't know if she'll be around. I don't know if she knows. I log on. She's online. My world hums and slows. I have no intention of saying anything to her, unless she says something to me. I wait, and wait, then the *uh-oh* chirp of a new message.

I don't blink or breathe or swallow but click to open her message.

"Hey Erin," it says, simply.

It's impossible to interpret. *Could she not know?*

"Hi," I reply, cautiously.

"I heard."

I relax a little, automatically, surprising myself. I'm tired; I don't think I have the will—or ability—to wordsmith my way out of this. Plus, she won't buy anything I say. Nor should she. I don't know what to say. And I'm not ready to talk about it. I'll never be ready to talk about it.

I wait.

"The only question I have is why?"

"I don't know," I type back right away, my feelings suddenly flowing like a clogged hourglass shaken free. I start typing more, but a new message interrupts it.

"We stood up for you! We got mad at other people when they thought it was you! I don't understand why you would do this!!!!"

I did this, I think, angry at myself. I'd never thought about the repercussions. My feelings had eclipsed absolutely everybody's. Now I'm seeing the truth and it's far, far too late.

"I don't know," I type again, meaning it. "I just... I just really liked you guys and wanted to be friends with you. I know I went about it in a totally fucked up way... I just didn't know how to stop. I'm so so so sorry," I type, meaning that just as much.

"I just don't understand. If you wanted to be friends with us, why wouldn't you just say something? It would have been so much better for everybody!"

"Fuck, I know."

Suddenly, everything is clear. There's no more rationalizing. Without the intoxicating anticipation of Soela looking at me ever again with kindness in her eyes, there's only myself to look at, to blame. What had filled my gaping hole, though tenuous, whooshed out of me with the words "It's you." Now, I know, I'll have to pay.

The *uh-oh* chirp.

"I still don't understand. I hear you have to get help… you really need it."

Her words make everything ache, and I know them to be true.

"I'm not going to talk to you anymore. And I'm deleting you as a contact now. Soela is my best friend. I just hope you get better," she types.

And that's that. No more "sweetie," no more "hon."

I copy the conversation into a Word document and print it out. I force myself to remember it. To feel the impact of Kristie's words like a punch to the stomach again and again and again, more air whooshing out of me every time.

And now, I eat.

8

Addiction: You do something to feel good, and when you stop doing it you feel bad, which makes you do the thing that makes you feel good again and again and again. And if you get cut off from that thing, well, there's no shortage of replacements. There are healthy things, wholesome things, neutral things, hazardous things, devastating things. You may have choice with what, but there will be something. An empty space screaming to be filled.

After the ICQ conversation with Kristie, I go into the kitchen and open the fridge. My parents are still out and I know I have at least an hour before I have to hide away again. I pull out the brick of Costco mozzarella and grate a molehill of it on the cutting board. I push down, hard, again and again until my bicep aches, my shoulder aches. I grate my knuckles. Wipe the spritz of blood off the cheese. Grate more. Open the fridge again. Pull out the jug of Pace Picante salsa. Pile the cheese high into a bowl. Stir in the salsa. Grab the tortilla chips. My mouth waters. I shovel the mixture into my mouth. My tense body relaxes, a bit. I'm chewing and carrying the chips and bowl into the living room. I turn on the TV to nothing but daytime crap. A sizzle of guilt—we were raised not allowed to watch TV. Especially during the day. I settle on *Judge Judy*—watch her berating some stringy-haired single mom. I pull up the recliner, the chips nestled beside me and the bowl on my lap. I let myself get absorbed in the drama and my body relaxes. I put chip after chip into my mouth, swallowing without chewing fully. One after another after another. I finish the bowl and get up, grate more cheese, pour more salsa, watch more of *Judge Judy*. Smile when she softens for a moment. I'm calm now. My world's tiny and manageable. I refill the bowl until my fullness hurts and I'd throw up if I put one more thing in my mouth. I turn off the TV midway through my third episode. It's been an hour.

I'm slow going back upstairs, stuffed full. I don't even make it to the top of the stairs before I'm blasted. My negative thoughts are piercing and relentless, coming from no obvious place, like bullets from a sniper who could be taking aim from any number of sky-high buildings around a busy downtown square.

I'm so gross. I'm so ugly. I'm so disgusting.
Piew. Piew. Piew.
I'm a freak.

Piew.

My parents aren't home yet—I go into the bathroom and look at myself in the mirror. My face, my face people say is pretty, is like a too-small carving on a jack-o'-lantern.

I'm disgusting.

I pull up my hoodie, grab at my white rolls, twist them red. Then I hear a car and the *booph* of a door shutting. Another door. I tiptoe to my bedroom, quietly shutting myself in.

☊

Back to school, like a blur. I have eight weeks left. Eight weeks to uncurl, unfurl myself every morning at eight thirty, endure seven hours in a hyper-anxious state, devoting every speck of energy to avoiding Soela and her friends, then get back home to my room. I steal a small box television from its storage space in the garage and rig it up at the end of my bed, hidden in a bookshelf I hollow out by removing a shelf and pushing all its books under the bed. I disguise the TV with thin pieces of wood I also snag from the garage, and masking-tape bunny ears to the inner top of the bookshelf, creating a clear picture with one fuzzy horizontal line cutting through its centre. It becomes my light, and my comfort and my womb, and I sneak heaping plates of food when my parents are watching TV in the living room or not home yet, and I zone out on boring sitcoms like *Everybody Loves Raymond* and *That '70s Show* and whatever else is on so my body can relax.

At school, I regress to who I was at my first high school. Back then, in science one day, a flashing-beacon classmate in the centre of the room rings off names of fellow students and what animals they represent. Carl is a dog because he's faithful. Maya is a lion because she's regal and demands attention. I'm already origami folded in on itself, and I sit there waiting my turn, that nervous pang in my body that's always there exemplified. She turns to me.

"And Erin, you're a mouse. A little mouse. You just sit there all timid."

She hunches her body into an oval and chews her bottom lip deliberately. Laughter accents the room and the pang gets louder and Little Me's face goes red.

And now, going back to school after April 13, I'm not just a timid little mouse. I'm a timid little mouse who has been almost stepped on, almost poisoned, tortured, trapped. I'm a timid little mouse living in fear that anything I touch could be the imminent end of me. Timid little PTSD mouse. I scamper from class to class, just trying to keep my head down.

All the "firsts" are humps after which the road gets surprisingly smooth.

Or, at least, unsurprising. I now use my knowledge of Soela's schedule to avoid her. But on my way to earth science a week later, she's in an unusual corner of the school. The hallway is sparsely speckled with other kids, and we're unavoidably heading straight for each other. I want to avert my eyes but I can't. I see her see me. Her face stays neutral, like she's looking at a dishwasher. Nothing in her eyes or her expression dances or recoils—then she looks past me and is gone.

Kristie is the same. She just ignores me, at first, which is the best I can hope for. Then she starts staring me down every time I pass her in the hallways, her expression glacial. As if any actual connection we had was on a whiteboard scrubbed clean. Then there's Soela's other best friend, who I've never talked to and never had any classes with. She, too, gives me the stare down, but it's bigger. Louder. More aggressive. When I pass her, the whites of her eyes follow me and she looks like a cougar that could pounce at any second, to slash me with her nails and bite into the artery in my neck. It's her I'm most worried about— that David will see how she's acting and ask why. I start getting around school by going outside through the doors at the end of the hallways, and then back inside through the closest side door to each of my classes. I no longer linger in hallways, or ever put my guard down. David doesn't seem to notice. Once, that other friend mutters aggressively at me when we pass her holding hands. He looks at me expectantly.

"She just hates me. I don't know why, it's weird," I tell him, which he seems to accept.

The psychologist my parents choose is in a second-floor office in a strip mall near Cash Converters and T&T Supermarket. His greasy natural black hair is parted far to the left and he's wearing an ugly sweater that'd be the butt of a joke in some contexts. He's gangly, wearing equally wiry glasses. He sits about fifteen feet across the room from me with a clipboard and dives right in.

"So, Erin, I hear there were some letters?"

My wall's up. His wall holds framed certifications layered with dust, slightly off-kilter. I wonder if that drives some clients bonkers. To his right is a four-foot-tall, tropical-looking plant and it's fake.

"Yeah, but there *was* a guy." That's a safer place for me to tread. It's what I say when I'm cornered. "I didn't really like to talk about it, but he was real. His name was Trent."

He doesn't react and doesn't press me further. I relax into talking about David and Twyla and how I like English class and that I kind of want to be a teacher eventually. I smile and shrug and talk a lot, showing him I'm truly okay.

There's never a follow-up appointment, and my parents never again bring up Soela or what happened—both they and I prone to avoiding the squirming discomfort of facing something so emotional and complicated.

⌒

I'm young—probably four or five or six. Morning, in bed, I hear the murmur of what happened: my dog, Kegger, hit by a car, on the living room floor across the house. I know she's dying. I trace my pointer finger along the trim of my wood-en headboard—warm brown wood, rectangle after rectangle after rectangle, just the size of my small finger. I rest my forehead against its smooth downward curve, somehow warm. Maybe somebody comes to get me, to let me know, my mom or dad or brother. Maybe I pretend I'm sleeping. I don't go out there, though, don't see her like that. I imagine it, but I don't look. Like how eventually I won't go to the hospital. Not that second time.

⌒

Sometimes the space inside pulls, hard—a black hole. Sometimes it's rambunc-tious, like a drunken extrovert at a funeral. Most of the time it just aches. Filling it with food blurs its sharpness; then, paradoxically, so does taking food away completely.

⌒

In the summer between grade eleven and grade twelve, I limit my calorie intake to a maximum of 450 a day.

It makes my feelings simple. Stick to under 450 calories? Feel good about myself. Go over? Feel bad. I have all the power over how I feel, so I know who to blame when necessary. On the good days, I build up that version of myself. I buy pants that sparkle and colourful, trendy shirts from Carli's, a boutique shop my mom finds across the Fraser River. That summer, I lose thirty pounds. I also get comfortable with drinking, craving the feeling of heaviness in my legs after a few guzzles of wine. I start messing around with other boys—always at David's house with him right there. Everything I'm curious about, I try, and being drunk makes it seamless. No teenage awkwardness, just whatever.

Summer is easy with its warm nights and no schedule and alcohol stashes parents aren't noticing the watering down of. Probably, it just seems easy.

9

On my first day of grade twelve, I walk through the front doors of the school a lighter version of myself. I've shed weight and fear and have long straight hair. I can place my fingers in the grooves of my rib cage. My hip bones jut out like never before. I'm starving, but in total control of my calorie intake. It's like I've shed the old Erin, the Little Boy, the self-conscious weirdo forced to skulk up obscure staircases and keep her head down. I'm tanned. Wearing sparkly pants. The summer's brought me confidence. I feel vindicated right away, get complimented before I reach the foyer.

My Polish acquaintance: "Oh my God Erin, you look so good!"

She doesn't know—a thought that makes me curl a bit; a thought I hadn't had to think for weeks.

"How did you lose so much weight?"

I shrug, casually. "I just really watched what I ate this summer."

Her eyes are piercing blue and ours meet, then I look down. I signal a subtext, a call for pity. The curl inside deepens. She's shorter than me, and smart—always at the top of her class. Her dark, straight hair makes her eyes shine.

"What classes do you have?" She pulls out a folded paper with her schedule. I pull out mine, and we hold our sheets side by side. She smells of beautiful perfume. "Oh, we have law and comparative civilizations together next semester! Oh, and literature this semester! I guess we'll see a lot of each other." She says this without reservation and it makes me smile.

"I guess so."

This is what high school should feel like. This is what normal should feel like. The pace in the hallway picks up.

"I've got to get to class," she tells me. "Welcome back, Erin." I watch her like a dog watches its departing owner get farther and farther away, until she blends in with the other bodies in the hall.

Whirring from our encounter, I take a left down the foyer, head down the main artery of the school. To my right, a clog of Soela's friends. Guys with backpacks and first-day-of-school haircuts and Felicia Penn, splayed like a praying mantis atop a row of lockers.

I don't see her mouth moving, but I know exactly where it's coming from. And I know exactly who it's meant for. It pierces the murmur of the hallway.

"MURDERER!"

Familiar feelings seep into me, round my shoulders and deflate my chest.

"MURDERER!"

I glance to my right—memorize her hard, sneering look. The eight sets of eyes around her, all disgusted or angry. I keep walking, but my legs are weak—they could crumple under me at any second. I thought I was a lizard who shed its skin, a colourful proclamation on the cover of a glossy January magazine: "New Year, New You." I thought I was the sun, kissing the mountains late into a summer evening, stretching farther than and longer than anyone expected. But I'm not any of those things. I'm just a timid little mouse, scampering. I'm just Little Me. How silly, I think, that I felt I could use the front door.

⌒

It's not long before the taut strings of my willpower give way. One evening, still in September, I enter the kitchen to find the soft-coloured light above the stove illuminating a half-full pot of ravioli. I smell it before I see it—its cheesy, garlicky, satisfying aroma. It's a ticket to easing the discomfort crusting my corners, and it's just sitting there, a beacon. How do you beat instant gratification in a moment of yearning?

My parents are in the living room distracted by *Survivor*, oblivious to my presence and even my strict, summer-long calorie counting. I'd just pretended to go to the gym, pretended I was making healthy choices. Bobby's chaos, which had gotten louder over the summer, eclipsed mine. He'd always been "popular" in school—tall and handsome and alpha—and this brought more drinking, more graffiti, more late nights and locked doors and end-of-ropes and anger. My parents stopped affectionately calling him Mr. B and I moved in the shadows with ease.

Now, I get closer to the pot of ravioli. Pick up the lid. Its inside is layered with drops of condensation. I pull it up. The meaty pieces are stuck together, covered in olive oil, which reflects the light above it in shimmery lines. I reach my hand in and nudge a piece from its group—no longer hesitating, no longer weighing anything—and bring it up and into my mouth. My body's instantly warm and grateful. I take it slow and chew it completely—lusty, appreciative chews—and pull out another one. This time I don't finish chewing before I reach in for a third. And I'm off—like a galloping horse untethered, I pick up speed, taste less, eat more, and soon I'm ravenous. I open a cupboard to a huge case of chocolate chip cookies from Costco and I eat one, another, a third, a fourth, the taste of garlic still lingering in my mouth. I open the fridge—it's like I'm out of an underground jail and am feeling the wind and smelling the world and hearing its sounds for the first time in months. It's so overwhelming I can't tell if I'm feeling everything or nothing. I cut a hunk of jalapeno jack cheese off its block and shove it in my mouth, barely chewing. I open a zip-lock bag of sliced provolone and crumble four slices into my mouth. Still chewing, I part, like curtains, a container of Pace Picante and a huge bottle of ketchup to find my next target, my head whirring, my body warm. Then, like an alarm, the recliner of the couch where my parents sit snaps into place. I close the fridge and imperceptibly slip out of the kitchen and back upstairs, closing my bedroom door silently.

I feel the weight come back a lot faster than it actually does, and although I'll make several attempts to reclaim my low-calorie lifestyle, I'll never make it even another full day without eating. At least by trying to not eat.

David gets a job at the Husky gas station near the south end of Fraser Heights, where he figures out how to deceive the system and leaves every shift with a wad of cash and a pack or two of cigarettes. He always gives me a pack. My brother keeps coming home late at night with the whites of his eyes tinged red and his lids at half-mast, reeking of distinct, pungent marijuana. One night, not long before David starts at Husky, I can't sleep and my room is a mess, so I sit on the dark front porch, the heels of my palms imprinting into the cobblestone as I stare absently at the orange of the single street light across the road. It's cool enough to feel jarring, but not to send me inside. A black shadow rounds the corner in front of me, obscuring the light, and it dissolves into my brother, who sits clumsily beside me, forcing me to move over. Bobby smells like alcohol and pot and his eyes are glassy and distant. He opens the lid to a pack of Benson & Hedges Gold cigarettes, pulls one out and lights it. My little brother, smoking. My little, big brother.

"When you have a smoke after a joint, you get 10 percent higher," he tells me, his voice low and slow and knowing.

And around April, two months before graduation, David, Twyla and I start smoking pot. It's the beginning of three long roads for the three of us, roads that will wind and snake and intersect and veer far, far from one another—but roads that all run through the same place.

⌒

Once again, I'm living a double life. Being stoned, I have no worries. There's no weight or vanity or Soela. It's April, and within weeks, high school is over forever. At the end of the evening on 4/20, David hands me the silver tin mostly still full of pot—dry, THC-caked shake—and puts his hands over my hands, around it.

"You can have it," he says. It's the first time I have a stash, and it's like a curtain lift revealing who I truly am. The person who can't stop unless she's cut off. I start using it every day, and when I'm out in the world—at school dodging danger, or in the back seat of my parents' car getting groceries or visiting my grandparents—I crave it. Out in the world, I'm on sensory overload—it's loud and full of distractions and I'm at the mercy of it all, like a plastic bag flitting about in a gust of wind. But when the rest of my family is asleep or not home, I pull out my crushed, flat cream soda can and poke holes in the top of it, sprinkle on the weed and light it, sucking in through its drinking hole and blowing the smoke out my window. Everything blurs and slows. The high comes over me and it's like my ears and neck are cradled by delicate, beautiful summer flowers, and my world is as small as the room that holds me, like I'm in a womb.

At school, I'm keeping it together, somehow. Keeping my head down and reading my textbooks slow enough to absorb their information puts me at the top of a few of my classes. I ace my law exam, getting the highest mark in the class. I finish comparative civilizations with 99 percent. Doors are opening for me, all around, but I linger in foyers, drawn instead to the dark and wild unknown of the surrounding forest.

"Work hard, play hard," I tell myself, repeating it for years to come—rationalizing my tendency to fall down while holding myself up.

10

Twyla migrates toward PamAndNancy, an inseparable duo of poofy-haired, heavy metal stoners who laugh a lot and hang around older punks and tattooed metalheads in bands who party with cocaine. David and I, together like a three-legged race team, expand our social horizons. Candy has dyed black hair and a smile you have to work for. She's in my English class, and during our poetry unit, we'd both read aloud personal poems with intensities beyond the realm of typical high school. Alyssa is quiet and, Candy aside, is a loner with long blond curls, Gap sweatshirts and a pink purse. The two are inseparable and project an air of we-don't-need-anyone-in-this-dumb-school-besides-each-other.

It's a Wednesday night and the four of us meet at a small playground, down the short path beside the dollar store. This is what blazing has brought us: people outside our go-to acquaintances with mystery and intensity. The humid path to summer has already begun, and we sit in a circle on the millions of lady-bug-sized pebbles of the playground's floor and pass around a joint.

"Oh man, we should do jib again," Candy says, looking only at Alyssa.

Alyssa covers her mouth with slender fingers and laughs and shakes her head. "Only if your dad goes away again—that lasted so long."

They both giggle and I notice how rarely I see Candy's face like that. Neither David nor I know that "jib" means crystal meth. I shift uncomfortably and feel as separate and strange as I did one day back in grade eight when I heard my locker neighbours talking about getting "stoned" with "roaches." I can't fathom, of course, that "jib" is coming for me too, or, rather, I'm coming for it. Later, I search "jib" on the internet but find nothing.

Sitting there on the playground with Candy and Alyssa, everything around us dim shades of grey, my head soft and light, I'm making rounded pyramids with the rocks. Dirt residue covers my hands and I cup the pebbles and let them drop through my parted fingers—soothing like a rainstick.

Then, matter-of-factly, a question from Candy: "Erin, are you a lesbian?"

They all look at me. I'm surprised by the question. "What? No," I say, my voice skydiving on the "no." "No!"

I'm not hiding anything—I'm not a lesbian. My feelings for girls, the fact that I fall in love with girls, has nothing to do with me being a lesbian. Lesbian is that geeky Hannah girl from my first high school with the stringy hair and magnifying-lens glasses. That's lesbian, and I'm not that. Those feelings I have, well, that's just this thing about me.

Our conversation on the playground departs from the topic easily, but the question hangs in me. I'm not a lesbian. *Lesbian.* It sounds so weird. I'd never thought about it that way before. Am I a lesbian? No. No, I don't think so.

⌒

It never gets easier, going back to school after April 13 of grade eleven, but it doesn't get harder than that first day back. I just have to weather the storm, and I know it'll howl around me and beat at me and try to wear me down, but I figure there must be an "other side," so I stay patient.

The vibrant love I'd felt for Soela flips over, heavy with shame. And that shame sticks to me like an alien tumour deep in my gut. It's stuck to me when I walk naked down the hallways, through the doors, up and down stairwells. It's stuck to me when I throw my journal into the garbage—hundreds of pages of obsessing and agonizing and fighting with myself and cherishing Soela, my constant mourning too painful to look at. Years later, when I finally let someone see that cobwebbed corner of me in the tiniest flashlight glimpse, she'll say, "It sounds like you were lost and in a lot of pain." Only then will I feel one speck of compassion for my younger self, and only then will I feel a few specks of regret for throwing away that journal.

⌒

Before I walk out of high school for the last time, I have one final interaction with Soela, at graduation. In typical rich-neighbourhood-suburb style, it's held at the Hyatt Regency hotel at Canada Place in downtown Vancouver. It's mid-June and warm. The sun reflects orange and white on the water of the bay, a pretty, golden-hour backdrop to dozens of children in tuxedos and thousand-dollar dresses. We all line up and smile in pictures that we won't see developed for at least a few days. For the occasion, I buy a cardboard-encased point-and-shoot camera. Looking back on my photos I seem light and happy, and maybe I am.

David's my date, and he bleaches his spikes platinum at my request, more rooted in curiosity than anything else. My dress is burgundy, under $300, and beautiful. Most of the neighbourhood kids take limos but we take David's silver Hyundai. He arrives at my house and puts a burgundy corsage around my wrist, and my mom, an avid photographer, takes dozens of photos of two lovebirds on a milestone day. Today, I laugh looking at them. There's us in the kitchen, him on his knees on the floor, tenderly holding my hand. There's us in the backyard, me on the ground with my dress like a Christmas-tree skirt around me, us gazing into each other's eyes. There's us standing in the front-door nook, me a few inches taller than him, his arms gingerly around my waist. In all the photos we look like we're acting, which we are, but it's also clear that we're having fun. Which we are.

At the downtown hotel, I take off my shoes and we dance, and the perpetual nervousness in my chest gets swapped for excitement. I'm barefoot and head up a centre aisle for water, still feeling the music, a rare moment with my guard down. Before I have anywhere to turn, I notice Soela walking toward me, unavoidable in the thin aisle. Maybe I know this could be the last time I lay eyes on her. Maybe I'm just feeling better than usual. Maybe in this one minuscule bubble of a moment, I just don't care. I look her in the eyes, smile and nod. She looks back at me, in her baby-blue dress and her beautiful makeup and without any underlying disgust, anger or sadness. She looks at me, looks me in the eyes, smiles and nods back.

Then, high school's over and it's that summer. That summer when David and I start smoking pot and cigarettes every day and try magic mushrooms and drink white rum out of the bottle, and that summer when Twyla migrates ever closer to PamAndNancy. Shortly after graduation, my parents buy me Super-Beast, my first car: a 1988 light blue Volkswagen Golf with warbled speakers and purple reverse lights. It gives me freedom. Then, that summer night with Blossom and the bathroom floor, along with the realization that maybe, just maybe, I'm not straight, and then there's Melinda, who helps me know it.

That summer I shift, and by the time September rolls around, everything's different.

Storms

craving
/ˈkrāviNG/
noun
a powerful desire for something.

11

We move. From one thing to the next, we move. Like the world is full of magnets. Like the space within us is a magnet too.

For a while, I'm the "smart stoner." At least to PamAndNancy and their friends. They're still in their final year of high school, and everybody they hang with works labour or retail, so the fact that I'll hotbox SuperBeast at noon with seven other stoners and then drive to Burnaby for university always impresses people. I just smile and laugh and bask in the admiration and ignore the fact I go to campus to smoke more pot in the parking lot, slowly walk the quad and smoke cigarettes on the school's giant steps. In fact, I'm nearly four weeks into university and there are classes I haven't yet attended. On the first day, I carpool up with a couple of girls from high school: Zofia and Missy. I drive, and we're nearly late. On the drive up, I blast my System of a Down tape, probably to sharp pangs in their ears, and when we arrive at the Simon Fraser University campus on Burnaby Mountain, we have to circle the lot to find a spot. We speed walk, the three of us, to the closest doors to the quad, cooler September air biting at our extremities, and I realize I have no idea where I'm going. I picture myself stepping into a lecture after it already begins, hundreds of eyes on me, and feel a stirring of panic. Entering the front doors, a brand new environment, Missy's anxiety is like an electrical storm, yet Zofia senses mine. She looks at my sheet that says I have African History, her pointer finger trying to help me decipher its location.

"We're going to be late!" says Missy.

Zofia looks at me apologetically and I brush it off. "It's okay. Go."

And they're off down the hallway. I already know it's too late for me, and as soon as that thought occurs, my clenched body relaxes. I find a bench and settle in to read my Kurt Cobain biography. It's not like high school, where the hallways clear after the first bell. I'm incognito; it's comfortable. I find my linguistics lecture later that week and sit at the back of the theatre, watching the young professor dance across the stage. I'm bored and uncomfortable until I notice short pink hair and a punk-rock vest adorned with spikes several rows in front of me, and suddenly, school gets a bit more interesting. I don't really know what a "lesbian" looks like, but if I had to put money on it, I'd bet on her—she has freckles and no makeup and is bulky and tough looking. She smokes, too. Her name is Mary. Within an hour we're both smoking outside the closest door to the lecture hall, about seven feet apart. I take a drag, blow it upward, glance at her. She seems to be doing the same. Everything at school is monochrome, and though I get stoned, the moment I walk through the doors, I'm the same. Human shaped, but invisible. But then she glances at me, and this ruby-coloured whirring zips up my core and I'm no longer just going through the motions.

She talks to me for the first time shortly after I notice her. I'm alone on the gargantuan steps that connect the quad to the rest of the university. It's still warm for autumn, at least when the sun hits you, and the sky's blue. Her shadow darkens the book I'm reading. I knew she was coming, so I was just looking at the page. I look up at her—she's blocking the sun from my eyes.

"Hey, do you have a light?"

Her voice is husky and butch. Mine's high and excited and way too exuberant for the question. "Yeah!"

Everything suddenly sounds different. On the *Unplugged in New York* version of "All Apologies," Kurt Cobain's raw calling out of "Mary" becomes about me, about her. He's really singing *married*, but I never sing it that way, even now.

Meanwhile, I get a job at Java Hut and a slew of new friends. One noon hour behind the coffee shop, I open SuperBeast's door and let the pot smoke from eight stoners billow out. The car's undercarriage sags low toward the ground and I can barely breathe. The cool-air rush heals my lungs and I gulp it up and round the corner to the coffee shop.

At the counter, I buy a coffee with my 50 percent off discount, and my stoner co-worker gives me a knowing look and a gigantic smile.

"How's it goin', Erin?"

I know I reek, and in a way, it makes me feel cool—part of a community underlying the hubbub of affluent housewives popping by for noon-hour coffees, grabbing a bite after the gym with their girlfriends. I grab a lid from the counter and cover my steaming cup without adding anything, just how my parents drink it. The smell of freshly ground beans brings to mind Saturday mornings as a child, my parents bleary-eyed and in terry cloth robes, four hands, two mugs, asking, "What'll we do today?"

Hot coffee in hand, I round the building and light up a Benson & Hedges. The circle of smoking stoners widens to let me in and I smile along with the cadence of conversation—not saying anything, not knowing what to say, but part of something. Undeniably that.

The drift between Twyla and me begins, and it's cinematic. Like she's on a ship and I'm on shore and I watch her get smaller and smaller until she's a little dot.

"I did blow at Pete and Steve's," she says matter-of-factly during her lunch hour from school on a Monday. I've just finished my shift at Java Hut, and we're at a little two-seater on the coffee shop's patio. She's drinking a blueberry smoothie from a clear plastic cup, stirring it with a thick straw between sips. Cocaine. I light a cigarette. There are lines I won't cross and this is one of them.

"Why?" I ask, my voice dead and condescending, not actually looking for an answer.

"I don't know." She ignores my tone. "It was just there. It was fun," she says without enthusiasm.

"What was it like?"

"Oh, I don't know, nothing too crazy. I just talked a lot."

"Hmm." I shift in my chair and take a drag of my cigarette, blowing the smoke up and toward the sidewalk to avoid pissing off a nearby table of middle-aged housewives. "Well, I had a pretty crazy weekend at Danny's," I say.

I'm always at Danny's these days, thanks to David, who has a few classes with him. Danny's an artist and a stoner—scrawny with messy hair—who lives in his parents' fully finished basement in one of the richest parts of Fraser Heights. His girlfriend, Elise, welcomes me from the first moment I walk through that sliding glass door, and so does Delia, her best friend. Grey, Delia's boyfriend, towers above us all in height and hair and still has a baby face.

"Yeah, we all got super wasted, and I actually blacked out." I study Twyla as I say this and relay the rest of the story. I was swigging Bacardi from the bottle while we all crowded outside the sliding glass door, smoking pot and cigarettes. The more we drank, the more we spread out into the backyard, onto the grass, onto the rolling hills of the greenbelt behind the house. I remember staggering up a grassy hill to the bench where I knew everybody else was blazing—I could hear their muffled chatter and laughter—but my memory stops there. I woke up in my own bed, vomit pungent and caked onto the same clothes I was wearing the night before.

I shake my head and butt out the cigarette I'm smoking in three stiff downward motions, wiping the resulting residue on my socks. "Apparently I did a handful of mushrooms. I don't remember at all."

"How'd you get home?"

"Uh, apparently my dad actually came and picked me up. I couldn't walk and I guess my pants fell down on the front driveway. Apparently."

A day or two later, my dad will enter the kitchen just as I'm pouring a bowl of Vector—him smelling like car oil and sweat, hands stained grey, baseball cap that says "Starbucks" worn on its brim. I sit down at the head of the kitchen table, heat vents warming me from the ground. He pours coffee into a large-handled mug and lingers for a second and we nod at each other and he opts to take the coffee back into the garage where it'll cool in a flash, I know, and the night he picks me up wasted—and what, puts me to bed?—becomes the latest addition to the Things We Don't Talk About repertoire.

To Twyla, I shake my head again and smile, feigning embarrassment, searching her eyes for something.

"Fuck. They're all so cool though—Danny and them. We're getting really close."

The truth is, we'd never hung out sober.

"Yeah," says Twyla, "I feel the same way about PamAndNancy and them. Hey, you should come out with us. There's a party at Pete and Steve's Friday. There'll be good music and shit. Pete and Steve are in a band."

That Friday, I join her wearing a teal tank top that just shows off my stomach, still flat from starvation. I drink Bacardi and it doesn't take long to settle into the rhythm of the party. Everybody's older, except our group, probably at least twenty-three or twenty-four. Somebody's playing guitar and drums in the garage. The deck is smoky and crowded and I smoke my Benson & Hedges and blend in seamlessly. I'm sitting on the edge of an armchair, talking to a guy with tattoos about the Smashing Pumpkins, observing his eyes soften into fondness. Twyla spins into the room and grabs my arm. "Come into the room; Mike's cutting up a line."

I know I'm not going to do it, but I follow her anyway. "I'll just come with you."

Tattoo guy says, "I want to see you again." I smile at him and recognize something. If he were a girl, he'd clink through my brain like a pinball. Back and forth and back and forth until he becomes this catalyst for feeling—for goosebumps and flutters and cravings. But he's just a hot guy who likes me, which makes me feel good, sure, but that's it.

In the bedroom are Twyla, Misha, PamAndNancy and a couple of guys I don't know. One of them has a loud presence, like a television, and he's holding the CD case with the coke. Pulling two cards from his wallet, he divvies the white powder into several lines. Default plays in the background and he sings obnoxiously, changing the words: "Stop wasting my line, stop wasting my line."

My body rings with nervousness and I'm drunk, but I know I'm not going to do it. I refuse to inhale anything up my nose. That's my line. The guy rolls up a fifty-dollar bill horizontally, putting one end to the CD case, his nose on the other, breathes in with an easy breath, then rubs his pointer finger over where the line was and rubs his top gums.

"Blow's numbing," Twyla tells me later, knowingly, her eyes and mine meeting at their corners.

Each person in the semicircle repeats what the first guy does and the rolled bill gets passed to me within minutes. I shake my head. "No. Thanks."

Saying no makes me feel strong. The room is moving but I feel somehow superior to the rest of them, all chatting over one another like seagulls. I have a line, and I refuse to cross it. But that line—that line is smudged and it's tenuous, and lines: they're so easy to cross.

⌒

Working at Java Hut puts me at the epicentre of the neighbourhood happenings. The pot smokers swoop in and out, dumping too much sugar into coffees they don't particularly like, disappearing for hours or days. The smokers who don't really drink set up on the patio, drinking cup after cup, smoking cigarette after cigarette. I tend to the regulars—the extra-large mocha in the morning, the students hovering over textbooks, the soccer moms who gossip as much as their high school children. I take it all in from behind the counter, wearing my burgundy apron.

I watch the smokers who don't really drink on the patio. Some I've known for a long time, peripherally. Others I know by name, but that's it. But all their faces grow familiar, as familiar faces do, and I grow fond of seeing them. Sometimes, when I finish a shift or take a break, I join them on the patio to smoke and chat. The things they talk about barely skim the surface in comparison to the deep explorations we get into over at Danny's, but it's light and it's easy.

I'm drawn to Melinda, who's the first "bisexual" person I've ever met. She's not turn-my-head attractive, but there's a soft sensuality about her. A huskiness to her voice. A hidden depth I can feel. And she seems to be the same person around everyone, which intrigues me. Sitting across from her on the patio after work, our eyes meet and linger through drags of cigarettes and conversations around us. Even when neither of us is talking, our eyes meet—and linger.

By this time, I'm smoking pot every day. Sometimes, after my shift, we'll pile into an old burgundy Aerostar van for the shadows of J.R. Park. Melinda and I have been eyeing each other for a while, and amid my crumbling academic career and this faint inkling that I just might be hooked on pot, our dance is an oasis. She starts calling me Sexy more than Erin and I revel in it. And unlike how it was with Soela, it's sexual. At J.R. Park, there are six of us scattered in micro-groups. It's dark and the autumn air cools my face, the smell of damp cedar bark, wet air, despite no rain.

"Give me a hug, warm me up," Melinda says to me, push-starting a roller coaster in my stomach, and I wrap my arms around her, press my cheek against the top of her head. I know who I am. I know I'm not straight. Girls eat up the recesses of my mind. I think about tattoo guy at that party with Twyla, how my stomach didn't flutter; I didn't hold my pillow at night and think about him; I didn't wake up the next morning with his face running through my mind.

I breathe in the scent of Melinda's thin hair—cigarette smoke and shampoo. Feel, viscerally, her arms wrapped around my waist. I bury myself in our embrace, then break it and trip headfirst over my words. *Just say it!* I scream this silently to myself. And then, out loud for the first time, using the best word I know to define what's growing ever more apparent to me; "I'm bisexual," I tell her, the words freight-training past my frantic hesitations.

"Okay," she says. That's it. I can't read her. It's not the reaction I'm hoping for—a big part of me wants her, needs her, to grab my face with both hands and pull my lips to hers and press her body against mine like I'm a long-lost love, finally home. Rather, a beige door opens and we walk through, not even holding hands. But it's a threshold crossed—albeit without fanfare—and I have no idea where I, we, will end up from here.

12

Danny's palm is outstretched and full of shrivelled, curly, grey and brown mushrooms. David and I are eager and seduced by the warm living room, by the bright paintings that pierce you with apprehension only when you spend too long looking. It's the richest part of the richest neighbourhood, and the spiral staircase that separates the basement from Danny's family life makes it feel like he lives here alone.

"The only way to do mushrooms is in the forest," he tells us, and the lot of us venture out into the damp coolness of late afternoon, after choking down a portion of the handful. The mansions of the neighbourhood end a few streets over, and the forest feels like it goes on forever. It occurs to me that the forest is something you can never really know, yet at the same time, it's predictable. Thoughts like these reverberate in this secret place deep inside me and give me goosebumps, and I keep them to myself.

Soon, time warps into a dismissible man-made construct, syphoned away by the wonder of the forest. It's like wearing much-needed glasses for the first time—the green is so green, the droplets of condensation on leaves are so important, so fundamental, I marvel at how I could ever have obliviously brushed by them. At one point, a faint whirring of engines—distant ATVs or dirt bikes—nips at the corner of my consciousness. I'm thinking about something under layers of thought, a kernel of frustration piercing my mind and travelling downward in circles, a gumball rounding a spiral dispenser. And then, I start laughing. Laughing and laughing and laughing. It's not that feel-good relief laugh; I'm out of control, laughing without the anchor of reason. I laugh until my stomach hurts from the tension; I laugh until my cheeks ache, laughing, desperately wanting to stop laughing. Tears are running down my face when I'm finally able to quash it and look at David, a few metres from me. He turns toward me, his face serious and big eyes even bigger, black pupils overtaking the green of his irises.

"We need to get out of here," he says, my body instantly ringing with nervousness.

"Why, David?"

He says, "I'm scared the dirt bikes are going to get us."

My stomach cranks and we run, brushing past all the leaves, from squishy ground to asphalt, past the looming mansions and back to the bright warm basement at Danny's.

My brain feels sluggish and strange, like a computer that needs defragging. "I don't like mushrooms," I say, and Danny sniffs and giggles.

"I found this sweet place in the forest," he says. "This ravine with a little waterfall. We could build it up and party there."

The Pit, we'll call it, and it'll become Fraser Heights famous. Every weekend we'll get a bonfire going and we'll sit or stand around on the tiered seating, hang out in Thor's Blazing Hut across the bridge we'll build over the ravine. I'll celebrate my nineteenth birthday there, and meet Ava there. This peculiar secret place in the forest will become our own.

☾

Though they're to my back, the cars vrooming by Fraser Heights' busiest intersection are loud and distracting. I'm on the concrete partition between Melinda and another friend, Cynthia, facing our warbled reflections in the glass wall of Quiznos, occasionally distracted by the movement of Twyla in her little half hat, behind the counter making sandwiches. It's warm for October, the sun making my half-sleeve knit feel like it just came out of the dryer. Cynthia's chain-smoking—her only vice—and Melinda takes off her hoodie, the skin of her bare shoulders against my knit. Twyla's smiling at a family who just walked in, and I turn to face the traffic. I take a little risk. I reach my hand out, gently cup Melinda's head, behind her ear, and run my fingers through her hair. The sensation of soft strands running through the curves of my hand that rarely feel touch makes the seconds stretch. When my hand regrettably reaches the end, I gently let her hair go and its tips whisper at her shoulders. I could sit here forever, happy. She exhales heavily, sexily, and cranes her neck toward me, her chin still pointed up.

"You're giving me shivers," she murmurs so softly Cynthia probably can't hear it, and my entire body feels her words.

☾

I join the smoker crew heading to the party in Langley only because Melinda's going. We all squish into the Aerostar and on the way there, behind the comfort of tinted windows, I sip Bacardi out of the bottle, it sloshing every which way. The party's full of people who only drink—geeks and nerds and I'm not sure whose friends they even are. But the party's easy, and the usual pressure that weighs down in social situations isn't there, so I make small talk about university, pretend that I'm like them. After the conversation I'm having fizzles into awkward nodding, I realize that I haven't seen Melinda in a while, so I set out to find her, poking my head into various rooms. The third room I push into, one lit solely by a dim red light, she's just about to exit and we nearly crash into each other. I have confidence fuelled by alcohol and a montage of a thousand flirtatious encounters with her.

"There you are," I say, looking down at her, our bodies close.

"Hey sexy," she says softly in her raspy voice, not backing up.

She's wearing a tight, white tank top and I put my hands on her hips and push them to wrap around her back. She looks up at me and touches my cheek, softly. There are people talking, laughing, on the bed adjacent to us, oblivious to time screeching to a halt around them. The whirring in me is in overdrive but outwardly I'm practised like a lifetime of routine. My mind's no longer blaring questions—I'm simply present in this moment everything in my life has been leading up to. My body's weightless, light, as if all my energy is suddenly without gravity while somehow still grounded. I crane my neck down. Our lips meet, and we kiss. Every cell hanging in my body somersaults. We pull our bodies closer and kiss and kiss, and I'd kissed countless boys—enjoyed it, I thought—but it's nowhere in the same galaxy, the same universe, as this visceral pummelling. I suddenly know what love can be and I suddenly know where to find it. I know what it was all about with Soela and I suddenly know, really know without a shred of doubt, that what I feel for boys could never come remotely close to how I feel for girls. Without a shred of doubt, I know.

We kiss and kiss, caught up in the feeling of each other's lips, four hands running along the curves of each other's bodies. I kiss her until I'm not even kissing her anymore, but everything I've been missing that I didn't realize I've been missing, and a new banner over my life exclaims: Things Will Never Be the Same.

⌒

As I spend full days circling campus, smoking on the steps and in the parking lot, sometimes sitting in the library, time obliterates the faint voice inside that ensures I'll fix this. I'm taking five classes, the sun is nearly set on the semester, and I've never been to African History. I went to English once and Linguistics only a couple of times. I half-heartedly started reading *Heart of Darkness* for class after the teacher scrawled a passionate case for the concept of "writing is rewriting" on the chalkboard, but I missed every exam I was supposed to take. I'm going to fail all my classes and my parents have no idea.

Zofia and Missy also seem to have no idea, and I shut out inquiries when I drive by blasting System of a Down so loud they'd have to grab my shoulders and shake to get my attention. When they drive, they talk about their classes, their papers, their professors, and I just sit there silently in the back seat, a child along for a road trip. If I told them I didn't know how to find my classes, they'd look at me like I'd turned a eulogy into a fart joke and ask, "Why wouldn't you just ask someone?" And then I'd ask myself, *Why didn't I ask anybody?* And the thought would turn my body nervous. The longer it goes on, the more hopeless I feel, and picturing myself walking into a lecture or study group for the first time, weeks into the semester, scares me infinitely more than asking for help in the first place. Eventually I learn that it's better to take a deep breath and do the thing I know I have to do, no matter how scary or hopeless it feels, but that version of me won't emerge for a long, long, long, long time.

So I continue my spiral, shame as present within me as my heart, my lungs, my kidneys, and I avoid those little risks that could improve things. I sit outside in the autumn air until I shiver, smoke cigarettes until my throat hurts and daydream about Mary or Melinda. Nothing ever does happen with Mary—near the end of the semester I see her hanging out with a shorter, skinnier girl with a tuft of natural hair and glasses. *A lesbian*, I think. And soon they're together more than Mary's alone and I watch from my tunnel, surrounded by blackness, a world of colour streaming through me that nobody else ever sees. This dulls school further and I just start waiting for the inevitable, and when I don't carpool with Zofia and Missy, I don't go at all and stop teasing myself with the notion that I'll get better.

13

Working at Java Hut at least gives me a schedule—a place to be and a time to be there, so staying in my PJs until mid-afternoon isn't an option. Staying awake all night isn't an option. Putting on my burgundy apron and eye makeup means I'm at least tethered to something, though outside those part-time hours I float.

I'm on the clock, wiping down a patio table outside, when Melinda comes around the corner, whirring in a way she normally doesn't.

"I told Jeff. He flipped," she says, referring to her boyfriend, looking straight at me, her eyes unusually frantic. Normally, she focusses her gaze on me and it's soft and comfortable. Now, her brow is furrowed.

On one hand, I'd have expected Jeff in his muscle shirt and slicked-back waves of Italian hair to say something like "Well, you can do it but only if I watch," but instead, he gets that I want her with a fierceness that eclipses him. I am a threat, and he sees it.

I look down at the cloth in my hand. She moves closer to me. I'm not sure how I feel. I'd been meaning to tell David for weeks now—I'm surprised she beat me to it.

"He doesn't want me to see you but I told him I'm not going to stop," she says.

I fiddle with the cloth and hang my head. The hunk of me that had been floating through the neighbourhood on a magic carpet ride nosedives into the asphalt. It was easy and carefree and everything I needed it to be, and now I feel forced to make a commitment I'm not ready to make.

Our relationship solidified something in me—something I can't go back from—but I have no burning desire to make her my one-and-only.

"I still want to show you my body," she says, looking up at me.

Her words electrify me, and they'll ring in my mind long after they're spoken. I look down into her eyes and bite my lip.

"C'mere, sexy," she says, and we wrap our arms around each other.

It's part of our wind-down, this moment; from here on out, endings. Over the next year, we'll make out intermittently between her string of boyfriends after Jeff, but I'll never feel more than I did when we kissed in the red-lit room.

The high of the first time. The high of newness. The high of obtaining after wanting.

Despite the endings, though, I know I have to tell David. Because this, I know, is so much bigger than Melinda.

That same evening, David's waiting for me outside the glass walls of the coffee shop. It's early November now, dark, get-inside-your-bones cold and ten o'clock. Java Hut is the last thing to close for the night on both sides of the street. We sit along the side of the Tim Hortons. The plaza is quiet, the parking stalls empty, the businesses darkened, save for their neon signs.

"Brr," I say and sit close to David. He pulls out two cigarettes, lights them simultaneously and hands me one.

"Chilly," I say. "It's chilly out here."

David looks at me playfully and responds musically, "Out here!"

I smile and turn my words into a melody, him effortlessly gliding along beside me in melodic silliness. "Chilly… it's chilly in there."

"In there!"

We keep it going as long as we can, then laugh and hug and relight our cigarettes; they've both gone out.

I know what I have to say and prepare for it, turning sombre. "David, I have to tell you something."

His eyes are still crinkled into smiles at their corners and I can tell he's feeling lighthearted. I know I just have to come out with it. "I'm bisexual."

He peers into my eyes and smiles a bigger—borderline unnerving—smile and laughs before he speaks. "Ya don't say."

In his reaction there's a disconnect, like the resistance between two strong magnets being pushed to touch. I don't get why he seems so happy. And then his face shifts to serious and it's apparent. "I'm bisexual too, Erin."

His musical interlude, his backing me up, his part of the song.

I feel giddy and weird.

I tell him about Melinda, how our kiss felt. "No offence to you in any way," I say gently.

"None taken at all! I'm kind of jealous actually. I really want to kiss a guy."

He tells me he's happy for me and I shake my head, disbelief. He puts his arm around me and I lean my head on his shoulder, contemplating our new reality, and in the comfort of his embrace, I lift my head. "David, oh my God, we're your parents!"

He bursts into laughter and I laugh too.

Our relationship dissolves shortly after this night, and after an awkward transition period, we rematerialize as best friends—a place in each other's lives that solidifies easily. A place, for us, that's sustainable amid our flutters of the heart and all my burning, burning desires.

⌒

They took away my bumper pad when I was a toddler—my parents. They raise this, enough times to pay attention, over the years. They both shake their heads, question whether the parenting advice of the day was right to follow. I was obsessed with it, apparently. Too obsessed. I bawled like I'd never bawled before when they took it away, apparently. If something as ordinary and cream white as a bumper pad could bring so much comfort, so much anguish in its absence, couldn't it be anything that we need so desperately?

⌒

I've already decided I don't like mushrooms, with their uncorked laughter and murky reality and lack of control. I expect acid to be the same, but as David, Delia, Grey, Elise, Danny and I exit the bubble of Fraser Heights for downtown Vancouver, I still feel excited—part of something. Just off Davie Street, we meet up with a dealer David recently met. Between buildings and bus shelters, I catch glimpses of the ocean. We stand in a tight circle around the dealer—a short lady in a black leather trench coat, *Matrix* sunglasses, rings on every finger. She makes eye contact with each of us, like she's instructing a weekend course.

"Try not to touch the surface. Just hold it by the edges and put it under your tongue. Keep it there for longer than you think you should."

"Like, for how long?" David is earnest, thrives on detail.

"Like thirty minutes, definitely." She does another sweep of our faces and smiles, revealing a mouthful of crooked teeth. "Have fun, dudes. It's wicked shit."

We wander the streets for a long while, those little squares under our tongues, all with sudden lisps, which we laugh about, carefully. It's that beautifully warm time of year when it stays T-shirt warm late into the night. My brain's saturated in anticipation when Delia holds out her arms horizon like, stopping us all. "What the fuck is that?"

A block ahead, its stomach crouched low to the ground, appears to be a skunk.

"A skunk!" says David. "They live down here!"

"Jesus fucking Christ," says Delia, slowing down and backing up. Grey moves toward it and it freezes. The street's otherwise deserted. "If you get fucking sprayed, I'm going home," Delia tells him. We all pause and so does the skunk until it slinks away.

We head to the beach. A lightness infiltrates my being and I know a switch has been flipped. I look at Delia, whose face is turned up in every way possible, and she's laughing. And laughing. She hangs on to Grey and they both laugh. Danny prods at the sand with a stick and I jump onto a log, inhaling the ocean, looking out at the barges on the horizon and the sky's reflections on the water. There's nothing lingering at the edges of my world—no guilt, no school, no Melinda, no nothing; everything is now. There's a crispness to acid I appreciate.

I turn toward the city, toward the neon lights of the Sylvia Hotel sign. The words turn into moving swans and I laugh and laugh. And we're now a gleeful group on a great adventure. We wander from the beach and back into the city, where everything's funny and bright and crisp and I feel fully in control. Positive energy bursts from my chest and we make home in a steep half alley that ends with a door for a truck and a door for a person.

"This is perfect!" says Elise, and we're all on her wavelength—we all know just what she means. We settle in and light cigarettes. Danny passes around a Colt 45 in a brown paper bag and it tastes better than it ever has. We talk and laugh and entice passersby to come in and talk to us.

We stay there for hours until my exuberance fades, then wilts, then dries up like leaves on a tree in November. Uneasiness settles back into my stomach and I'm still tripping out on street lights through the small window to the world at the bottom of the alley, but now I'm freezing and notice the filth all around me. We're no longer in a circle but rather coupled up, facing out toward the rectangle of the world. David and I are behind everyone, and I feel nothing other than a vicious need for pain. Tears are suddenly flowing out my eyes. I push my head toward David's as close as I can get, and his stubble scratches my forehead, feeling like sandpaper, like relief. He's quiet too now, and solemn, looking out onto the street.

"Just kill me," I say softly, out of nowhere, and that makes me cry harder. I pull his arm around my neck hard, squeezing it against me, needing it, him, someone else, to cut off my circulation. "Just kill me, David, please."

He tries to pull his arm away and I can't stop and I'm flooded.

The others are in their own worlds and I feel my desperation bursting to exit my body in screams, like an out-of-control costume party, its guests frantically rushing the front door. My body rings and I need to be hurt. I fucked up with Soela, fucked up with school, fucked up everything with my parents and my life and I'm in this dirty alley high on a drug I hate and I just need, deserve, pain.

I mutter with a wavering voice, "Just fucking kill me, David, please just do it."

I don't know what I mean, really. It's this heavy boulder of pain inside me suddenly reverberating with sound, waves of it pushing through my body, words coming out my mouth.

And then I look at him. The costume-party guests—the clowns and bananas and Grim Reapers and knights and cheerleaders—freeze mid-frenzy like time pauses. And silence. And stillness. And I see him. And I see me. He's crying too and looks so small and sad and desperate, and I immediately soften and put my head between my curved knees and take in a deep breath. When I look at him again, his green eyes are shiny and he looks at me like I just kicked his dog. Then I just feel bad.

"Fuck, I'm sorry."

Then to everyone else:

"Can we just get the fuck out of here?"

14

Failing school is in my long-term weather forecast for so long, by the time it actually happens, I've already battened down the hatches and curled my shoulders inward and nestled my face away from the wind and the rain. The day I get the letter stating I'm on academic probation ends and then the next day arrives and so on, and it all just feels like a normal part of everything. I'm told, in the letter, that if I fail another class I'll be kicked out. It's simple like that, and I see before me a clear path to redemption, and a clear path into chaos. If there's even a choice, it's easy. My parents just figure I took too many classes and got overwhelmed, so for the January semester, I sign up for just two: English and philosophy. I promise myself, as the weather gets inside my bones, that 2003 will be my year.

At Java Hut in the evenings, when my boss is probably at his kitchen table helping his daughter with math homework, I'm whizzing around the coffee shop like its sole proprietor. On my smoke breaks I join those bundled on the patio—linger above them and laugh on cue—and I don't have to work hard to socialize. The suits from the security company adjacent to Java Hut walk by regularly, monitoring us. They make anybody who doesn't have food or a drink on the patio leave. "Agents of the landlord," they call themselves, and tensions rise. Kids take to calling the bald one Cue Ball. He ramps up his evictions.

Meanwhile, my confidence has a surprise bloom. Through the glass of the patio, I watch everybody, feel their energies, even from a distance—recognize their human power struggles. I watch the bodies of those who dominate in conversation look bigger, and I watch those who contract, like I do, when in a big group. Nobody notices, but I do. This pretty goth girl I recognize from my first high school is like that—she smokes when everybody else does and giggles with a hand covering her mouth. When she enters the coffee shop, my stomach jolts.

"Can I get a medium coffee, please?"

Her eyes are the blue of forget-me-nots.

"Room for anything?"

"Nope."

A shy smile. I consciously hold her gaze—practise that. She looks down.

I slip her cup into a sleeve and push it across the counter toward her. "It's on me," I say.

She does a double take, then brings her hand up to her mouth, her eyes smiling into mine. "Really? Thanks!"

I hold her gaze. Smile back. Like this all comes naturally. Like I'm suave, for real.

It's a glimmer; confidence with no crutch.

⌒

I'm still making promises to myself of a better 2003 on New Year's Eve. I'm on English Bay Beach in Vancouver and just accidently swallowed my tongue ring with a slice of ham and pineapple pizza. I'm drunk, and so's David. "Work hard, party hard," I'm telling myself like it's something to be proud of. Like it's actually possible. The sun has long since dipped below the horizon and the lights on the barges in the distance and the lights reflected from the city twinkle on the surface of the black water, the tiny waves of the bay, far from the open ocean.

I think about the impossibility of whales there, the sheer delight seeing one would bring. I think about how nature forces us humans to stop our sprawl, how this is the edge of the land and how it always will be and how it always has been. The expanse of it all builds in me and I feel inextricably part of it all. Like everything that is, should be.

David and I wander the beach and when we come across this odd grouping of twelve metal chairs, I'm still puffed with feeling. They're immovable and facing the water, a clear group without precision. The metal of their seats is cut into phrases—phrases that hold me in that part-of-it-all feeling the shoreline whirred to life.

This day ends no matter what.

He came early, she came late. So they met.

Some of them are in French.

I sprout goosebumps. Then spring into action, excitedly showing them off to every passerby.

Girls with straightened hair and shiny lip gloss holding Smirnoff Ices look at me expressionless. A long-haired hippie guy drapes his arm around my shoulder and we move chair to chair, him less interested in what I'm showing him than in me. A couple in their fifties crinkle their eyes into smiles, hold each other close.

I'm on fire.

This day ends no matter what. This day ends no matter what.

I feel it where I felt Soela, where I know who I am in a way I've always known. I feel it in the promise of that path to redemption, in knowing where to go and how to get there.

The couple in their fifties ask my name.

Twenty minutes later they're back, and they hand me a baggie of weed. The woman, still wrapped in her husband, looks at me with kind, crinkled, blue eyes. "We like you, Erin."

I'll always wonder whether they were the artists behind the chairs, thanking me. Seeing me. Seeing me seeing them.

Years later, another stranger—a customer at the restaurant I'll work at—a woman with smooth, brown, old-soul eyes and a daughter named Crow will tell me she sees so much light in me. And that it's blocked by so much darkness.

I'm standing at the fork, 2002 nearly swallowed into 2003 like the last gulp of the moon's crescent during an eclipse. I take one tentative step down the wrong path. And then another. Then another.

∩

Danny holds out his hand with five pale red pills, each stamped with a mini-crown. David and I glance at each other. E. Ecstasy. "Take it," he says, his scratchy voice encouraging. "It makes you feel really good."

From Danny's, we sling on our jackets and toques and trek to the Pit. It's dark and lightly raining; we haul wood pallets for firewood. Before leaving the basement suite, I call Twyla, who's with PamAndNancy and Misha. "We'll meet you guys," she says. It's around suppertime Thursday night. I carry a mickey of Crown and my pack of Benson & Hedges in my hoodie pockets, my hands competing for space. At the pit, Danny and Grey build up the fire while the rest of us watch. I light a cigarette to counter the pang in my stomach. It's been thirty minutes since swallowing the pill and I'm not feeling it, I think. Though, when I tune in closer, my body feels light.

From above, branches crack and leaves swish, and shadows move across the wall opposite to where I sit. I look up and on top of the path down, Twyla is lit orange by the fire, a twelve-pack of Budweiser in her gloved hands. My body feels good—I notice that now. My nervousness is gone, my stomach neutral. Twyla forges her way down the steep mud staircase and PamAndNancy and Misha all materialize behind her, all lit orange as well.

"It looks so good down here!" Twyla steadies her body on a tree branch and pulls herself closer to the fire. It's her first time at the Pit. We smile genuine smiles at each other and I push myself up to give her a long hug.

The other three, usually I'm nervous around. Quiet. Now, I look them in the eyes, nod and smile easily. "Welcome to our humble abode," I say dramatically, and, for once, I keep up the small talk.

By this time, I feel like I'm beaming positive energy, wide awake and warm and revved to life. The fire crackles in my peripheral vision and nine smiling faces watch me. The brambles normally between my brain and what I say are cut down and cleared away. I'm on fire. I tour them around like a realtor.

"The water from this little waterfall here is actually being piped right under our feet." They look to the ground. I extend my arm and point past the fire and into the darkness of the other side. "It comes out there." Their heads follow my hand and I feel more like a leader than I ever have.

"This is amazing," says Pam, looking around.

"Oh! Wait until you see up here!" I lead them back toward the fire, its warmth a breath, then up—quickly, effortlessly—to the top of the gully. I'm connected to everything around me. Meant for all this. They follow me, though slower, more careful. "This is the bridge." Gauging their faces, their flickering orange faces, I offer assurances. "Oh, it's as stable as can be. Really… finely engineered." I nod and look at each set of eyes wryly and they all laugh and follow me across.

On fire.

"Thor's Blazing Hut, I present to you."

"Oh, Thor," says Twyla.

"Light 'er up," says Nancy, and Misha rummages in her purse and pulls out a fat joint.

Danny and David and the rest of the group are murmuring around the fire, nearly inaudible. Inside, I round a corner.

"You know what? I know I'm so quiet all the time."

This grasps their attention and all eyes, once again, are on me.

"It's just that sometimes my mind literally goes blank. I just literally don't know what to say. But hanging out with you guys, like, hanging out with you guys has been so great. Even if I don't say much."

I feign bashfulness, but I'm not bashful. Not now.

"Aww!" Nancy reaches in and gives me a quick gangly hug. "Erin, you're awesome."

I feel like the person I am inside. Like the burdensome layers of shyness, of nervousness, of self-consciousness are gone and shrunken Little Me inside has suddenly grown to normal size. I can say anything to anyone, and I do. I talk and I talk and share everything normally kept behind closed doors.

"I love you guys, you know," I tell Danny, Grey, Delia and Elise later on. David too, but he knows. We're in a circle, around the fire. "It's just crazy—I feel like you guys really 'get' me, and I haven't had that before. Like I don't have to say anything. You guys just know."

"We love you too, man." Grey reaches his arm long enough to touch my shoulder.

"Yeah, our group is perfect. I feel the same way," Elise says. Danny just smiles his big smile and Delia stares into the orange glow, thoughtful and slack-faced.

"I do want to talk more, though. This is great actually," I say and laugh.

David stands up and wraps his arms around my shoulders from behind.

"Love you, Chud," I say, genuinely using the pet name I developed for him that probably began as a joke; he squeezes me.

The fire is crisp and beautiful and the cool air on my back and sudden soft rain make me feel one with everything on the earth, in the universe. The high lasts for hours and by the time I walk home, appreciating everything, feeling love bursting out my chest, I know I've stumbled on something special; I know who I can be, which means I can't continue being who I was. It's like the song "Mayonaise": *I just want to be me... when I can, I will.* For me, it's now. I've found it: everything I need in a surprising, tiny, pretty little pill.

The next day isn't even horrible. Later on, when my new "normal" fully develops, somebody will tell me words no lover of the good times ever wants to hear: "However great you feel when high, that's how bad you'll feel when you come down."

But the next day, that doesn't feel true. My head feels scrambled; I feel what I'd call sketchy, but overall it's not nearly as bad as a shitty hangover that has me throwing up with a splitting headache all day. In fact, it's kind of fun. Sketchy, but fun.

The emotional implications, though, had already taken hold, like a virus in my bloodstream, as easily as touching a railing, then touching my mouth.

15

It rains all the time, but January feels particularly cruel. It rains and it's a wet cold and it's always dim, except when it's dark. Yet, I start my second semester optimistic. With my bright red backpack still new, my unchewed pens, my binders neatly filled with lined sheets of paper. Hundreds of blank slates. I find both my classes and sit there studiously before the bell goes off. Two classes, two days a week, a couple of hours at a time. I can handle that, I tell myself.

Work hard, party hard.

Then, cocaine. It's easy—surprisingly easy. Like something you've put off forever because you didn't know how to really do it, but when you finally do, you shake your head at yourself for thinking it would be anything but. Easy. As easy as standing in that same circle with the same people. As easy as reaching my hand out when the rolled twenty-dollar bill gets passed my way. As easy as putting one end to my nose and the other to the CD case. As easy as breathing in.

Unlike with ecstasy, my chest isn't the conduit for all the love on earth. But its gnarly mess of nerves is gone. I'm alert.

Misha grabs my arm with both of hers. "I want to talk to you for a minute," she says.

I wonder, is this how people feel most of the time? Like, they don't worry how their arms hang off their bodies? No inner brakes, no overthinking, just—themselves?

I follow Misha into a corner of the living room. Tattoo guy is sitting near us, in the same chair where he talked to me last time. A line of Christmas lights dangles from the middle of the curtain rod and reflects in the window. All the knick-knacks match the grey carpet. She lights a cigarette and smiles a big gummy smile at me, sweetly. Genuinely sweetly.

"Twyla told me about you," she says.

I look hard at her. Fucking Twyla can never keep a secret.

"Don't be mad at her. I just want to tell you it's okay."

My face softens. Tattoo guy looks out of it. I can see my reflection, vaguely, in the window. Pink lips, not ugly. I don't say anything and Misha continues.

"You know, I've kissed Pam many times."

I look at her with surprise. Is she a lesbian? Could I love her?

"The thing is, it didn't mean anything, you know? The difference with you," she says, looking deep into my eyes, "the difference with you is that it means something."

I'm cradled, softly, like she's whispering against my cold cheek with warm breath, "It's okay."

⌒

Then, the cusp between winter and spring—cold and rainy, speckled with flowers. On school days, I grab a medium dark roast from Java Hut and crack all the windows of SuperBeast to keep it from fogging up, slowing down through the massive puddles along the way. I absorb everything I learn in school, particularly philosophy, and carry that intellectual bent to the concrete patio outside Danny's basement, where, rather than huddling over textbooks at home, I spend most nights.

"Don't you guys see it?" I'm buzzing, standing up with a cigarette between my fingers, the rest of them in a semicircle on the concrete. The high of ecstasy like an uninhibited scream coursing through me. "So we're in the womb and we have everything we need. Like, we're not hungry. We're not cold. Everything just comes to us. Everything just *is*."

Five sets of eyes, captive. I'm talking fast and I consciously slow my voice, like how my philosophy professor gets his points across in these slow, silky statements like ribbons as he paces the auditorium.

"We are all created within a dependency. But then we're born, and we suddenly want and need. The world is bright and fast and scary and loud and we're crying because nothing is how it's ever been. And then…"

Grey brushes his hair away from his left eye and looks up at me, a gangly cherub.

I lose a bit of momentum as this deep sadness laps me into its ocean.

"And then. We're left searching for that place where we're warm and comforted—actually at peace—forever."

I pause again. Delia hangs her head. Elise lights a cigarette.

"Some turn to Jesus, some turn to heroin. It's a Joni Mitchell lyric."

Grey looks up at me, his black hair like curtains over his face.

"I love you man," he says.

That night, I go to bed feeling full, like I suddenly see a truth that's had me invisibly wrapped up my entire life. The feeling, real. It has to be. But my binders and textbooks still sit unopened in the corner, and the ecstasy still courses through my body.

16

Warmer days are coming around more often when the first of three bad things happens. I'm still holding on to school, but with an ever-loosening grip. When I am sober, Soela's on my mind, saturated with guilt that I let it seep into my bloodstream. I deserve to think about it. About her. It pulls my insides into this hard, impenetrable tree knot, a quid pro quo for what I did. For being the sinister stranger lurking in the shadows.

E cradles me. It's complicated, sure. But it cradles me and holds me in a place where shame can't, won't seep in. I'm just present and observant and, well, me.

It's Saturday night when our new friend Brooklyn shepherds us to a party she knows about in Delta, another suburb of Vancouver, uncomfortably far from our neighbourhood. Fraser Heights shelters us with its big houses and granite countertops and pristine landscaping and professional parents. Ecstasy is pretty, unlike crack and crystal meth. Brooklyn lives in a dilapidated house surrounded by dilapidated houses in Whalley, the part of Surrey that gives it its infamous reputation for drugs, gangs and poverty.

"I'm so happy I met you guys," she tells our group when we do E together. "You keep me from doing shitty drugs."

Cynthia drives David's car packed with the four of us, plus another couple of guys from a larger group of Fraser Heights acquaintances who come around sometimes on Saturday nights. Brooklyn puts a fuzzy pink cowgirl hat on my head and touches my cheek and chin. I don't love-her like her, but I could, maybe. It's the weekend, so we each pop a cap and a half of ecstasy and pack mickeys of Bacardi and Crown Royal.

I don't know how long we're at the party—looking back on it, my memories come in clips. Brooklyn and one of the guys fucking against a kitchen wall. David smoking in hurried drags outside around a circle of strangers. Cynthia sitting captain-like with the collar of her jacket touching her chin on a couch, talking to whoever sits near her. Brooklyn and the other guy on the hallway floor. The house is dusty, brown, unkempt and full of strangers—boring strangers, drunk and loud. I'm high but uncomfortable and just can't find my groove. I sit against a wall, resigned and not caring. It could have been a minute later or an hour later when Brooklyn approaches me jingling a set of keys. I focus first on them, then her face.

"Let's go for a drive," she says.

My gaze focusses and blurs on her face and focusses again, my mind not piecing something together.

"David gave me his keys."

My brain is scrambled with ecstasy and booze and heavy with an evening that feels off. I should question her further, but I don't. "Yeah. Sure," I say instead and pull myself up. In the living room I see David sleeping on the couch. Brooklyn grabs the pink cowboy hat off the corner of the couch and puts it back on my head, crooked. I get into the passenger seat and take it off, put it on my lap. I'm a dream version of myself, lulled along like an indifferent Eeyore. Whyyyyy not. Ohhhhh bother. It. Doesn't. Matter.

"Do you know how to drive?" I say to Brooklyn.

"Oh, yeah, of course."

She's perky and alert—the opposite of me.

She pulls away from the house, the first hints of daylight turning the darkness away. I roll down the window and light a cigarette, laugh a bit. The cold air feels good and so does moving fast. It's that secret time of day when the partiers are done for the night and the morning people are still sleeping. The streets are quiet and deserted and the light's getting softer every minute, pink and gentle, and I'm coming down and feeling reflective watching the houses blur one by one. Where we are, what time it is, I'm not thinking about. Only the shade of the sky hints at time passed. Once we see our first car, though, I'm nudged back into reality.

I look over at Brooklyn, who's driving fast. Who lets the steering wheel turn itself back when she turns corners, I notice. A first pang of nervousness. We've been in our own worlds, not talking, for—how long? Hours? Minutes? It's lighter now; there are more cars.

"We should go back," I tell her.

She exhales. "I've been trying. I can't find the house."

I feel for my phone in my jeans pocket and pull it out, dial David. It rings forever with no answer.

"Fuck."

I look around and we could be in any neighbourhood, anywhere. We're in Delta, aren't we? I don't know Delta at all. I was in the back seat making out with Brooklyn when we drove to the party. The only thing I noticed was David's hurt eyes in the rear-view mirror. I feel sick about it now. I try David again, then Cynthia, then the one guy whose number I have. Nobody picks up.

"Fuck!"

We're in Delta or Newton and I have no idea how long we've been on the road or where we've been. Brooklyn is laughing and I want to punch her. She takes her hands off the wheel to light another cigarette and looks like she doesn't give a fuck about anything.

"Get to a main street," I tell her. "I'll recognize something."

She pulls out of a neighbourhood and I recognize Seventy-Second Street. I'd know how to get back to Fraser Heights.

"Turn around; I know where we are," I say.

Brooklyn turns abruptly into a car wash, but this time her turn doesn't recover itself and we smash hard into a fence. My body lurches forward, stopped abruptly by the seat belt.

"Fuck!"

I swing out of the car and around to the front. The entire front end is a gruesome tangle of silver metal. I rush around to the driver's door and open it. Brooklyn is laughing, doubled over the steering wheel, and looks up at me with tears in her eyes like somebody just told her the funniest joke, like why am I not laughing?

"Get out. I'm driving."

A man wanders out of a business kiosk across the parking lot and is heading toward us.

"Get out!"

She complies and gets into the passenger seat. The car is still on and I drive away, heading toward Fraser Heights. We don't speak until my phone rings and it's David. "Where are you?"

"Where are *you*? I've called you like twenty times! We went for a drive and couldn't find the house again and I couldn't get hold of you!"

"What do you mean you went for a drive? Why the fuck would you take my car?"

I glance at Brooklyn who's looking out the window. I know what I knew. My voice drops. "I thought you gave Brooklyn your keys."

"Yeah. To get Crown out of the trunk."

I shake my head. His voice is saturated with anger and I haven't even told him the worst of it. "Fuck, David, we got into an accident."

A painful pause.

"What happened?"

Procrastinating on the things you have to say just prolongs the pain and I'm as weary as a seal swimming hard all day for food and I just want to get onto a rock, off the road, out from behind the wheel.

"The front of your car is smashed in. We hit a fence."

Another painful, painful pause.

"Where are you?" His voice is cold. I'm retreating into myself, trying to focus on the road. Brooklyn hasn't turned from the window.

"Just driving up King George, near Gateway," I say quietly. It's fully light now and there are cars all over.

"I'll just meet you at Soo's Grocer," he says. "We'll go there right now."

"Soo's Grocer?" Soo's Grocer is on the cusp of Whalley and Guildford—far from Delta, close to Fraser Heights. "How did you get *there*?"

"What the hell are you talking about?"

"We were in Delta. How did you get to Whalley?"

"Are you fucking kidding me? We left Delta at like 2:00 a.m. How do you not remember that?"

As soon as he says it, I remember.

"We'll be there in like five," I tell David, and he hangs up.

"Did you know that?" I say to Brooklyn. "That we started in Whalley?"

"I don't know," she says nonchalantly, without turning her neck. I look at the side of her head—her dark hair—think about her on the dirty floor, against the wall. Her hair is greasy and I hate her. I despise her. Probably I despise me, but sometimes it's just less labour to project.

As we pull up at Soo's Grocer, David's face says it all. I watch him staring at his crunched silver Hyundai, flanked by Cynthia and the two guys. I get out as David lights a cigarette with tears brimming in his eyes. He inhales quickly, frantically, dramatically.

"David, I'm so, so, so, so sorry." I'm crying too.

He walks around the vehicle without looking at me. Brooklyn gets out.

"Sorry, Dave," she says, still not sounding like she gives a fuck. "I can walk home from here."

She turns and walks away, not looking back.

David looks at me.

"I'll give you a ride," he says.

⌒

The next two bad things that happen reshape my world. Like I walk through a door and it disappears behind me. So I walk through another door. And that one disappears too. As if my life since graduating high school is a maze of doors that just keep disappearing behind me. That I keep walking through.

⌒

I get my final grades first. The notice of expulsion next. I hand it to my mom in the kitchen, the gurgle and putt of coffee brewing, she in her bathrobe. She looks at me, the morning light accenting the creases in her face. The darkness below her eyes.

"Didn't make it, huh?"

She's not surprised. I'm not surprised.

"I guess I just wasn't ready," I tell her, a marble of indignation rolling down my spine.

Maybe to her it seems like I just took a giant white erasure to my future, furiously pushing back and forth and then blowing the black specks remaining away with an aggressive breath. Poof. Be gone.

To me, it just means I can relax. I can stop worrying about failing school because I failed school. I can stop putting five dollars in SuperBeast to drive to Burnaby to smoke on campus steps. There are things to look forward to. Like the big Pit party planned for the weekend. Like my nineteenth birthday next month. I tell myself I'm really living. Door closed.

⌒

Not long after that, on a sunny spring day, just before 1:00 p.m. and after I'd hung up my apron for the day, I join Twyla and Misha outside Java Hut. I'd barely taken a bite of the sandwich I'm splitting with Twyla when Cue Ball passes by and comes to a jolting stop.

"You need to leave," he tells Misha, who's smoking a cigarette, with no food in front of her.

"Why?" she asks in a tone that oozes, *You're fucking ridiculous.*

"Did you buy anything?"

"We're sharing," I say, just as snottily. "I just got off work."

"Not good enough," he says, chest puffed. "You're loitering. Leave now."

"No," Misha says.

"Leave now or I'll have you removed from the property."

He moves toward the table, his sunglasses protecting whatever his eyes might be saying, his body language disguising any apprehension.

"No, this is ridiculous!"

"I'm going to count to ten."

Misha bursts out laughing. "Okay, Jesus Christ. I'm phoning my mom."

She gets up and puts a quarter into the adjacent pay phone, punching in seven numbers. Before it has a chance to ring, Cue Ball and his crony approach her and grab her, one on each side. They pull her, struggling and yelling, to the entrance of Windsor Security, push open the glass door and drag her up the stairs.

"What the fuck!" I say to Twyla, whose face says it all. She runs over to the dangling phone. Misha's mom is on the line. Within five minutes she's in the parking lot and out of her car, her face shiny red, her body stiff.

"Where'd they take her?"

We follow her upstairs and wait while Misha's mom pushes her way into the firm. The crony comes out a minute later. "You two need to come in here."

In the boardroom with no windows with dull white walls and dull grey carpet and a dull blue speckled table, they push a sheet of paper in front of us both. On my sheet, my name. On its header, "Property Ban." The property is the entire central plaza on both sides of the road—the gas station and the grocery store, Java Hut and Quiznos and the bank and Tim Hortons. Banned from everything. For a year.

I scan down to a section that reads "Reason for Ban." Underneath, a line with no writing.

"What the hell is this? Why would we be banned?"

I'm in as much disbelief as I am swirling with red guttural anger.

Cue Ball, whose eyes are now exposed and void of anything resembling compassion, is silent. Just his crony speaks. "We are an agent of the landlord and we have the authority to ban whomever we deem fit for such a ban."

"Yeah, okay, why am I deemed fit for such a ban?"

"I just said, we have the authority to ban you."

We're going around in circles.

"I work at Java Hut. I have to go to work!" It's like I have a boa constrictor around my neck. But I still feel like I can fight it off.

"If you're banned from the property, you can't work on the property."

"What the *fuck*!" says Twyla.

We're both starting to lose it and the suits are keeping their cool. Misha's mom senses the dynamic. "We should go for now girls," she says softly.

"This is bullshit," I say as I get up, clanging my chair. "I'm *not* banned."

My boss is confused and assures me everything will be fine. But later he calls apologetically. Tells me to not come into work.

The next day, I go to Java Hut anyway. I order a coffee and sit at a table outside, the sheet placed square on the table in front of me. Within minutes, Cue Ball is there, telling me to leave.

"I'm not leaving until you tell me why I'm banned."

"If you don't leave I'm going to call the police and they'll remove you."

I'm calm; I don't raise my voice. I don't get excited and I refuse to cry. I sit there, matter-of-fact, responding to everything he says with my simple demand.

Sometimes, there's an internal click that allows me to swallow external chaos and present stoically. Like on one of our summer vacations I left Whitey, my favourite stuffed animal—a white kitten with blue eyes—on a remote beach of kid-fist-sized stones, warm on our bare feet, threatening to our ankles. After an hour or two, we walk the path back to our orange Volkswagen and drive the gravel road that got us there. It can't be more than twenty minutes later when I realize I left Whitey on the beach. I imagine her alone on the log I left her on, on the deserted beach. Wondering where we went. Wondering if we'd come back. The tears behind my eyes and in my chest, though, I stuff down. I stuff them down into my gut, the tension of this like pushing down a French press. Down into my depths. Stoic in the face of chaos.

"Just tell me why I'm banned."

Cue Ball calls the police and soon a constable with a mix of pretty and hard features looms above me.

"Can I just show you this, please?" I'm speaking politely, sure she'll acknowledge the injustice. Sure she'll help me.

"Just come over here," she says, motioning to the adjacent parking lot. I comply, collecting my paper and leaving my coffee, which has cooled anyway. I explain everything to her. What happened the day before. That I work at Java Hut. I show her the paper.

"Look! It says nothing under 'Reasons for Ban.'" I sigh and lean back against a parked car. She'd turned her gaze to the sheet but shifts it abruptly and explodes into aggression.

"Don't lean against that car," she spits, then lunges and grabs me. In a single motion she pushes me to the ground, stomach down on the asphalt.

"What the fuck!" I yell, stunned.

She presses her knee into my back and handcuffs me, still on the ground. Pulls me up to my feet, my arms behind my back. I'm a rag doll through the wash and she stuffs me into the back seat of her car. Maybe she has something to prove. Maybe I have a black mark on my record. But as we cross the bridge out of Fraser Heights, it starts to hit me. That I won't go back to work. That I won't hang out with friends. No Melinda. No pushing coffee across the counter to pretty goth girls with forget-me-not eyes. No laughter and smoking cigarettes, no buying cigarettes, no munchies from the grocery store, no sitting beside Tim Hortons. By the time we get to the police station I feel like I've been socked in the gut by someone I love. They lock me in a tiny white room and take my mug shot and press my fingers in ink. Eventually, they let me go. And another door disappears behind me.

17

I pick up odd jobs as an extra in Vancouver's bustling movie scene, which keeps the money at least incrementally rolling in. And it keeps my parents off my back. The work's easy. Play a part, do what we're told, put on costumes, be somebody else.

Like how there are two types of people in the world: Those whose insides match their outsides; like what you see is what you get, what they say is so clearly also what they think. And those whose insides are a mystery—the ones I'm drawn to, the ones who can be maddening; also my category, though I want my insides to match my outsides. But I cower at the response of the world.

Working as an extra is like putting on disguises: dress like paupers, let them spray our hair into beehives, cheer, boo, dance, let them brush foundation across our necks. Sometimes shoots last late into the night, which fattens the paycheque I pick up in downtown Vancouver the following week.

By the time my nineteenth birthday rolls around at the end of May, I'm doing ecstasy four times a week. The small, chalk-like pills always feel a bit different, depending on what they're cut with. They're also different colours and have various prints like stars, roosters, eyeballs, lightning bolts. And various names like red rooster, red star, white rhino, green dragon. With how pretty and fun they are, it's easy to be swayed.

For my birthday I decide on a Pit party and write a long list of friends and loose acquaintances I want there. Most of them show. I pick up a mickey of Crown Royal and a brand new pack of Benson & Hedges Gold tall cigarettes and pop a cap and a half of buzzy red rooster E. I wear my jaggedly ripped short jean skirt and black hoodie and start out happy and unconstrained. Things can only get better.

David and I show up early. The sky's dim, but crunching through the forest, our way is still illuminated. We get to the top of the Pit, and I pull myself down the steep embankment by clasping my palms around aspens. It's darker here; I look around and notice a large square of plywood propped against Thor's Blazing Hut on the opposite side of the ravine. On it is a huge green spray-painted pot leaf with the words "Happy 19th Birthday, Erin!" At the bottom of the ravine, Danny's on his knees blowing at a collection of newspapers and sticks that's sending smoke in a swerving line up into the sky.

David rubs my shoulder and carefully pulls out the tissue from his smallest jean pocket with our ecstasy. He kisses my cheek and hands me my share, our extra half cap already sliced down the middle. I put it in my mouth, a peck of tang on my tongue, and swallow it with a swig of Crown, wincing at its brashness.

"Happy birthday to me," I say with a laugh, excitement revving in me.

As the dark corners of the Pit elongate, as the sky moves from pink to grey to blue to black, as the stars dot the sky and the fire grows more crisp, the crowd thickens. More bodies shadow the ravine, more faces lit orange by fire. More laughter, more buzz. I meet strangers and see friends. It's my birthday and I'm nineteen.

And then, Ava.

I meet her as the ultra-confident version of myself that ecstasy welcomes into existence. I'm happy and it's dark and I'm still working on that mickey when I climb to the top of the ravine and cross the bridge to Thor's Blazing Hut. I nestle the bottle into the ground and light a cigarette. I know if I'd seen her before, I'd remember. And not just because of how she looks—dyed black, chin-length hair, a lip ring on each side of her bottom lip, wide-set eyes like an anime character. My stomach pangs. I'd remember how I feel before fully assessing what it is I'm feeling. Like how it was with Soela. But more intense? The kind of instant magnetism that makes me shake my head at every old crush, every "the One," every "perfect for me, couldn't want anything else." That thing that happens sometimes that makes me wonder about swirling energies. About all those things that *are* us and are all around us that we feel—we feel viscerally—but can't put our thumbs on, pin down, write in a textbook. It's that feeling I remember. It's the end of the runway; it's liftoff.

She's sharing a joint with Alek. In hindsight, that's the first glimpse of a red flag far from my flight path, barely discernible. Blended in with the red hearts popping everywhere. The light from the fire barely reaches the hut and her eyelids hang low like she's stoned. But I can tell her eyes are blue-green.

"Like the ocean," I'll later whisper into her messy morning hair.

She looks at me for the first time, smiling. "That's a really long cigarette." She kind of laughs it out and when she turns her body fully toward me, I notice a rainbow on the front of her hoodie. I'm beaming and hitch on to her laughter, elated.

"I know. It's my birthday and I wanted to do something special."

Alek hands her the joint and instead of taking a toke, she hands it to me, meeting my eyes again. I somersault from a place of cozy contentment to one with energies so entrenching I am pure colour. I am vibrance.

"Happy birthday," she says, and I take the joint from her. The tips of our fingertips touch like a jolt and our eyes meet again. I hold her gaze, the ecstasy doing its thing.

She asks how old I am, tells me she's eighteen.

Alek and the others—there are others in the hut—cease to exist. I take a long drag on the joint and blow the smoke upward. We stare at each other like we've both been waiting for this.

She tells me her name is Ava.

And there's no going back. From the first moment our eyes meet, from the first touch of even the most insignificant part of her body, I'm infatuated. I'm hers. I know nothing about her yet, but I present her my bloody beating heart in two red and sticky cupped hands, bowing down in surrender, take me, take me, take me. I don't know, at the time, how long I can hang on to the tiniest star of hope in a black sky with no gravity, but soon I'll learn. Eventually, this skill? This stubbornness? This madness? Eventually this will serve me well. But with Ava, I won't walk away. I can't walk away.

☾

It's not long after my nineteenth birthday party that I'm nervous in my drive-way, chain-smoking and practising keeping my shoulders straight and square for Ava's arrival. It's around 10:00 p.m. and dark. To my delight, she lives just ten minutes away. She rounds the corner and just as the cymbals inside me start their clamour, a black Oldsmobile pauses parallel to the house and my brother gets out of the back seat.

"Hey," he says with a buttering-me-up tone, the whites of his eyes tinged red. "Can I use your car?"

I bristle and try to greet Ava by turning to her apologetically while jug-gling this unexpected hitch. "I'm literally just about to go somewhere. I need it."

Ava's silent and my brother doesn't acknowledge her.

"Please? I won't be gone long and I have a bunch of acid I can give you as a trade."

"What do you mean a bunch of acid?"

He pulls out what looks like a sheet of thick paper, with perforated lines making about one-inch-by-one-inch squares, and hands it to me. It looks noth-ing like any acid I've ever seen.

"Acid?" Ava has a gigantic smile on her face. "Sure!"

Bobby half turns toward her and smiles.

I crumple for her for the first time, hand him the keys. "How long are you going to be?"

"Not long, like thirty minutes or an hour max."

Ava and I walk a few houses down to where a path bridges the sidewalk and alley and sit on the curb, our bodies close enough for electricity to move between them, but not touching. I talk about the Smashing Pumpkins at first, then about how I used to date David. I tell her about Melinda and that my family doesn't know I'm bisexual.

"Do you think they'd care?"

I tell her about watching *ER* with my parents not long before. About how Kerry, the lesbian on the show, kissed another woman, how they turned away, how one of them said, "Why do they have to show that?" Words like little daggers.

"I've never been with a girl," said Ava. She leans her body into mine and I press back and have a feeling this might be the best night of my life.

"Do you feel anything yet?" she asks.

It's been at least an hour, if not two, since we pressed what's probably just paper under our tongues. No brother, no high.

"Nope. You?"

"I feel something."

I look at her and she looks at me and leans in. She'll have this way of saying these tied-up-with-a-bow phrases that just make me shatter and come together stronger in the same single second. I lean forward and she does too, and we kiss. We kiss gently, we kiss fiercely—our tongues press together and we're down on the dewy grass, the weight of my body pressing against hers. I touch her face and kiss her neck and finally ask if she wants to just come inside. Fuck my car, Bobby can have it.

"I have candles," I tell her excitedly in my room, trying to keep my voice low and out of earshot from my sleeping parents across the stairwell.

I light a slew of tea lights on my table, then change into my PJ pants and a T-shirt in the bathroom and brush my teeth. I'd been teetering on the edge of this world. Now I'm steady on the ground, transfixed by its swirling colours, its allure, its comfort. I dip from my knees and then spring into the most graceful swan dive, like it's the most natural thing in the world, like I can anticipate my landing. Back in my room, I press play on the Smashing Pumpkins' *Mellon Collie and the Infinite Sadness* album and squish into my single bed with Ava as the title piano track bleeds into "Tonight, Tonight."

She takes off her glasses and I look into her eyes and kiss her face and the dip below her throat, the centre of her collarbone, and she smiles and stretches out her body. I pull at her shirt and she wriggles out of it, candlelight illuminating her smooth, perfect skin orange. I kiss her stomach, her hip bones and slowly up her torso. It feels familiar, like some ingrained instinct in me is guiding my hands, my mouth—no overthinking. No worrying about doing something wrong. She's pushing up her hips, stretching her arms above her head. Lust blooms in me a field of wildflowers, a door finally unlocked, and me, slinking through it, soft skin, petals, black bra strap slipped down a shoulder. I push my fingers up her bicep, pressing down with my fingertips, tiny wells of shadow in the orange glow. Press my body against hers. We're wrapped in each other, moving together, heat on heat, tongues, lips. Her hands move toward the band of my PJ pants, but I have my period and am wearing a pad so I gently interlock my fingers over hers and pull them away. We're gentle and we're fierce, our breath audible in our throats, faster, louder, and I want it all and I have it all. We lie there, after, intertwined and quiet, and finally Billy Corgan sings "Farewell and Goodnight" and the candles flicker out and turn the room dark and we fall asleep.

I wake up feeling like I'm on ecstasy—my entire body is warm and comfortable and there's no nervousness, just calm peace. My face is nuzzled into Ava's neck and she's breathing in that rhythmic way that signals sleep. I shift my body and she opens her eyes into a smile and a stretch. I smile back at her and kiss her cheek, hold my lips there.

"Good morning," she says mid-stretch, emphasizing the "good."

I notice there's a slight gap between her front teeth. I kiss both sides of her chin, warmness embracing everything. "Hi."

We kiss again and I'm happy. She long-yawns and stretches again. "Did your brother bring your car back?"

"Shit!"

I move to get up, to look out the window, but she pulls me to her and I don't resist. She kisses me deeply again on the mouth and then my cheeks, then along my jawline.

"I have to get up," she says.

SuperBeast is in its usual spot, parked at a slight diagonal. Ava's up and scouring for something. Then, I notice. I notice like I'm about to peacefully fall asleep and a sudden drop startles me awake. On the thigh of her dark green corduroy pants is a four-inch-thick vertical blood stain. My period. Immediately my insides clench away the warmness. And then the doorbell rings. My parents are at work and Bobby must be sleeping, so I pull on my T-shirt and new pants and run downstairs. It's David and Alek. Lunch hour at Fraser Heights High School.

"What are you doing? Want a smoke?"

In me, horror wrestles with elation. But I bound up the stairs and try to read her face.

"Alek and David are here."

"Really?" She sounds excited. Like she's somehow not disgusted with me. Or she hasn't noticed. Or there's something about Alek for her. Though that last thought doesn't actually occur to me.

I watch Alek's and David's faces when Ava follows me outside. They both look surprised. Alek's eyes hide behind the two pink furls of hair that droop down both sides of his face. But still, they dart between Ava, me and the ground. David's no longer jovial and puffs his cigarette in the telltale spurts that say he's going over something in his mind.

"We did acid last night," Ava tells them. She seems immune to the air of weirdness.

"Oh, yeah?" Alek shifts his weight from leg to leg and looks at the ground between cigarette puffs. Something's off, but I can't quite place it. It hitches on to my nosediving sense of how perfect everything felt when I first opened my eyes.

"Yeah, but it didn't seem to work. Right, Erin?"

I'm staring at my blood on her thigh. She pushes the side of her body into mine, which cradles me out of the blacks and greys. She doesn't mention it. She never mentions it. Alek and David don't mention it, ever.

"Yeah, I don't even know if it was really acid. It was on, like, perforated paper."

I push my body back.

"Perforated?" Alek says, coolly. But I don't even care. The perpetual roller coaster of my emotions is going upward and I can see nothing but blue sky and feel the warmth of sunlight on my face. The excited tic-tic-tic-tic-tic of an upward journey. I linger there. Ignore the promise of a fall.

David's still tight and quiet. He blots his cigarette like he's angry at the cobblestone. "We're going to Java to blaze. Want to come?"

I have to work on the set of *Scooby-Doo 2* at four. I say "I can't" at the same time Ava says "Yeah!" We embrace goodbye, a hot make-out session on the private side of the door, and she leaves. I have an hour before I have to get ready so I crawl back in bed and hold my pillow with closed eyes. Reliving the best night of my life, so far.

18

Twyla and I are lounging in her backyard at a dirty white plastic table early afternoon on a weekday. I want to be anywhere else but have nowhere else to be. She's a few provincial exams away from the end of high school and is going on about people I barely know.

"Yeah and Elliot got a new girlfriend. She's so pretty. And Misha got a boyfriend and they're going on a double date!"

I look at Twyla, who seems genuinely happy. Months before, I thought Elliot looked like Billy Corgan, thought I had a crush on him. That seems like so long ago now—and laughable that I thought I knew what a crush was. I'm restless and anxious and haven't smoked pot all day. "Do you have any weed?"

"I have some roaches," Twyla says, getting up and pushing open the sliding glass door. Sitting quietly with myself, the restlessness pushes me up. I open my pack of Benson & Hedges. Only two. A grey blandness fills my insides and the world is monochrome. The backyard's ugly with patchy grass and dog shit land mines all over the place. The fence is faded salmon with curled-up paint. I light my second-to-last cigarette and all I smell is dog shit. I check my shoes. When I have money, the last cigarette of a pack isn't ever the last cigarette. I never wait until afternoon to get stoned. And I don't have to strategize about how to get money. My parents stopped leaving their wallets lying around for me to slip out twenties when desperate. The cheques coming in from movies are sporadic and the money goes too quickly. Why am I so goddamn unhappy? It's like I'm unable to smooth out a corner of a sticker that's lost stickiness. I press and I press and I try to smooth it down, make it stay, fix it, but I can't. It's this black hole inside me. If I just feed it, it'll stop its pull. But I know, believe, on the level that houses uncomfortable truths, it will always pull. I know its nature is to want and when it gets, it just keeps wanting. More. More. More. Would it always be drugs? Pot and ecstasy? But if I need drugs to be happy, am I actually even happy? And what the fuck is happiness, anyway?

My mind turns to Ava. Her eyes closed and her candlelit neck craned for my open lips. Her hot sighing. The pull of that, too. The glass door opens and

Twyla shows me her palm, which cups half a dozen roaches. She holds her glass pipe in the other hand.

"Merry Christmas," she says and pulls out a chair to sit down.

I smile easily for the first time all day and already feel relief from my restlessness, relief from the heaviness of those big questions. "Sweet."

She stuffs the pipe and we get stoned and suddenly the curled paint doesn't matter, the mediocre landscaping.

⌒

I had boarded a ship with a giant heart on its flag. One that sails smooth waters in warm, inviting air. But that ship, it doesn't actually exist. And I find, at the most inopportune time, the ship is in fact a raggedy vessel with holes in its stern so subtle, they've gone unnoticed for far too long. And it's about to sail, unavoidably, into a storm.

Ava disappears from me for a solid week after she walked up to the corner with Alek and David, and I can't figure it out. I try calling every day, but each time I get only an answering machine. And no matter how fucked up I get, I can't temper the uncomfortable nagging.

I'm at Danny's on a Wednesday night with the group and we've each popped a half cap. I feel its elation like I'm a bird tethered to a rock. We're slumped around the living room space, a subdued evening. Maybe there's a downer laced into this batch. I'm slumped inside myself, turning over thoughts about Ava.

"Hey, Erin, want to go have a session?" Elise is looking at me with big blue eyes, reminding me I'm here.

"Yeah, sure."

Maybe pot'll help. Another guy moves to get up as well, and Elise turns to him.

"I think I want to go with just Erin," she says, her words holding tingling electricity. I look at her. I really like Elise. She's smart and doesn't demand attention, but isn't meek like me. She says what she feels when she feels it. She pushes the glass door closed behind us. "I can tell you're feeling shitty. What's up, dude?" We both sit down, cross-legged.

"Ah, fuck. I feel myself wanting to feel better but there's just something stopping me. Did I tell you about Ava?"

She smiles. "You said you guys had an amazing night."

"We did, exactly! And now it just feels like she's gone. I don't know." I take a hoot from Elise's pipe and hold it in for a few moments before passing it back to her. It hits me like a pick-me-up, but the tugging doesn't relent. "It was like—the most passionate, amazing experience I've ever had." I shake my head and look down. "And now she's just gone. I don't get it. Like, if she doesn't want anything to do with me, I just wish she'd tell me. I keep going over everything in my head and going back and forth. Maybe she's just busy. She totally regrets everything. Or maybe she just likes hanging out with the group but doesn't want to be involved with me. It's just, ahh."

I shake my head again, and everything curls inward. My shoulders, my neck, my stomach inside my flesh and muscle and blood. I'm a beetle in defence mode, just an inward ball. I push my thumb hard along the scratchy cold concrete. Raise my eyes to Elise.

"You know what, Erin? If she doesn't want anything to do with you, she's an idiot." She speaks with so much authority it's jarring. Ava's not an idiot, I am. It's me who fucked up; I just can't figure out how. "You're such a cool person, you know?" Her tone softens. "You really are so smart and passionate and pretty. Like honestly, fuck her if she doesn't want you. Really, just fuck her."

"Well, that was the hope," I say with a wry smile, not sure how else to react. She gives me a hard look and a half smile.

"You know, I've thought about this before. I think you and I, we're really alike. I see so much of myself in you."

Within the same moment, a tinge of something more for Elise. A flash flood of warm feeling. I shake away the former. The latter, had I dug in and investigated, would help me see that there's power in vulnerability. In connecting in a way that lays a person out clearly stencilled, probably naked, definitely open. The feel-good drugs take me there, usually, but isn't what I really want, always, to connect? To be seen and accepted? Do I normally live hidden by thick grey storm clouds, afraid if anybody were to look, really look, they'd turn away with some form of disappointment?

My shyness is a blockade to speaking my truth, most of the time. Lined up at its indefinite stop are my true reactions to everything. Saying no. Sharing unpopular opinions. Telling people what they don't want to hear. Speaking before thinking. All these things that make me "me" are lined up, car after car after car. And for what? I use drugs to take down the blockade and get them moving. And yet, had I dug in, I'd see I could also just take down the blockade. I could also just hold my breath and spit it out. But I refuse to recognize that, at this point. Or maybe I'm just not ready to get off the ride.

19

How long do I broil inside before steam gives me away? Since Soela? Since I met Ava? Since I was a toddler who sucked her thumb for soft and soothing calmness? I'd been broiling inside maybe forever. Then the steam, then an explosion that changes my setting, my scene, that leaves me staring at a white wall.

The steam: "I'm not into drama."

I'm trying to piece together her words into something I understand. Ava's unwavering. We're standing awkwardly in my parents' driveway, at 11:00 a.m. on a Friday, my Golf and her rusty red hatchback beside each other. Inside, I'm divided into three. One part revels in the electricity between us. The other part tries to digest what she's telling me, which is nothing I want to hear. The third part is a tendril already reaching ahead to the night. A night I'd been planning for weeks, where I'm going to drink Kokanee beer and do coke-and-E. I let that third tendril grow like an overcompensating limb, weakening the others, giving this moment a destination.

I tell her I don't understand.

She tells me David's still in love with me.

The steam hisses.

"When I went up to the coffee shop with him, he told me everything. I'm just not into that. I don't want to come between people."

"Ava, really, you're not coming between anybody. There's nothing to come between! We're best friends, that's it!"

I shake my head, reach for her. She backs away. She'll always be backing away, and I'll always be reaching for her. I'll reach for her until that weakened limb shrivels up and dies and it turns into a phantom limb and still, I reach for her.

"I really want to be friends," she says. "Let's be friends."

I look at her sullenly, feeling shrunken and light and useless, a torn plastic bag. I don't want to be friends. I can't be friends with someone I want to hold, want to kiss, want to find the bottom of knowing. Someone I want to prop up and ooze within, want to stare at forever, want to memorize.

"Well, I definitely want you in my life," I say, instead of anything else.

My emotions leap from my body and cling to her like she's the last thing standing between life as I know it and the giant question mark of everything else. They cling to her as she turns away from me; as she gets into her car and closes the door; as she looks out her back window and backs up into the street; as she puts her car in drive and she disappears from sight. She doesn't turn to look back at me, and I just stand there, grey. A body, a mind, automatic movements. I sip my coffee and it's cold and it doesn't faze me. I think ahead to Kokanee and coke-and-E, its allure muted. My mind fizzles into a bleakness akin to a cold hot dog. But, automatic movements. I drive to David's. I try to channel enough passion for a confrontation, but that too fizzles into a shrug.

"Yeah, I told her that. It was impulsive," he tells me. "I know you like girls and I've sort of seen you with Melinda and Brooklyn but it just threw me off actually seeing her in the morning. Knowing you guys slept together."

A slight yank.

"But why would you tell her you're still in love with me? She doesn't want to see me, David."

"It was stupid. It was just what I was feeling in that moment and I was impulsive. I don't actually feel that way and I know we're broken up. I guess I was just jealous."

It's impossible to argue with honesty.

"Can you just tell her it's not true then, David? Can you tell her you don't actually care?"

"I guess. But do you really think that's the actual reason? If I like somebody, I like them. I wouldn't let a jealous ex come in between. Maybe it's an excuse."

I sigh and settle back into my blahs.

And maybe he's right, but I don't want to believe it. I sigh again. This time, when my mind reaches ahead to the night, a tremor. Kokanee and coke-and-E.

"Plus," David says, "you know Alek likes her."

I turn and look at him sharply. "He likes her?"

"That night when they met at the Pit, he asked her out and she said yes. I think they've even hung out."

Alek is fifteen—I'm sure she wouldn't actually go for him. I want to be sure. I decide, in the bubble of the moment, that I'm a better choice and I shake it off, focus on the tremor. Focus on the night. "So, Stryke's selling coke now, so that should work out easily."

"Can't wait," David says in a singsongy voice and nudges me. I can't help but smile.

And so Ava ping-pongs in my life and I'm always the paddle, always there to meet her, never missing a shot. Sometimes she doesn't return for weeks, and I stand there as my arm grows painful and then numb. And she does return, at least for a while, and then, again, she disappears. I live for the connection, its allure a beacon. If I could zoom out on my life and look at the anxiety woven into me, the smack of a high that never lasts, the stale anticipation every other moment, I'd tell myself to walk away. I'd tell myself the crack is but a spark that'll always fizzle before it makes fire, that it mimics a bonfire in a glorious illusion, but that it isn't, ever, real. If I could zoom out I'd tell myself that, but I'm not sure I'd listen. I'll walk away from pot, alcohol and cigarettes. I can put down ecstasy and cocaine, crystal meth and heroin. I'll scoff when they say, "Once an addict, always an addict." But give me a taste of forbidden love, show me an untameable wild heart, and I'll burn down my life for her. Again and again and again. They say addiction is the pursuit of something even when all indicators blare *stop*. So, do I take what I'll learn from walking away from all the things society says I shouldn't be able to walk away from and apply it to my most human corners where I feel most alive? Say, "You are heroin. You are crack. You are illusion." And saying it will break my heart into pieces, but it, too, will mend. Until next time. The crack of connection followed by the sucking void in which I wait.

◠

Ava and I are headed down a steep embankment in the dark, branches with wet leaves snapping as we go. We come to a stop where the ground juts out and nestle underneath a tree, bodies pressed against each other, the ecstasy and my love for her wild and rushing in me. Bigger than gravity, it feels. She's wearing glasses, as she does sporadically, and I pull them gently up from her eyes and touch her cheek gently with my fingers.

"I love you, Ava. I…"

I want to say more. Say everything. Give name to the supernova of white light bursting inside me. But she laughs and smiles and pulls me into a hug so brief, I crinkle for more.

"We should get back," she says.

I could have stayed there, with her, wet from the rain, dirty from the ground, on slippery sticks atop this awkwardly sloped hill, all night. I could stay like that and be happy, I tell myself. Would that prove true? That's another question. But I follow her back up, where Alek has his hands tucked into his pockets and David's on the phone with Stryke, the dealer, trying to get more ecstasy. His forehead is crinkled and his palms are up, asking why. He hangs up.

"What?" I ask him apprehensively, half knowing. I'd quietly graduated from getting ecstasy handed to me, to picking up when I had money, to devising ways to get high more often.

"Stryke says we still owe him money."

"We?" asks Ava.

I was the go-to, the one who collected the seventy dollars we owed Stryke and supposedly paid him. Six eyes on me. "I can pay him. I just… it was just a shitty time. I have a cheque coming. I mean to pay him."

Ava stares at me, cold. I move toward her and she backs up.

"Ava, I—"

"Fuck off, Erin."

Her voice is flat, colder than her look.

"I'm sorry. I'm so sorry. Look. It's not that big a deal. You guys have already paid and you won't have to pay anything else. I'll make sure he gets the money!"

I'm addressing them all, but talking to Ava. Alek and David stand back, watching but quiet.

She won't soften and the weight of a waterfall pushes down on me. Muddy and dirty is exactly where I belong. The tears flow with the helplessness. She says nothing.

"What do you want from me?" I'm crying and desperate. I want everything from her. I need everything from her. I'd do anything.

She suddenly pivots her body, a jerking move, and speaks. Her words come out emotionless but assertive—final. She speaks chillingly slowly. "I want you to die, Erin."

She turns her face toward Alek and David, then her body. Inside, the black hole sucks in everything dark and uncomfortable, right where it belongs. And I wait, in this state, for her to come back. Her candlelit torso, her smiling blue-green eyes.

Then, as if those words didn't quite get their message across, the next morning I exit my house around lunchtime and something catches my eye, black and shiny, slumped atop SuperBeast's driver-side windshield wiper. I look closer, my brain a rapid microfiche of questions, settling on a mixtape with all its tape yanked out and curly and abundant, "For Ava <3" neatly penned by my own hand. The spectacle of it screams viciously at me in the midday silence.

And yet, I'll wait. Because something in me signals that underneath this garbage heap of pain, there's something warm and comforting to be found. I swear it.

When I see Ava next, at a Pit party, she's attached to Alek like they're a couple and this sick feeling oozes into me and stays, no matter how much ecstasy, cocaine and booze I try to counteract it with. My vices just hit and roll down the feeling's exterior like I'm throwing eggs at a house. And however fucked up I get, it stays, a black box in an airplane, indestructible.

At home, without vice, I'm just grumpy. This particular morning, I wake up around noon and part my blinds to blue sky, heat waves distorting the air above the asphalt. Downstairs, my mom bustles about the kitchen and looks at me as I come through the archway, but doesn't stop puttering, doesn't smile.

"So what are you doing with yourself? You must be really bored."

My Ava-induced sick feeling has softened enough to flow to my fingertips, around my organs, settle in me as if it's my blood, my nervous system. It makes me defeated and non-combative—Eeyore registering negativity like it's to be expected. *Ohhhh, bother.*

"I'm not bored, Mom."

"You don't have a job; you don't do anything!"

She's now wiping crumbs off the counter and looks at me merely in glances. I harden.

I don't know, then, that she's unsure how to talk to me. I don't know, then, that she doesn't know how to say what she means. I don't know, then, that she means: "I love you and I'm worried about you."

"Why do you even care, Mom? If you don't want me around, I'll just leave! I'm nineteen years old. I know how to take care of myself!"

I so don't, but now's not a time for reflection.

"Fine, Erin. You do that. You move out and try to take care of yourself."

So I do. I pack the few things I care about into boxes, into my car, indignantly telling myself and anybody who'll listen that I was kicked out, and I move into David's mom's house in Fleetwood. I'm still washed with the grey blahs, the nagging and tugging stronger than any narcotic I throw at it. Right away, in the three-storey townhouse nestled against and around three-storey townhouses in a neighbourhood with a gate, there are things I miss.

A house with no music, I write in my journal. I always rolled my eyes at it— my mom's incessant blasting of Van Morrison, Joni Mitchell. The way she listens and opens in a way that nothing else prompts her to. But this isn't something I actually notice, then. I just roll my eyes at her music, her obsessive collecting, listening.

But here, now, it's too quiet and I miss it in that way we miss things we didn't realize we'd miss until they're gone and we do.

Linda, David's mother, who's trying to make sense of David's erratic comings and goings, starts eyeing me as the problem, and one evening while David's working at the Husky gas station in Fraser Heights, she confronts me. Tells me

I need to respect the rules of the house. Look for a job. Not drag David down with me. She tells me this sternly and unsympathetically and I stand in front of her, a head taller than her, and stifle the inclination to burst into tears. I feel turned inside out and like she could blow on me and I'd turn to dust, scattered all over the carpet, un-put-back-togetherable. I hang my shoulders along with my head and say nothing.

"I think you're a bad influence on him."

If I weren't looking forward to her imminent out-of-town trip, I would have picked up my still-packed bags and left right then.

"Just get up at a reasonable hour, look for a job, don't stay out late drinking and don't pull David down along with you and we'll be fine."

"Okay, Linda."

"Okay?" Her voice takes a softer tone. "You'll be just fine."

She briefly rubs my shoulder, leaving me pulled in opposite directions.

Upstairs, I sit on the corner of the neatly still-made bed and stare at the white wall, still and restless in the house's unsettling quiet. Sometimes the things we think will bring us warmth and comfort don't.

20

Ava and I. We crash together, then pull apart. I flail, legs in the air, tumbling, and then, somehow, draw nearer to her until we crash together again.

The crash. It's pouring rain and she's in the passenger seat of SuperBeast, the inside windows fogging up. The drumming of rain on metal, she and I hot-boxing the car. Me, inside, a wild garden of flowers twisting and blooming. Listening to a tape I recorded from CDs. Songs I love. Songs of love and beauty. "November Rain"—that almost, not-quite, fleeting-love vibe. We kiss and I touch her face. "It's been so long," she says.

"Ava, I love you," I say. Happiness.

Flailing. It's been days since I've heard from her. Four days, probably, or longer. It's midnight and I'm wasted and high at David's mom's townhouse in Fleetwood. Bottles of hard alcohol crowd the counter. Bobby and his friends dropped it off and hung around. Everybody's at the party. But not Ava. Delia, at one point, senses my turbulent emotions.

"Come here," she says. "Come upstairs." She takes me to the computer room and on LimeWire downloads "Sometimes It Hurts" by Stabbing Westward. "Sit down. Listen to this," she says and presses my shoulders down into the computer chair. I comply and she turns the volume knob on the computer speakers.

I sink in. My head and body are heavy with the thought of Ava and the buzz of alcohol. And with friendship and music and with feeling seen. The song, about how much it hurts to lose love.

Then, as if the music swirls with my yearning to summon her, a text from Ava: "What are you doing? Want to hang out?" I turn to Delia, who's already looking at me, her face slack and unimpressed. "Ava," I say.

I can't hide who she is to me. A click in my brain. Yes. Yes. Yes. I could be mid-sentence of an important lecture, I could be holding my grandmother's hand on her deathbed, I could be about to board a plane for a much-needed, long-awaited vacation. Yes.

Yes, above everything. Yes, above me. Because Me isn't really Me without the thing that's missing. The thing that's currently Ava.

Things happen in clips. I'm downstairs, ripping past my brother and his friend and Elise and Grey and Alek with his pink hair curled into his eyes. Somebody, I don't know who, in a surprised tone: "Where are you going, Erin?" I'm outside, the relief of cool air. I'm in SuperBeast turning the ignition. Backing up. Then, a commotion in front of the townhouse. Everything's blurry, then, clear in the headlights, David. Tears in his eyes, standing in front of the car, a crowd from the house around him. I don't understand why they've even noticed. I don't understand what's happening.

I roll down the window. "David. Move!"

"No. You can't drive."

"Move, David! This is none of your business!"

He holds his ground and I stare at him. Fuck. We're at an impasse and I need to be with Ava, near the only person in the world who can bring me the kind of happiness I'm trying to get to. Get near. And she's just a couple of miles away, at her brother's place near the hospital. And she wants me there. She wants me. I feel the rage broiling in me, spitting and seething and fuck, I push the car in park and swing out the door, leaving it open. "Goddammit, David, move!" Rage courses through me, at David—the only thing blocking me from her, from peace, from happiness. I lunge at him. "Move! What the fuck is this! Move!"

He ducks around me, around the open car door and in one motion reaches inside, grabs my keys and darts into the house. I follow him in a rampage, raging now, set after set of round, confused eyes seeing my layers and niceties scraped away. "Where is he? Where are my keys? Give them to me!" I yell at them and him and everybody to no avail, so I rush out the front door, slamming it as hard as possible behind me. I stomp, hard, on the concrete, raging mad, and kick the side of the house once, twice, and storm away from the house, the party, the neighbours peering out their blinds from dark rooms. I storm away and speed walk to where Ava is, where she wants me, thirty minutes away.

The walk calms me and when I arrive she opens the door and smiles and hugs me and the last hour dissolves like darkness in an early morning sky.

21

The morning after I rage at all my friends and storm down 152nd Street at midnight to close the space between Ava and me, I go back to David's mom's house. On the front porch, two garbage bags with everything I left my parents' house with, slumped against the beige siding, my keys on the ground beside them, neatly placed. David didn't kick me out—I told him I was leaving. And I told him I didn't want to see him. SuperBeast is parked in a slot in front of the townhouse. I push the bags into its hatchback trunk and take off. Good riddance, I think, the hero of my own story, the indignantly wronged, on to the next adventure, come what may.

I end up staying with Tyson, an acquaintance who lives with his single dad and little sister just a left turn and slight swivel from my parents' house in Fraser Heights, the relaxed atmosphere exactly what I need. I can come and go as I please and eat bagel bites for breakfast, lunch and dinner. Friends stream in constantly—a meld of the smoker crew and the pot smoker crew. We smoke pot and drink Colt 45s on the back deck while Tyson's sister's at school. But this summer, things feel different. At the corners of each social gathering, a darkness that beer and pot are powerless against; a darkness that pulls me toward the uninhibited warm-headedness of ecstasy. This summer, nothing's quite normal without it. And although my highs aren't as extraordinary as they once were—I'll stumble on my words now—nothing feels like it's as it should be without it. It's hooked me from the insides and when I resist its pull for a lack of money or ability, its tug is painful. Reserved for me, only, and painful. But it gives me something to attribute my bad feelings to. Putt, putt, putt along the surface and it makes sense and it's tied with a little ribbon.

Tyson's dad is everything my parents aren't. It makes my insides feel like a plain white hallway. TV on all day? Yep. Sleep in as late as you need to? Yep. Drinking at noon? We all do that around here. I can do whatever I want whenever I want and nobody challenges me. It's like if I didn't exist within this microsystem, everything would function exactly as it already does. It's *that* kind of loneliness. Sometimes, during the day, when the house is quiet and nobody's home but me, I'll tiptoe around anyway.

I wake up one morning on the pullout couch, home alone and awash with bland grey, and step into the kitchen, my bare feet cool on the large white kitchen tiles. I turn on the stove to boil water for perogies and muse about touching the red-hot glow of the stove element. Would it make me snap to? I have two cigarettes left. If I had money, I'd find something to look forward to to occupy this space in my brain. With people around, these doldrums are bearable, but without, an unshakable restlessness.

The water's boiling and I watch it, not thinking about much, then dump the frozen pieces into the pot, pulling my hands away quickly to avoid the searing droplets that spit at me. Sometimes, I let myself get stung. One of the kittens born to Tyson's unspayed cat circles the living room fast. It defies gravity, cascading horizontally along the couch, and I watch with mild amusement. I drain the water from the perogies, add a dollop of sour cream to the corner of the plate and sprinkle it with salt. I open the drawer and grab a fork, then something strikes me. Fork still in hand, steam rising off my ready-to-eat meal, I creep up the stairs, one quiet barefoot step at a time, my senses on high alert.

I've been at Tyson's for just a couple of weeks. His younger sister's room is big and messy in that kid sort of way. A neat bed with toys scattered all over the place. I survey it, knowing what I've seen. Neatly in a corner is a stack of DVDs—about a dozen of them. I look through them and separate them into two piles, slowly, then back into one. I scoop them all up and take them downstairs and shove them into my backpack as quickly as I shove the perogies into my mouth and take off with them and the rest of my stuff, still in garbage bags, in SuperBeast to Cash Converters, where I can turn the DVDs into money and plan something to look forward to.

If there's ever a place to remind a person how pathetic and desperate they are, Cash Converters is it. Located in the wounded heart of Guildford, the store is staffed by men with slicked-back hair, practised in the art of being non-reactive to those looking them in the eyes, begging for a break, a fair amount of cash. Sellers to Cash Converters are fuelled by desperation—the need for a quick fix. My body doesn't yet need a drug to function, but my mind sure does.

I'm standing in front of a bulky man in his thirties with too much gel in his neatly spiked hair. I tell myself he has no idea what "need" means and what discomfort with reality means, and those facts make him great at his job.

I push two neat stacks of DVDs side by side in front of him, trying to hold my shoulders like somebody who is calm would—somebody who doesn't have to say yes to whatever piddly offer is bestowed upon them.

I watch this genuinely casual man open each case and inspect each disc. He frowns often, which feels like little jabs. He stacks the cases back into two piles—one taller than the other. When he finishes, he pushes the shorter pile toward me.

"I'll give you two apiece for these," he states.

I nod, expecting that. "What about the other ones?"

"Fifty cents each."

I hold my frustration inside and keep my voice steady. "Why?"

"These are kids' movies—not worth as much."

I know from learned experience and his demeanour that these quotes aren't negotiable. I collect my $19.50, already working out my plan. If I can persuade others to do ecstasy with me, I'll be able to buy a discounted cap and a pack of cigarettes. As I pull out my phone to call Ava, it rings. It's Tyson, which is unusual—he never calls. He knows.

I was never good at concealing the truth, never good at lying. I can pick up, play ignorant, play it cool, apologize profusely and give him the $19.50. But I'm no good at confrontation and I'm no good at exposing weakness and I'm no good at admitting when I'm wrong.

Now… what if? What if—despite my mistakes and yearnings and cravings and desires and wanting and hoping and daydreaming—I'm already… complete? What if this idea that I will always need Some Big Thing like a person or a drug is a trick of perpetual dissatisfaction? I can see it, too. Like when I put on Joni Mitchell's *For the Roses* album and her melodic voice is so light and deep in my ear, touching me in places I can't locate, exactly, feeling things I can't explain—the transcendence of poetry, of music—and in those moments, those fleeting moments, I do feel complete. Goosebumps sprout down my legs, down my arms, waves of positive feeling. So, does completeness come in those fleeting moments? Is that what I'm feeling? Completeness in simplicity? Or are those moments when I realize that I'm already complete? Oh God, maybe we never stop questioning. Even when it feels like we've drastically evolved. It's confusing.

I silence my ringing phone and let it go to voice mail.

A Line Allows Progress, a Circle Does Not

addiction
/əˈdikSH(ə)n/
noun

**the fact or condition of being addicted to
a particular substance, thing or activity.**

22

Here's how it goes: you're on a train, looking out your window at the world speeding by. You're settled in well enough and have no plans to make a big scene, to push over your breakfast tray, to kick out of your sleep cabin yelling, "Stop!" You boarded this train, paid for your ticket, see value in your purchase. So you just sit there looking out the window. You see gardens of wildflowers reaching their heads toward the sun. You see bodies slumped in alleys. You see newborn babies squinting at the lights above them, you see a crow on the ground with a broken neck, you see the sun rise over half-built houses, you see life disappear from eyes, you see drowning in dark water. You focus on the wildflowers, the sunrise, the babies. You focus on them hard until you lose them in the blur of the darkening landscape. And that's how it goes. But you stay on the train. You stay on the train because you're used to being on the train.

Taking those DVDs from Tyson's sister casts a darkness across my land. I let all his calls that day and those that follow go to voice mail. On it, he pleads with me to call him. He tells me he knows. He's my disappointed dad. I ignore phone calls from Alek, who eventually texts me to say everybody's worried about me. Whatever that means. I reply back, finally: "I'm fine, don't worry." Everybody knows I'm a thief who stole from a child, from a house I was staying at for free. It's shameful. I can't see them. I can't ask for anything from anyone. I won't.

My family is on their three-week summer vacation, so I park SuperBeast around the block and plug my cellphone into the electricity socket in the backyard. When my phone rings and I see it's Ava, I answer. She offers me a tent, which she drops off in a hurry later that day. It's a quick *I care about you* whispered ever so faintly into my ear. I want more, crave so much more, but at least I have a place to duck into where nobody will bother me.

After spending a second night alone, curled up in the five-person tent underneath my clothing, I can no longer bear my hunger, so I nervously walk the back roads to Java Hut and, watching out for Cue Ball, slip inside, discreetly stuff both my hands with packets of peanut butter and scarf them in the bathroom stall, peeling each little green wrapper, my finger as utensil. I'm getting out of there, having thankfully avoided running into all the people I could have run into, when I hear a friendly "Hey!" behind me. My body pangs before I see it's Twyla, holding hands and giggling with Kevin in that new-couple-love sort of way. *They can't know.*

My friendship with Twyla has been a spotty phone call—she's there, clear, then she isn't. She'd joined at the hip with Kevin, who lives on the brink of South Surrey and wears thick silver chains. He's short—surprisingly short enough for Twyla to lean a craned-up chin atop his head—and has this baby face and big smile that yin-yang with beady black eyes and the forced-masculinity demeanour so typical in Surrey.

They look at me untainted and I'm thrilled. We hug, hard, and I realize how much I miss human touch already.

She introduces Kevin like he's a prized birthday present.

His voice is alto and scratchy, making me wonder how far ahead of puberty he actually is.

"He's turning seventeen" is how she frames it.

"What are you doing tonight?" he asks me, and beady eyes aside, he's dreamy, friendly, dark-chocolate hair cropped.

I look at him and smile. "Absolutely nothing."

"Let's hang out," Twyla says. "Do you have any money?"

"Yeah, like thirteen dollars." Still the DVD money, minus a pack of Canadian Classics cigarettes. I was waiting for an opportunity like this, having not quite crawled over the ledge of the get-high-alone landscape. "I was hoping to get some E. I could call Ava too, see what she's doing."

"Could we go to Tyson's?"

I study Twyla, who doesn't appear to be testing me. "I'm actually staying in my parents' backyard right now." They both look at me. "Long story." I smile and shake my head.

By 10:00 p.m. we're making plans in the tent when the gate sounds and Ava's voice pleasantly calls, "Hellooooo?" She and I hadn't been romantic for at least a month, but she looks at me with a softness that stirs. I can feel the buzz of her body like I've forgotten for a moment to exhale as she sits close to me in the tent. And as we gather our plans, she leans into me like she did that first night when the candles lit her skin orange and strands of black hair shadowed her face.

"I can't call Stryke," I say. "I owe him money."

I glance at Ava, knowing this is a sore spot, but she doesn't flinch. As if "I want you to die, Erin" never happened. I'd been living on high alert, scanning streets for Stryke's red sports car, ears as watchful as my eyes.

"I might know somebody," says Kevin, borrowing my cell and making a barrage of calls until time starts to feel like Dalí's melting clocks.

Uneasiness flicks my insides, rhythmically, damped only by the current I feel off Ava. Maybe this is the only balance I'll ever know. The rest of them are uneasy too, and tension slows the chatter, makes us fiddle with our hands, with the clothes scattered around.

"Got it," Kevin says, finally, after flipping closed the phone for the dozenth time. We pile into Twyla's car and drive to Guildford, to Tim Hortons for Kevin to meet the dealer. He pops out of the car and returns within minutes, but not with ecstasy. He hops into the front seat and shakes a dime bag at us, about a quarter full of clear shards that look like glass.

"Crystal," states Ava, knowingly. Crystal meth. Twyla and I exchange glances.

"You couldn't get the E, babe?"

Kevin shakes his head and avoids her eyes, I notice.

I'm uneasy. I don't know much about crystal meth. Only that it's long-lasting and more common in shadier parts of Surrey like Guildford and Whalley. It's also much cheaper than ecstasy.

We drive a handful of blocks to Green Timbers—a massive park in the bull's eye of Guildford—and the summer sky is already lighting up, revealing the horizon. Revealing tops of trees and tops of buildings. It's still cold, though. Damp cold.

"We have to smoke it on glass," says Kevin, once we're in the park. "I don't have anything for that. I think we should snort it. It hurts, but only for a second."

I'm suddenly quiet and apprehensive. Moments in which I wonder what I'm doing, why I'm doing it and what it means for the Me of the future sometimes jar me. I suddenly yearn to be fast asleep in a warm bed in a clean room at my parents' house. Not in a park on a Tuesday in the middle of Surrey at daybreak, about to try a dirty addictive drug for the first time. *What the fuck am I doing?* But now, there's no alternative. My warm bed is obstructed by a locked door. My parents are who knows where in the USA, totally unreachable, even if they were willing to unlock the door for me. I miss the security of a front door and even David's white, clean house without music and the kind slackers at Tyson's who held me up when I'd otherwise crumble to the ground. I miss it all. I miss them all. But I blotted out every single option I had. I did that, and now I'm here.

It's summer but it's cold and it's dim. I'm aching tired. Last summer was golden light and green afternoons and laughter. Woven with simplicity. When I wasn't distracted by love, I drew. I drew detailed black-ink scenes with giant suns and crouching gremlins and music staffs and eyeballs and buildings and mushrooms. I'd draw in meticulous detail and add silver highlights. Danny, an artist himself, one day loomed over me and asked to see them. He flipped through my notebook. "Erin, these are so good! You should take them to HMV and get them to make posters out of them!" It gave me the kind of feeling I long for. The kind of feeling I use drugs to trigger. The kind of feeling I caress Ava's cheek to trigger.

Kevin's pressing his social insurance card onto the shards on top of my Deftones *White Pony* CD, using another card to scrape it back down. He repeats until the crystal meth looks as fine as cocaine, then he splits it into four thin lines. Nobody has a bill, so Kevin digs around in his wallet and rolls up a bus ticket. He snorts the first line and it makes his eyes water, forcing his hand to grasp the bridge of his nose. My stomach turns as I watch Twyla do the same.

"Waaaah," she looks at me through teary eyes, suddenly nodding profusely. "Whoaaaaaa."

She hands me the case and the rolled-up bus pass.

I hesitate but before launching into an internal debate, I snort the line. It feels like a mouthful of wasabi—my head stings, my nose stings and there's an immediate foul drop in the back of my throat.

Danny noticing my drawings wasn't the first time someone saw something in what I doodled. That first summer after graduation I crossed the Port Mann Bridge into Coquitlam and discovered an idyllic scene of a flowery park with a paved path circling a pond full of lily pads and ducks and summertime insects hovering in the warm air. I'd packed my notebook and my ink pens and circled the pond, warm but not hot, with a renewed feeling of freedom, which had been eroding with every joint I smoked—every dependency I clutched. I nestled into a natural seat on a boulder in front of the pond and opened my notebook to work on my current drawing, my face and head warm from the beaming-down sun. I'd glance up every so often at orange duck feet paddling. At pointy feathered bums. I was as light and carefree and in the moment as I possibly could be. Maybe it was the joint I'd smoked before adventure called. Maybe I was just happy. A rustling behind me caused me to look up to a guy and girl, both around my age, maybe younger, behind me. The guy was young-buck handsome—the kind of person who meticulously slicks back his hair in the morning and twirls into sprayed cologne behind the privacy of the bathroom door. The girl looked a bit older, a bit rougher around the edges. Her hair was dark and thick and a bit messy, and she wore a navy sweater that hung below her hips and had a few obvious holes. The sweater, well loved, must be her safety blanket, I thought. The guy was eager.

"Hey! What are you drawing there? That looks really cool!"

"Oh, you know, I don't know. Just doodling."

"Do you draw a lot? Do you have others I can see?"

His energy was electric. The girl smiled friendlier than I expected and I handed over my notebook.

They both craned their heads in and nodded, flipping through the pages, the girl looking over the guy's shoulder, squinting in the sunshine.

"These are really good," said the guy.

"They really, really are," said the girl. "Are you professional?"

I laughed. "A professional bum," I replied, lightening up. "I just draw for fun. Nobody has even really seen them aside from you guys and my really good friends."

"You know what?" The guy looked like I could press a button and he'd shoot straight up into space, laughing gleefully as he burned through the atmosphere. "Our uncle is an artist and he's having a garden party right now, just around the corner. That's where we came from. There's tons of food and a band, and I bet my uncle would look at your work! You know, like give a professional artist's opinion."

I studied his face for a hint of something nefarious and saw only an eager teenager. The girl smiled another genuine smile and I followed them away from the boulders, the pond, the path and into the adjacent neighbourhood, where, sure enough, there was a garden party. Sure enough, there was a three-piece band playing, and sure enough, there was a well-manicured lawn and well-manicured people mingling with hors d'oeuvres on mini-plates and glasses of champagne. The uncle was sitting in a position of importance in a gigantic chair that must have been hauled out of the house by strong and loving family members.

The young buck, still holding my notepad, handed it to his uncle. The man embodied the artist uncle archetype with wild white hair and round spectacles. He turned each page, studying each drawing with squinted eyes, as I stood there uncomfortably as though I'd been invited to walk a carpet and stand before a king. The towering house blocked the warmth of the sun and the pot had worn off. My anxiousness readjusted itself into its prominent position inside. Eventually, he spoke.

"There's a lot of potential here. The design is excellent, it really is. They're just raw." He looked up at me, above the curve of his glasses. As he handed back my notebook, he looked squarely into my eyes. "Keep at it. I think you really have something here. Otherwise, enjoy the party! There's food, there's a ton of art. Stay as long as you'd like."

Before tracing my way back to the simplicity of sun and blank pages, I thanked my new friends whose names I never knew.

In Green Timbers, at daybreak with Kevin and Twyla and Ava, my mind is now ruthlessly anchored in the moment. The wasabi pain subsides and everything changes. Instantly I'm wide awake. Instantly I know I can sprint like a champion or fuck like a porn star or be anything I want to be. Instantly I'm exuberant. I watch Ava take her line, then turn to me with squinted eyes. She laughs and pushes my shoulder and I'm malleable and happy. I grin back at her and all my doubt and apprehension are gone. All my longing and desire to rewind life are gone. And none of that stuff will return for a long, long time.

23

I'm tired. It's been nearly three months since I slung those garbage bags over my shoulder and left my parents'. The bags are now settled on the bottom bunk at an acquaintance's house down the street from Java Hut, and I'm sleeping on the top bunk, and I can tell my welcome's nearly expired. My only call for extra work was to audition for a toothpaste commercial, but I got too high and came down so hard my insides rattled, so I didn't return Trushel-Thompson's voice mail, which likely caused her to lose my number for a while in a stack of more reliable, eager extras. I'm starving and broke and can barely afford gas and cigarettes. And SuperBeast is breaking down. Its fan belt broke off and I replaced it with tied-up neon pink fabric from Ava, and it's a job that has to be redone multiple times a day. And it still spews smoke from its engine, even when I stay within the neighbourhood's borders. So I sputter to my parents' house, ribs protruding, deep exhaustion, a tiny, meek version of myself. A tiny, meek version of myself that even drugs can barely jostle.

My mom's car is in the driveway. I approach the door a stranger, a possible guest, and knock. Footsteps grow louder, and she opens the door. She looks smaller, somehow, and has bags under her eyes. The stinging promise of tears grips me. Instincts take over and I turn around and round the corner.

"Erin," she says, gently, to my back, and it stops me. My body pangs with guilt and exposure for this weakened version of myself, this drooping flower. She's still standing in the doorway and I'm lingering at the corner of the life I once knew, the life I'm tumbling into and a life that might be. But I'm all twisted up, staring at a confused road sign with arrows pointing every which way, and everything feels like a total crapshoot.

"Mom, I just don't have anywhere to live."

Then tears, from both of us. And it feels like a succession of marbles from my gut to my throat. My mom cries only in sad movies and hides her face from the rest of us while I watch from the corners of my eyes, from behind my own wall that hides negative emotions.

"Negative," "positive," "good," "bad"—our emotions are our whispers, our signals, our energy, our humanity. And when we resist, when we feel like we should shut one down, rather than revel in it as part of what makes us human and alive and beautiful, we use drugs and we yearn and we take step A and step B and step C to get closer to the "positive," the "good," the "okay." But we'll never be okay. Not if we resist. We are but vessels they'll board regardless. And fuck us up if we're not careful. So we must lean in and lean in and lean in to feel everything. I don't see this yet, though.

"Do you want to come in? We can talk about it."

She sets down rules: "You have to look for a job. You can't just float around without structure."

I nod firmly. This I know.

"And you have to respect the rules of the house. You can't just come traipsing in here at 5:00 a.m."

"I know. I really, really know, Mom."

I agree to everything and mean it.

Maybe I'm distracted by Ava. Maybe the pull of crystal meth already has me all tangled up in its ropes. That day, late into summer, my mom tosses me a life jacket. She tosses me a life jacket so within reach, its droplets splash my face when it lands in the water. But I don't reach for it. I float on without it.

⌢

Maybe they call it crystal meth because it clarifies muck. But there's a hitch. It clarifies muck but for a holy moment. My job becomes to grasp it and hold it, slippery fingers be damned. I'm filling notebooks with scribbled musings on passion, on addiction, on human nature, on love. I'm ripping apart cigarette packs and turning them inside out to have somewhere to write the revelations that pang through my body before they evaporate into nothingness. *It's not about finding the meaning of life. It's about finding meaning* in *life.* I capture these snippets, but so often—too often—my brain untethers itself from my hand and gallops away and I'm left limp-handed, knowing I'd held something life-changing within my grasp. Knowing it's irretrievably gone. Crystal meth reveals cocaine and ecstasy as mellow siblings, and after I stay up for twenty-four, forty-eight hours and feel the hollow comedown slump me into sleep and ache, I vow to stay away from its shimmery terror.

24

Summer cools into fall and when it's not blue-sky crisp, with leaves openly beginning their beautiful decay, first shining with auburn light, then turning matte, it's socked in. David moves to New West, into a hobbit hole you have to duck to enter. And I start another great crash and pull, this time with crystal meth. I try not to buy it. I try to tell myself coke and E are good enough.

I'm in the habit of visiting Kevin and Twyla at his house in Delta, in the backyard shed past the cool air and rakes and shovels and lawn mower and smell of gasoline from jerry cans. Into the crystal-meth-clean heated space with couches and shelves. Where Kevin holds a glass pipe to my lips for the first time and I watch crystals melt like ice cubes in Sprite on a hot day. Where I exhale a cloud and buzz like I am passion itself and I write and I wait for eleven hours for the next hit and I curl inside like old paint and I watch Twyla on her hands and knees searching for more meth and I am on my hands and knees swearing I see chunks in the carpet and Kevin gets mad and hits himself in the head with a hammer and rips off his shirt and Twyla says "Baby, calm down" and I leave the shed expecting it to be nighttime but it's blue-sky noon. Yeah, I'm in the habit, but I'm trying to break it.

Ava disappears again but turns up with Alek, and I feel like half of my soul has ditched my body to go along with her, wherever she may go. So I buy a soul prosthesis with drugs. And she herself is a soul prosthesis, too.

⌒

I'm bored and chain-smoking bummed cigarettes from Cynthia on her patio in mid-October. A sun-faded grey umbrella shades the dirty glass table that supports our lazy arms and overflowing ashtray.

"Ashleigh likes you," Cynthia says between drags, and it perks my ears like a dog hearing the rattle of a leash, hours into a lazy afternoon snooze. Ashleigh is a "girly girl" on the periphery of our friend group who I assume I have nothing in common with. She's into clothes and makeup and shopping and isn't into music. And she has a boyfriend, an ex-firefighter who was injured on the job and is on a steady supply of morphine for the pain, which Ashleigh helps herself to when she's not doing coke. Neon signs above the situation scream, *Nope!* But watercolour notions in my brain muse, *Why not?*

I soon start flirting with her on MSN Messenger and she's all-in.

"So what do you like?"

Her paragraph flashing across my screen stumps me. What *do* I like? My mind flashes to Ava's candlelit face, her eyes soft, my mouth on her collarbone, *Melon Collie and the Infinite Sadness.*

I type, "I like a lot of things." I stand and pace to the edge of the living room and back. I sit, cross-legged. Stumped and nervous.

Ashleigh: "I like being eaten out and lots of clit play."

I stand again. What do I say to that? "Cool"?

She types again: "Want to come over?"

I do want to go over there. But I also don't. I'm interested, but am I attracted to her? Not like I'm attracted to Ava.

"Ahhh I'd like to but I can't. Soon for sure though."

Smiley face.

Within a week I'm at her house, but with a buffer of Junior and Ashleigh's sister Mara. It's after 10:00 p.m. and we're taking lines of coke. Junior's a dealer from Whalley who Mara knew from way back. He'll keep you captive for hours with painfully drawn-out stories about people you don't know. You'll stop by his apartment for a quick pickup and he'll flip through a photo album from his trip to Disneyland in 1988 with a talking track so mumbled it's impossible to make out. He's lonely and he's maddening. People say he has a brain injury. He owns every room, every house he walks into with a straight back and the cockiness of someone who has the thing everybody else needs. I tolerate him because I have to.

Ashleigh's parents are out of town and we have the house—in its tall-ceilinged, immaculate, suburbia-real-estate-magazine-worthy glory—to ourselves. We stand around the granite island and take smoke breaks on the concrete patio, leaning back in reclining summer chairs, me looking up at the stars. Ashleigh plays 50 Cent through the television speakers.

Ashleigh and Junior go upstairs together. Mara looks at me. "Smoke?" Outside, I notice the cool air for the first time all night. And the black sky, bleached with orange city light, begins its inevitable morph into the deep blue of morning.

I surprise myself with a yawn. Mara looks at me. "Come on, Erin. You're not tired," she says, her demeanour an excavator to my passivity. "I want to continue this conversation. You're making it sound like everybody needs drugs or alcohol to be happy."

The Erin of three and a half hours ago had philosophized at them, leaving me to defend the position. I inhale a thoughtful drag and exhale up, into the bright motion light. Subdued does me well, though, with no overflow of brain-power for overthinking. No infused emotion in my voice for others to dismiss. I speak low and confidently. I speak my truth.

"I'm not saying everybody needs drugs or alcohol. I'm not naive. It's more about the fact that everybody needs *something*. Maybe it's coke." I give her a pointed look. "Maybe it's Christianity or it's sex or maybe it's painting or playing guitar or being a winning forward in soccer, I don't know. Maybe it's exercising or climbing up the corporate ladder. Or maybe it's being obsessed with Van Morrison or gardening or hiking or pot. It's like there's passion. And there's obsession. And there's addiction. And it's this tangled ball that society loves to pull threads from and says, 'Oh, wow, this is revered.' Or 'Oh, no, this is unacceptable.' So then we just silo ourselves and point our fingers and say 'good,' 'bad.' Good, bad, bad, bad, good. And we pretend like we don't actually understand each other. But we do. Because these are human needs. We all need and we all share that."

Energy in my chest, just like when I sing "Mayonaise" or another song I love, twists and turns and revs me back up. The motion light goes off and we're shadows in the dark, the only light coming through rectangle windows from in-side. Mara waves her arms and we're illuminated again. She's shaking her head.

"Erin, that doesn't make sense. There's a huge difference between being a cokehead and Michael Jordan."

"Right, but what's driving it? It's not easy for Michael Jordan to get up at whatever time and practise until, what, his fingers are raw, or whatever. And eat quinoa and shit. Maybe Michael Jordan just wants to order an extra-large pizza every night and eat it in bed. But there's something driving him. Something that says, 'Look, you do this now and you will be rewarded.' I mean, Michael Jordan is kind of a bad example, but what's that reward? What's the payoff? We're all chasing feelings. To feel bold, to feel *good*, to feel worthy, to feel like ourselves. We're all doing these things for these feelings. We're all fucking junkies of feel-ing. We get there in a million and one ways. But we do what we can to get there. We all have a tool box. We all learn what tools work."

"Nah, dude, I don't buy it. I'm not turning to anything at all."

"Well you're on coke right now and it's morning." I say it with as much kind sincerity as I can muster.

"Yeah, but I don't need it. I'm not trying to fulfill anything. I just... I just want to do it."

"Okay, I can totally accept that. But for me, this is true. I absolutely know this. Yes, right now I'm using drugs to fill that hole, but I could be using anything. Even if I stop using drugs, I'll definitely turn to something. I always have, I always will."

"What do you mean you always have?"

"Well, like love! I've definitely turned to this idea of love to somehow make myself feel, I don't know, better. But I also sucked my thumb as a kid. I wrote long stories. There truly has always been something, which is why I'm *sure* there always will be."

Mara waves her arm again and the light comes back on.

"Think about it. We're all created within a dependency. In the womb. It's like everything is provided for us. It's warm, we're fed. We're satiated. Need literally doesn't exist in our warm little world. And then, suddenly, we're born. It's fucking freezing, we've been ripped from everything we've ever known—absolute comfort and warmth—and now suddenly all this stuff we've always felt was part of us, we've always felt was just wholeness, is missing. That's the seeking I'm talking about. We're missing pieces. And it's like home, to all of us. This is something we all share."

Mara keeps shaking her head. "I'd love to ask you about this in five years and see if you still believe it."

"I will. I have zero doubt."

The sky's now a meek baby blue. My head and lungs are stuffy but the electricity sizzling through my fibres needs something. We haven't spoken in a couple of minutes.

"Well, that's the saddest thing I've ever heard," she finally responds.

⌒

In the full-blown daylight, Mara and Junior leave and I squish into Ashleigh's single bed between her and the wall, wide awake. She drapes her arm over my torso and falls asleep quickly. I'm tired, exhausted, in both body and mind, yet completely wired. Her breath is a pattern against my arm, warm and weird. Her dresser's crowded with bottles of perfume and cases of makeup. The sun is shining through the window. I push myself up, let her arm flop softly on the bed and whisper into her hair that I have to get home.

25

Days later or weeks later, Ava touches my hand. We're sitting beside each other on a couch at Grey's house, it's three in the morning and Halloween and we're coming down off acid and mushrooms and cocaine and ecstasy—our mismatched crew fully costumed and sprawled about the living room. Ava, a witch, has black lines of face paint smeared on her face. Me, also a witch, somehow able to polish my tarnished senses and tune in when she touches my foot, then my hand. This launches me back into walking a tightrope gingerly. Hot love on one side, fear of heartbreak on the other. And crystal meth epiphanies on one side and total addiction on the other. And I'm just trying to keep my eyes ahead, but it's socked in. And grey. I don't know what's there. Which means I'm going to fall. Or it means I'm going to jump.

I awake one cold November morning hoping that if I don't move, if I stay still long enough with my eyes closed as the reality of the room permeates my consciousness, I can savour the soft tendrils of my dream. In it, Ava approaches me with gentle eyes. She hands me a hat—a fisherman's hat—and smiles. I feel its scratchy canvas between my fingers and smile too and look down on it. Embroidered in red: *Tarzan Love Jane. Jane Loves Erin.* I look up at her, a hungry question in my smile. Are you Jane? She pulls me into a confirming hug and kisses me, backing up only to say: "I love you."

It's raining, in real life, and in its pitter-patter I grow more conscious of the nearly midday light illuminating the cracks between my blinds. I let go of the already dissolving dream and reach for my phone. It's 11:11, so I wish Ava will love me forever. There's an unread text message from Ashleigh, from hours ago.

"I dreamt about you last night," it reads, stirring not even a mild curiosity in me. Poor Ashleigh. She's probably lying in her bed or puttering about her house, waiting for me to crawl through the window she opened for me, but I don't. And I won't.

I don't text Ava but rather hope for my wish to rise into the fabric of the all-knowing and float down upon her like an imperceptible cloak.

Once fully awake, I head downstairs to find my mom tidying up. Feeling neither anxious nor confrontational, I meld with her semi-positive mood. She's leaning on the counter, flipping through a cookbook.

"Think you'll be around for supper tonight?" Her voice is light and her words deliver the entirety of what she has to say. Things between us have been strained between my late nights and long sleep-ins. Between my secrecy about everything and her saying about one-hundredth of what she could say. Between both our abilities to sense everything neither of us are saying.

Just days before, I'd spent the night and most of the following day in the shed, where Twyla now essentially lives, being spoon-fed baby portions of crystal meth by Kevin, stuck mostly in paranoid-listening mode, sick and uncomfortable, until I eventually pried myself away. On the bus home, two older women looked at me with disdain, not breaking eye contact while one whispered something to the other. A shift inside triggered my anger to crawl overtop of my hurt and throw its arms aggressively into the air. By the time I stepped in the front door around dinnertime, sharp red like an electric saw blade was spinning up and down my core. In the kitchen, my mom was chopping zucchini. My dad was watching hockey with the volume low. They confronted me about where I'd been all night and day and it supercharged the saw blade. The red spewed paint, splashing my mom's face like a slap. "I'm nineteen years old! This is bullshit! It's fucking bullshit! Why do I have to tell you where the fuck I am every fucking second of every fucking day?" Her surprised blue eyes. I saw her surprised blue eyes but I didn't let them sink into my soft sensitive place. Later, after I eventually confess my drug use to my mom, she'll tell me that that evening after I'd slammed the glass door so hard the surrounding walls shuddered, my dad had said, "Is she on drugs?" And my mom had brushed it off, scoffed at it, said, "No way."

The morning after my Ava dream, I don't have to tense up and force niceties.

"I'm actually not sure if I'll be around for supper. Maybe just make whatever you feel like? Like, don't depend on me?"

I glance at her acoustic guitar leaning up against the living room wall. I'd been eyeing it for a while and would sometimes pick it up, strum it, wish I were a rock star with eye-locking confidence and red lipstick. Hot sweat through ripped black T-shirts. An indie singer with a tall brown toque with a hole who was shy but would grasp audiences in places they didn't know were inside and who'd swirl those feelings around like a painter. I'd imagine these things, cradling the guitar I couldn't make an appealing sound with.

"Do you want to learn a little something?" My mom's eyes are crinkled into a smile, making them shine a lighter blue. She's pretty, but she's never liked how she looks. She's pretty and it shows when her brow unfurls—rare in those days. And she's a talented musician—can shred and pick complex melodies. But she always plays just below earshot.

She tunes two guitars and hands me one. And with it, a gift. She shows me how to read a tab—where the lines match the strings. She shows me a C chord and a D chord and a G chord. I feel the frustration bubbling to the surface when I awkwardly wrap my hand around the base of the guitar and want to put it down, do something easier, but I don't. It's like I'm just learning to walk, and my mom is patient. I make an appealing sound. And another. I learn a simple melody. And three chords. They sound awful. But I can now play three chords and a simple melody.

☾

Patches of forest in Fraser Heights are constantly bulldozed for new houses, which are being built bigger and bigger. Earthworms and voles have to get out of the way for concrete basements. Redwood, oak and Douglas fir roots are obliterated as families put down roots of their own—invisible and symbolic, defining home through structure.

Often, at night, our group visits these partially built houses, walking gingerly on crossbeams, drinking, getting high, watching diligently for nails.

On this particular day, the streets are iced on the back end of a freeze-thaw-freeze cycle. A light snow fell the night before and uncharacteristically hasn't melted by mid-morning when I meet Ava inside a half-built house across the street from my elementary school, halfway between our homes.

Inside, an industrial lamp emanates an illusion of warmth. I wear a knee-length scarf, which I've wrapped around my neck and shoulders, transforming me into a multicoloured Michelin Man. The house smells of fresh lumber and as I walk up the stairs, taking care with each step, I wonder about who would live here eventually. Whether they'd think about their family home in its skeleton state—now—when wind pushes through its spaces and strangers walk its floors, assembling it piece by piece. History is longer than we imagine. I hear what I hope is Ava coming through the space where the front door will eventually be.

"Hello?" She's loud and has no inhibitions.

Each of my footsteps makes a sound and I'm certain she'll decipher my keen pace as I head toward her. She's wearing a shark-coloured toque with prominent corners, her black hair an open semicircle around its bottom, and she smiles up at me. I notice those wide-set blue-green eyes, bright in the artificial light. I greet her, probably too enthusiastically. She closes in on me without hesitation and we embrace and I desperately want to kiss her but hold back, unsure how she'll react. These days we spend every day together, and while it feels like our touches and gazes linger, we've been platonic. We hold each other longer than friends would but stop just in time to make my head crazy. Still, I could burst with love. With anticipation. And yet, I tell myself: *This isn't fair. I'm in love with her, wanting so much more, and she thinks of me as a friend.*

She asks me what I'm doing today, and I'm moved to gush but I hold it in. I want to spend the day with her. I want to spend every day with her. Every second. And it makes me feel creepy. Almost how I was with Soela.

She tells me she's going for lunch with her mom.

My inner world is swirling and sparkling—light with feelings for her, winning the battle against my meek attempts at suppression.

"Ava, I—"

She stops me by drawing nearer with unmistakably loving eyes. Sometimes she looks so chill and relaxed and calm. She wraps her arms around my waist and nuzzles her head into my neck, the corner of her toque itchy on my skin. She then brings her face up to mine and looks unabashedly into my eyes.

"Erin."

I don't need to hear anything else. We kiss, lit by orange lamps, in cold December air. From my core, light shines as powerfully as a conductor's arms in the air during the climax of a symphony. And I'm home. This is home. This is need, fulfilled.

Then Ava pulls back, just slightly.

"Want to do crystal tonight?"

It's like the power goes out in the symphony hall and the instruments confusedly stutter to a halt. Gasps and murmurs. But what I say is "Sure." I'm surprised at how definitive it sounds.

26

David's new home in New West suits him in his eclectic nature and his shining green eyes and elfin ears. You have to duck through the front door and crane your neck through the kitchen before you can shake it off and stand up straight in the living room. I sit on his couch and stare at the white wall. So little daylight makes it through the small and sparse slit windows, it's hard to tell the time of day. David's flitting around, still settling in, placing knick-knacks symmetrically atop various surfaces. *Siamese Dream* is barely audible above his rustling about, but when "Mayonaise" comes on I lean back and stare at the white ceiling, my yanking sadness somehow a comfort. The song ends and David is still rummaging around, so I absent-mindedly sit up straight and open the box in the centre of his coffee table. In it, a half sheet of lined paper with some sort of list on it. I pick it up and pull it close enough to read. It's a list of drugs, some of which are crossed out. Marijuana, mushrooms, cocaine, *Salvia divinorum*, acid, heroin, ecstasy, crack.

"Hey, David, what is this?"

He comes around the bend fast and his body tenses for a moment, before shrugging.

"It's my list," he tells me. "Drugs I want to try or have already tried."

The casualness of his voice wrings my insides.

"Just like—for fun?"

And while I'm still having fun—more or less—something is also developing in the corners of my mind. A mild understanding that my free will is being assimilated. That getting high is becoming the only way to feel certain things: good about myself, about the way I look, about how I express myself. It's like a dark-magic beanstalk to Little Me trapped inside, enabling her to use my eyes, my mouth, my body, my laugh. It pulls her from deep down in solitary confinement. It becomes her only way out. And the cost, I'm starting to realize, may be far greater than a wasabi sting of the nose. David treating it like a conquest or a game cranks my insides, a knot twisting in a whirring washing machine.

And then, days or weeks later, it's spitting rain and the day's light is long gone by 5:00 p.m. Despite David's list, despite his parents often handing him money, despite his new job at the London Drugs on Fifth and Sixth in New West, he's able to take it or leave it, utterly puzzling me.

We're on his plump little couch and my insides are curling. A mixture of boredom, anticipation and a growing need to get high. David's off work for the next couple of days and so am I.

"So do you want me to call Mike?" I ask.

Mike. When I finally got my own crystal meth dealer, everything changed. It was like I suddenly found scissors in my own little dinghy and, without much thought or foresight, snipped the line between me and the bigger cruise ship with all its lights and its dark corners and its people dancing and sleeping and eating and complaining, leaving me adrift on the sea. Crystal meth is cheap and accessible and I can make twenty dollars' worth last days. Problem is, I don't always have twenty dollars.

"Nah," David responds passively. My body tenses immediately.

"Nah? What do you mean?"

"Nah, I don't really feel like it."

With no money, I'm at his mercy. I'm only sitting in his stupid little bunker because I thought he'd be up for it. Countless times he's flippantly doled out cash to get high. No hesitation. "Sorry, don't-feel-like-it how?"

The passivity in his voice grates me. "Erin, I just don't feel like it."

I stare at him. Agitation morphs into anger. *That fucking asshole*, I think. *So fucking selfish*. I feel the rage building in me. A lifetime of slamming doors and kicking them again and again, my anger broiling madly.

"Wow. Well, fuck it. I've got to get the fuck out of here then."

"Really?" He turns to me, looking genuinely confused.

"I don't know, David. I thought you wanted to get high. I have a million things to do otherwise, so if you're not into it, I'm not just going to sit around and twiddle my fucking thumbs."

"Okay, cool, because I said I don't feel like it. So I guess I'll see you later."

My anger's a train and David stands in its tracks, too close for it to stop. He squints in its headlights and holds up his arm and I scream at the top of my lungs, *Move, fucking MOVE* from the locomotive but everything's so loud, I'm mute.

"Peace fucking out."

With that, I pull on my jacket and zip up my knee-highs and duck out of there into rain and air so heavy and cold it hurts my head. A painful comfort of relief.

On the SkyTrain, I sit in the corner where I can see everyone and no one's behind me. A man in a worn baseball cap is trying not to fall asleep, a newspaper crinkled and unfolded in his lap. Another man with a scraggly beard and sunken eyes is shaky and wearing a construction safety vest and has a tote on wheels full of empty bottles and cans, its smell mingling with days, weeks, months without a shower, and I try not to breathe.

At Columbia Station, sleepy guy sets his newspaper on the seat and leaves the train, homeless guy behind him. Through the closest door to me enters a group of girls around my age or younger. Two have dyed black hair and they all wear thick eyeliner and emo-punk candy bracelets up their arms. Two are in each other's arms. I keep stealing glances. Finally, one turns to me. "What does that mean around your wrist?"

I'm wearing a pencil-thin rainbow cat collar bracelet, safety-pinned to fit. She holds eye contact and I fight the urge to look away. The SkyTrain voice announces my station and the train stops and I stare back at her saying nothing, screaming internally at myself to say something, anything. If I were high we'd already be settled into conversation.

"What does it mean?"

"I don't know," I mumble and exit the train, fast, intimidated, my anger at David, at not being high, at being an idiot and saying nothing at full boil. My anger at things just skimming along the perceptible corners of my mind. *I'm a freak.*

27

I've been awake thirty-three hours and counting when I finally pop the question to Ava, with confidence. We'd seen each other nearly every day all month. Plus, the holidays draw people together like magnets to cuddle up and quell the winter blues. To say "Ha, us too!" to all those love-centric Christmas commercials. But we're not skating in New York City. We're not laughing and kissing on a bridge over a canal, warm drinks in hand, half watching ice skaters below, enamoured with each other.

Being awake for so long invites a person onto another plane. I'm chilled from inside my bones, and while thoughts are generally fleeting on crystal meth, now they're sparks swerving up from a fire—fierce, then gone. My vision's full of gliders and my stomach is lurching and I feel hollow but stripped of anxiety, of worry, of uncertainty. I'm a shell, but in a way, I'm more real than ever. I'd spent the previous night and day with Ava at her empty home. We had sex on the car parked in the garage and again in the shower and again in her bed and she fell asleep naked on top of me and I lay there still and chilly as her new tall mohawk literally white-glued in place pressed against my neck. I was exactly where I wanted to be. When her mom came home late, we went to my house in the middle of the night and had sex again before she told me she had to go. She almost never sleeps over.

Two nights earlier at a party at David's mom's, I watched Ava standing close to Alek. Watched the two of them speaking in whispers. Watched her laugh—a laugh that angled her chin toward the ceiling and rang loudly, her eyes crinkled and tearing up in that I'm-here-now-and-feeling-it way. I watched all this but didn't take it at anything other than face value. When I headed to the kitchen to refill a drink, Bright Eyes was playing through the speakers—"A Line Allows Progress, a Circle Does Not"—and Delia and I collided into conversation.

"Yeah, stuck in a cycle," I said, referring to the lyrics. "That's exactly what it's like. You want to feel better—you had all these things, and now your world is so small. Like it's tiny. But you also know the world is so huge. There is so much possibility. But there's also no possibility. It's weird."

Delia looked at me, hard. "Dude, it's still a choice. You have a choice."

For a moment I felt something in me grow. Some internal vastness connected to a greater, external vastness. Like they were one and the same. Delia was quiet and I paused and Conor Oberst sang about the downward spiral of addiction.

And then, that space too open, too still, I filled with Ava, with longing, with pursuit and headed back to the garage. Everybody had circled around something I couldn't see until I pushed through the crowd. Sitting on a chair, smoking a joint, a towel around her neck, laughing toward the ceiling, was Ava. Alek stood behind her, shaving her hair off with an electric razor. Tuft after tuft of black hair drifted to the concrete, and the circle cheered and she laughed and Alek laughed and I laughed nervously. After, with just a strip of black running down the centre of her head from front to back, she came up to me and put her arms around my waist, which grew my love and eclipsed my apprehension.

"Like it?" She smiled into my eyes and I couldn't help but feel held and I smiled into her.

"It looks great."

After our two days of being together and awake, Ava puts on her clothes and collects her belongings and I follow her downstairs into the garage. With one hand on the doorknob to the outside, she turns, smiling an easy smile. Often, Ava's eyes dart about and she moves around a lot, like a restless kitten that doesn't want to be held. But tonight, she's still. Relaxed. She pauses in the doorway, looking vulnerable. The drug binge and lack of sleep have gnawed away my inhibitions and I can hardly hang on to a thought in the muddle of my mind, yet my body feels light. Her wide blue-green eyes and relaxed shoulders fill up that space—that vastness—that meant-to-be. Everything feels suddenly simple. Me in front of her, her in front of me. Everything else frozen. I let it carry me, this rare feeling.

"Hey. Ava." I look down and then at her and she doesn't tense up and I continue, hyper-tuned to any inkling of doubt like a dog whistle only I can hear and it's silent. "What would you say if I asked you to be my girlfriend?"

She looks up at me, her eyes bright and excited. A smile. A big, genuine smile.

"I'd say yes!" We collide and embrace and I soar—an eagle above a great canyon.

⌒

When Ava and I are together, everything else just sort of fades away, a Christmas carousel finally warbling to a stop, its employees retiring their dishevelled elf and Santa costumes for another year, just hanging them up.

Late into the evening on Christmas Eve, we sit bundled up together, side by side on her neighbour's front bench. The house is dark and they're away for the holidays. Both our cheeks are pink and our breath white and I have one bare hand tucked under me and the other in Ava's jacket pocket, my fingers interlocked with hers. It's another green Christmas, but that's no surprise. Ava has her notebook and a pencil in her free hand and we're marvelling over the mural of shadows the moon projects through the tree branches onto the side of the house. Take away the freezing cold, take away the high that'll keep us each awake through Christmas morning, and we're two kids lying on our backs, elbows triangled behind our heads, staring up at wispy clouds overtop a blue sky. Sun warms our faces and we watch the clouds forge steadily across the great sky, its puppet master teasing us with moving shapes. Poof, a dragon; poof, a jack-o'-lantern; poof, a mermaid with a devil's face. We giggle and lean into each other. Ava sketches what we see in the shadows and we giggle more and the high of love outweighs the high of crystal meth and I kiss Ava's cheek and feel happy.

The next evening after force-eating Christmas dinner, I meet Ava on the pathway adjacent to her house. The scraping cold of the comedown gnaws the insides of my bones and I want to see her, but more than that, I need more. She holds the pipe and its amber stains that'll give me the bump I need. Something in her has shifted. She's standoffish, again.

"I'm done with crystal," she says matter-of-factly. "I don't want to get high anymore."

Her face is slack and she has bags under her eyes. It makes something in me shift, too. And, through the cold, my pull to her strengthens. I wrap my arms around her and kiss her temple.

"Okay, I'm down. Sounds good."

I'm exhausted too. I need to get high, but I need her more. With her is the most real version of myself. Are all these things we turn to just a stand-in for love? Is the endless hunger actually about love? Is that the real space inside?

"What do you want to do?"

"Smash the pipe," she says.

She had carefully wrapped it in a sock, and its pull tugs at me. I want so many things at the same time. But Ava's my high. Ava's truly all that matters. In one swoop of her hand, it's smithereens.

"Merry fucking Christmas."

We both laugh.

28

I was feeling like a translucent red spectre before the words came out of Delia's mouth. I haven't used crystal meth in days and somehow I'm worse, not better. We're sitting on a waist-high workbench in Grey's carport smoking cigarettes. It's late afternoon and cold. With my free hand nearly frozen, I pick at the curled-up green paint all around me and avoid looking at Delia. She can be so indignant, so matter-of-fact with words that lance me.

"Ava says you're too emotional."

I turn toward her and she ashes her cigarette onto the concrete, her eyes trailing it. "When did she say that?"

Each of her words sink like a weight in a lake. "She came to Danny's with Alek like a week ago and we talked a lot."

I stare at the line separating one cold slab of concrete from the one beside it. Follow the line, easy and uncomplicated.

"She also said she doesn't trust you as far as she can throw you."

My chest cranks; I've had enough. I slide off the bench, cross my arms and face her. "Why would she tell you those things? What did you say to her?"

"I just asked her if you guys were dating and she just said all that." Delia shrugs and looks like she doesn't care, and I could shake her.

"Fuck! I gotta go. This is fucking ridiculous."

"Erin—"

But I'm already crunching through grass and heading up the sidewalk, stuffing my chapped hands into tight jean pockets. I storm up the hill and past Cynthia's house. Storm past Ava's house, where I pause but storm on, getting home sharp red and out of breath. I whisper-scream into my pillow until my body softens from anger to anxiety. I pick up the guitar, mess around for a bit, try to play Pink Floyd's "Wish You Were Here," which I'd been tirelessly, painfully trying to master, but this only props up my frustration.

So I call Twyla. Get the invitation I'm looking for. Grab my Discman with a burned Our Lady Peace CD and head across the freeway to the bus stop that'll get me to Surrey Central Station to catch the SkyTrain to Scott Road Station, then another bus to Delta. "Are You Sad?" comes on and my body starts to relax, the song somehow reaching past everything I try to hide and my skin and my muscle to boldly but gently caress my internal sadness. Plus, there's the anticipation of being okay, the high that lets me forget, the high that transforms my feelings into something intellectual. Something I can make sense of. Something I can pontificate about.

Things are about as they normally are in the shed. Kevin's rearranging speakers. Twyla's babbling about how to get an eight ball. I sit on a corner cushion quietly, waiting patiently. Over and over in my mind, Ava's saying what she said, and then some. "Erin's too emotional. I don't know why I'm with her. Alek is so much better in bed. So much cooler. So much better. I don't trust Erin as far as I can throw her. I don't trust her."

I want to shove my face into a pillow and scream-bawl. I think about Christmas Eve with her, sitting side by side and watching the shapes in the shadows. I think about driving around in the pouring rain, listening to "November Rain" by Guns N' Roses, feeling every hair on my body, electric. I think about candlelight and *Melon Collie and the Infinite Sadness* and her collarbone. I think about all this around a rot in my gut I can barely glance at. Where Alek leaves school at lunch hour and goes over to Ava's to fuck. Where she loves him. Where she gazes into his eyes. Where "You're too emotional" blasts, where "I don't trust you" blasts. Where everything else goes silent, leaving the words I most dread to penetrate me: "Alek. I'm in love with Alek."

Where that dissolves into: I am not good enough.

I'm losing grasp of what's real and what my mind is fabricating and I just need it to stop. Kevin and Twyla are still both fuddling about in their separate worlds. I want to get their advice. For them to tell me I'm not that emotional. That they can see Ava loves me. I want these things so much. But their eyes are hollow. And when I previously tried to broach the subject with Twyla, she brushed me off: "I don't know what you see in her. She's just going to hurt you."

Kevin surveys his rearranged room. I look up at him and, in the most polite and nimble voice I can muster, ask, "Any chance I could have a hoot?" One never really knows the version of Kevin and Twyla one is going to get in response to any given question on any given day, but this time it's a simple and upbeat and wholly relieving "Sure."

As soon as I exhale the white cloud, my broken merry-go-round of emotions, spinning out of control, comes to an abrupt halt. Metal clashes to the ground and rests. And now, just thoughts. Stripped of feeling, they're much easier to organize. The sun goes down and comes up and goes down again, and when I leave, everything is grey but everything is calm. What I don't know is that those feelings are just brimming at the rims of their containers. And they'll stay brimming there, needing me to carefully handle them, so they don't pour out and drown me in their depths. Because that's how it feels when I let myself feel. Like I'm drowning in a river rush of emotion.

⌒

It's almost over, then it's over.

Almost over: "I feel naked," Ava tells me. "Our friends know all this personal stuff about me and I'm a private person. I hate it."

I finally confronted Ava, the night before she planned to leave for the Sunshine Coast for New Year's. We're across the street from Java Hut, sharing my grey hoodie spread out over the cold and damp ground for a seat. I'm freezing in just a long-sleeved cotton shirt. Ava's rubbing my thigh absent-mindedly, and every movement of her hand echoes in my skin and my cells and my core where it becomes the biggest, secret smile.

"Look. I hear you. I think I just sometimes get so excited. I forget I'm invading your privacy." I shake my head, awoken. "I'm sorry, I really get why that sucks for you."

She looks at me—really looks at me.

"I'm sorry, Ava."

She's wearing a jumbo-sized skull bandana, which she takes off and rips in half. She wraps one half around my wrist and that gigantic smile happily elbows its way out of my depths.

"Can you get mine?"

I wrap hers around her wrist, caressing her hand with my thumb as I do. I look into her eyes, behind her rectangular glasses.

"I wish you were here for New Year's. All I really want is to kiss you," I say, the words popping out from behind their dozing guards. Romantic statements are always a risk with Ava. But she must feel at ease because she bites.

"What if we both kiss our hands at midnight?"

I agree and lean into her, giddy and full of blossoming flowers and we're back to that carefree love no longer strained by poor communication.

And yet, somehow, on New Year's Eve I wind up drunk in a half-built house with Alek and David. Midnight comes and goes without a countdown or confetti or champagne or cheesy hats or noisemakers. There are just lighters flickering until their metal burns our thumbs and bottles of wine with their corks bobbing in the liquid. It's just cold air whistling through raw wooden beams and me, lying between Alek and David, teasing them, touching them, trying to get them to touch each other. Maybe just to see if they will. Maybe just because I'm drunk. Maybe because I need to make the moment more daring than it is. I trudge home at 2:00 a.m. heavy eyed and heavy hearted and cry into my pillow and curl up into fetal position to sleep a long sleep.

And then, it's over. I hear that Ava fucked somebody at a rave on New Year's Eve. And then, unreturned phone calls. Waiting. Distant eyes. And then we're walking up the street from my parents' house, my stomach in knots, Ava unfolding a square of lined paper.

"I just have to read it."

> DEAR ERIN,
> I'M SORRY I'M TOO CHICKENSHIT TO ACTUALLY SAY THIS
> WITHOUT READING IT. I JUST DON'T THINK I'M READY FOR A
> RELATIONSHIP RIGHT NOW.

She goes on, but I get the message. "Look, I understand. You tried. It sucks, but thanks for letting me know how you actually feel." I put my hand on her shoulder and squeeze. "I should go now, though."

And there it is. I walk slowly back home with my head tilted toward the sky. Speckles of rain drop onto me, each one a tiny comfort. At least we tried. And the dark foreboding that's had me in its clutches for months dissipates. Sometimes it's just better to cut me off so I don't hang on forever.

29

It's mid-March and I get a job at Value Village as a cashier and floor person. When not working the till, I organize long rows of used clothing. I start with colour, then move on to shade. It's a good fit—particularly on the days when my anxiety bubbles up. Just me and a task at hand. Even the most disorganized mess is fixable with time and attention.

Plus, it's pretty hard to brood with a '50s soundtrack constantly on the speakers—"Walking on Sunshine," "Happy Together."

Having an actual full-time job liberates me from my parents' nagging, gives me somewhere to actually be on a regular basis and puts money in my pockets.

I get an instant mini-crush on my supervisor Hollie, who's a few years older than me and has a gentle yet assertive voice and a waterfall of brown, frizzy, piano-teacher hair.

Ed is my age and jovial and easy, with the build and bravado of a football player. Within days of my employment, we're smoking hash in the downstairs boys' bathroom during a fifteen-minute evening break, blowing the smoke up into the ceiling fan, and we giggle and get away with it.

Raj is a loss-prevention officer—older, probably mid-twenties—who skulks the rows in civvies trying to catch thieves.

Delia gets her high school work experience placement at Value Village, sorting the colours and shades, walkin' on sunshine.

And then there's Alice. I've nearly finished a row of ladies' sweaters when I look up and see her for the first time—lingering at the corner of the row and the aisle. She's taller than me, hip-bone skinny with a black tattoo, maybe an octopus, that crawls up her neck and rounds her left jaw. Her hair's platinum with a Joan Jett shag and she's wearing glasses with thick, black frames.

"I'm Alice." She doesn't smile when she says this, igniting my nerves, but her green eyes look into mine daringly. I notice her lips. Automatically, I match her demeanour. "Bird Dog" plays through the speakers.

"Erin."

"How old are you?"

"I'm twenty. Almost twenty, anyway. Nineteen until May. How old are you?"

"I'm twenty-two."

I wonder if she actually means "twenty, too," but I'm too nervous and self-conscious to ask.

She looks at me again, piercingly, seriously, not smiling, and I look back at her, unsure.

"Well, I guess I'll see you around."

She turns. I notice her silver belt is a string of bullets and go back to what I'm doing, putting fire-truck red ahead of burgundy.

⌒

A few weeks after my first day at Value Village, David, Grey and I are across the freeway and traipsing through the woods between Tynehead and 160th Street around 6:00 p.m. Our sneakers squish into the mulch floor and our hands are dirty from crawling over fallen trees. The wet smell of wood permeates the air, and the leaves we brush by leave streaks of water on our coats. In me, a burning need to talk. Thoughts boomeranging to Ava again and again.

After a dreary two months of not seeing her nearly at all, Ava called me around 9:00 p.m. the week before, her voice unusually soft and slight. A vulnerability only ever present in mirage glimpses saturated her voice, which stated, simply, "Erin?" surrounded by a lot of quiet that grabbed me by the core and shook.

"Ava, I'm coming over right now."

"Okay," she said meekly, unsettlingly. I threw on my shoes, ignored my jacket and the hurt and the uncertainty and the missing her and ran as fast as I could from my house to hers.

I was there in under five minutes, out of breath. I tossed a pebble at her window and it tinged, then skidded down the shingles. The outline of a head appeared, then quickly disappeared, and moments later she was at her front door, quietly shutting it behind her.

"That was quick." She laughed but I could tell she'd been crying.

"Ava, I…"

Her body was close to mine and the only natural thing was to put my arms around her. She reciprocated and we held each other in the freezing dark on her driveway. I kissed her head before realizing that was probably inappropriate.

"It's been so long." She was speaking softly into my ear, her armour down, and I didn't quite know what she meant, so I just held her, letting the words escape before I could think them down.

"I love you so much, Ava. I've always loved you so much."

She pulled back, eventually, and looked me in the eyes with her hands on my shoulders. "Thank you."

"You definitely don't have to thank me." I looked down, then back at her. Back at this softened version of the person I knew—*genuinely believed*—I'd always love. "There's nowhere I'd rather be."

I'd clung to our embrace for hours, for days, nights. And then, the poison of unanswered phone calls. The poison of her, once again, gone.

Traipsing through the forest, it's pulling at me—yanking my insides from the present. From the murmur of conversation with Grey and David.

"So Ava and I had a kind of weird but good evening a little while ago," I say to them awkwardly, my words stuttering like a rusty old jalopy.

"Oh, yeah?" David's singsongy and always wants the latest news.

"Yeah, she was feeling shitty so she called me. I literally ran over to her house."

I'd played the scene a thousand times in my head. I'd clutched my pillow and felt the warmth of the memory hold me each night since.

"You know she's dating Alek," Grey says matter-of-factly.

I look back at him. Mid-evening darkness absorbs his face but even still, it clearly exudes no bullshit.

"What do you mean?"

"They're together. I've hung out with them like the last four days. They're totally together, dude."

My dark tornado swirls. I'm standing on a log and I'm ready to bellyflop off it. Ready to accept sticks shoved through my gut, my head banging on another log. I'm ready to let go and see what nature has in for me. See, this is it. I've let her inside, shoving over all my organs and systems and nerves for her, and if she refuses to take up space, I'm less than half a person. I'm empty.

And then my phone rings. It's Delia. "Dude, guess what? I just got off from working with Alice. She likes you!"

"Likes me?"

I picture Alice with her white skin and tattoos and black clothes and punk-rock I-don't-give-a-fuck attitude lingering there at the corner of the coat aisle. I think about the smell of her perfume and how nervous she makes me. She's hard. And intimidating. And seemingly displeased with everything.

"Yeah, dude, she says you're hot."

"No fucking way!" I'm yelling. My tornado freezes, then drops. "Oh my God!"

I jump off the log in a ninja scissor and nearly twist my ankle on the landing. The impact crumples me to the ground. I look up at Grey and David staring down at me and I'm laughing, on the verge of tears.

"This timing! It's fucked! Somebody likes me! This super hot girl from Value Village! She thinks *I'm* hot!"

Grey reaches his giant hand toward mine and helps pull me up. This phone call changes everything. I'm ready to say goodbye to Ava, to my pining feelings, to unrequited love. And I'm ready to say hello to Alice. To sexy, pierced, alternative Alice. To Alice whom I know nothing about. Alice whom my tentacles will reach for and they'll wrap her up and squeeze her tight like I'm a squid and she's dinner. Me squid, you dinner. They'll squeeze her so tightly that I'll muffle her words but I don't care because I need warmth. I need someone.

I can't see that it's me. That it's me I need.

And so, without fanfare, we decide to become girlfriends. We get off shift at the same time and I wait and smoke outside the doors on the sidewalk in the cool spring air. It's dark and it's clear and all the other businesses in the Whalley strip mall are closed for the evening. A homeless person pushes a shopping cart with a bum wheel across the otherwise quiet and deserted parking lot and I avert my eyes to discourage conversation. A minute later, out comes my manager Hollie.

"Oh! You're still here."

"Yeah, I'm just waiting for Alice."

She studies my face and half smiles. "I see," she says, more knowingly than I would have expected. "Well, good night."

Then out comes Alice wearing a black hoodie with its hood up. She looks at me and it's the first time I've seen her smile. She pulls me into a hug and my limbs are uncertain and stiff, but I welcome it.

"So I'm bi." The word *bi* takes a nosedive and her green eyes meet mine and hold like she asked a question. "I can be your girlfriend and that'll be it, but… I still might want to date guys."

I return her look, not sure how to mould my face, and I'm sure it shows. She continues: "Look, I do really like you. I just know who I am and if I pretend to be monogamous it won't be real. I just need to be blunt and straight up."

I swallow this reality and quickly decide it doesn't matter. She wants me and that's what matters. However she wants me she can have me, I decide right there. I could have shared my apprehensions, or my surprise at her request, that this is uncharted territory for me—a different kind of relationship than the Hallmark love stories inked in my makeup. But I worry that anything I say against what was already in place would mean she'd cancel me like a lost credit card; just dial up a number and be done.

"Okay, sounds good." I look up at her. "I'm in." She reaches for me and we hug and kiss and I feel more nervous than anything, but I shrug that off. Alice is hot.

30

From the first night I spend with Alice, I'm nearly silent. After work, we go to Central City brew pub to meet her friend, who's as platinum as Alice and spunky and loud and confident—essentially the opposite of me. I sit, squirming, yelling at myself in my head, *Say something!* But I don't, can't. Depeche Mode's "Enjoy the Silence" plays as we sip our pints, me hoping for the alcohol to kick in enough to talk without reservation, to scrub out the filter, but it doesn't. But Alice's hand is on my leg and my hand is on her hand, so I'm happy enough and the song's upbeat synth and Dave Gahan's gentle and assertive voice sings about touch trumping words and I let myself believe that. Could this be real? Could this be everything I've ever wanted? I can't tell.

At work, we flirt in the long aisles of clothes. She approaches me—close enough to breathe in her deep, ruby perfume—and presses a folded, letter-sized paper into my hand. Gives me a wry smile. I open it to a picture of her, nearly naked and staring seductively into the camera. Later that night, on the hill across from Java Hut, I show my friends like it's an award.

"Even I'd fuck her," says Delia.

It's March and the air is starting to warm and the cherry blossom trees that line the city streets awake, ready for the season, bursting with colour, saying, *I'm here. See me.* Saying, *Be the most glorious version of yourself.* And at night, the cherry blossom trees nestle into the shadows, stripped of their vibrancy by orange street lights. See, getting high turns me into the cherry blossom trees in the morning sun. Coming down and being sober shadows me.

But could it be the opposite? Could it be that drugs are just a disguise for vibrancy, but they really shove me further into the shadows? Glimpses whisper this could be true.

It's nighttime in Vancouver and Alice and I walk hand in hand, in silence, down Davie Street toward Kenny, who's standing in the middle of the sidewalk with hunched shoulders and a wide smile, a grey hoodie casting shadows on his face. Kenny's a regular at Value Village—stepping through the front door every couple of weeks and zooming in on Alice among the cashiers before beelining it to the record section. I'd barely exchanged a nod with Kenny before now.

"Ready to party, girls?" He reaches into a zip-lock bag of chalky green ecstasy pills and hands one to me and one to Alice. "For you." He says it almost goofy like, which endears him to me.

Alice and I have our arms wrapped around each other when we check into a nearby motel. The clerk is curtain-eyed and indifferent, and inside the room the walls are thin and there are two double beds and we have no intention of sleeping. We've barely taken off our coats when Alice pushes me onto the bed closest to the door and crawls on top of me. Kenny sits on a chair wedged in the opposite corner between the window and the air conditioner and lights a cigarette. Him, shrouded in shadow; the orange ember, the glow-sticked wrist of a tired raver, travels weightedly from mouth to table, where he ashes it, to a resting spot on his leg. He blows smoke through the tiny squares on the screen. I try to stop glancing at him while Alice takes off her shirt and mine too and kisses down my torso, unzips my pants and pulls them off. In preparation, I'd used my staff discount to purchase red lingerie, which I thought would impress Alice.

"I got your thing wet," she says and lifts and drops a corner of the lingerie, slightly too big, near my hip.

My face gets hot and I glance toward Kenny, the orange ember now out. Alice's head is now between my legs and her tongue feels good and I'm torn between the shadowed presence in the corner and the first time this has actually felt good. With David, with high school boys, it felt sloppy and uncomfortable. With Ava, it was always my mouth on her. This feels different. I arch my back and press into Alice, who lifts her head, turns toward Kenny.

"You coming?"

He kind of smirks and laughs and she rolls off the bed, gets up and turns on a light.

"Uh, no," he giggles, again like a boy, like a nerd, and covers his eyes with his elbow. "I'm just enjoying the show."

"Yeah? Well, we'll bring it closer."

I'm high, positivity pumping through my veins, but still, a rumbling discomfort like gravel moving along the bottom of a clear river. Alice wipes her face—another jab of embarrassment—and gets onto the other bed, in front of Kenny.

"Take off your pants," she says, smiling at him from behind her shoulder. Quite likely under the same spell as I, he doesn't hesitate. "And your boxers."

Alice looks at me and smiles, motioning toward his giant boner with her head. I'm growing more apprehensive by the second and can see exactly what's coming.

"C'mere," she says to me and lies on her back, her head on the pillow, and I move from my bed to hers, naked, hyper aware of Kenny in the corner, but crawling on top of Alice and kissing down her torso, just like she did to me. I unbutton her bullet belt and move my head between her legs, pausing, nervous. Kenny makes a little gasping sound and she looks at him, then he's on the bed, still in his T-shirt and backwards ball cap, but no pants. I roll onto my back and she rolls on top of me and he pulls off her pants and underwear. She's on me, facing me, and he's behind her, my fingers where my mouth almost was and he's now in her, her torso moving on top of me; Kenny smiles down at where he's moving behind her. I'm turned on as hell and anxious as hell and insecure as hell as I watch her eyelids drop and hips move with his and then possessive thoughts infiltrate—*that's my girlfriend*—and take over and it's more gravel, less clear stream, and I feel like a bellyflop and push my way from under them, grab my cigarettes and pull on clothes and get the fuck out of the room.

I stand outside the dive motel in the cool air and stare up at the cherry blossoms, immune to their beauty. No drag brings me comfort but I smoke aggressively anyway. When I finish my cigarette I consider leaving, but the Sky-Train's closed and I have no way home. I wish Alice would come out to comfort me, to tell me I'm essential, but she doesn't. I smoke another cigarette so I won't walk in on them fucking against a wall like animals as I scour for my too-big, second-hand lingerie. By the time I head back in there, they're fully clothed and Kenny's back on the chair and Alice says "You good?" like there's only one answer.

"Oh, yeah. I just needed some air."

This isn't the first time I abandon myself, my needs, who I am, and it won't be the last. The secret, hidden in the shadows of the cherry blossoms, is to welcome it all. The silence, the awkwardness, the embarrassment, the heat, the laughter, the sadness. To welcome it all and decide who gets to stay.

31

"You've got to lay off the drugs."

It's summer, and fair enough, I'm now never without a baggie of crystal meth. Even just knowing I have more in my pocket keeps me satiated for hours. Trouble is, I miss things. Aside from sleep, from meeting with friends who aren't into getting high, from connecting with the real me who's growing more faint—more opaque—I misread my work schedule and miss two shifts within a few weeks of each other.

I'm at Value Village, working the fitting rooms, smoothing crumpled clothes and sorting them by colour on the smaller fitting-room rack. I had just two hours of sleep the night before and popped a blood vessel in my eye, making it ghoulish and red. My world feels cold and muted, like the long hall of a hospital ward at 3:00 a.m.

Raj, the ever straight-faced loss-prevention officer, does a drive-by of my area, staring penetratingly at me from just below the brim of his baseball cap. Like he sees me. Like he sees the version of me that encases the real me—the version of me that I fear is growing bolder, more real. The version of me that's hooked. He speaks the words "You've got to lay off the drugs" and is gone before I can process what he's saying. Had Alice mentioned something? Is the broken blood vessel a telltale sign? Do I just look like shit?

I can feel myself falling down. But it also feels like the ground is far enough away that I have time to free-fall—to experience the parts that rationalize the hollow aching, the gnawing, the shakeup. I like snorting a line and hopping onto the SkyTrain, sitting downtown at Starbucks on Davie, listening to Cursive and drawing. Or writing. Or people-watching. Or pulling my black hoodie over my head and waiting for people to talk to me. I like being down there. I like the world humming with colour. I like drawing what I'm listening to. I like feeling music in places so deep inside me I realize they're there. I like not telling my friends about what I always have balled up in my pocket. I like that they don't ask.

Summer is tentatively unfurling its tendrils when my brother moves to Barn-ston Island, a tiny knot in the Fraser River where Fraser Heights meets train tracks, meets flatlands. Either he or my parents can't take the yelling, the late nights, the crime, the punishment. A small free ferry crosses back and forth all day and much of the night. Sometimes the neighbourhood kids'll go down there for parties on beaches with big bonfires far from the eye of the law. And shortly after that, my parents pack the car and drive away for summer vacation one very early morning under just a murmured hint of sunrise, leaving me in the house alone.

The parties start innocuously, on normal party days, at normal party hours, with normal party people—at first. But as I pump more crystal meth into my system, my excitement mounts and I phone looser and looser acquaintances and the doorbell keeps ringing and people keep arriving and the house fills up. I'm smoking hash in the upstairs bathroom with two rough-looking guys from Whalley I'd never met. I'm playing "Push" by Matchbox Twenty on the guitar to a guy who was in my high school math class, my foot propped up on my parents' front bench.

"Wait, I'll get it, hold on, I'm going to start again," I say, him painstakingly staring at me, uncracked beer under his elbow.

Everything is abuzz and I'm like a moth in a room of halogens, clinking from one group to another, electric and sizzling and in awe of manufactured glory.

Crystal meth being a harsh and chemical paint remover to embarrass-ment, to shame, to guilt, to self-consciousness, I welcome a close circle of friends into my room, the wild and untidied version of me on display in full techni-colour. My room—a depiction of my messy inner workings—is a disaster of clothes piles, books and notebooks. My mattress, stripped of its sheets, sits in the corner.

"A refuge for my good friends." I smile at a handful of friends old and new, including Jess, a young stranger from the Kootenays whom I bond with instantly, who shadows me like a loved and loving dog. She's younger—probably fifteen—and I don't know who she knows or how she arrived and I don't ask. But she asks me questions about myself, and I feel seen.

It's like I'm fickle grey and look into the world as a mirror. A glance, skin and bones, a noticing, some colour. Being seen—really seen—turns me alive and plump and technicolour. This is how I exist in the world. This is how I use the world to gauge myself. Meanwhile, deep, deep in my gut, my inner compass that whispers "there, go there, do that, say no, say yes" has grown as spinning and indifferent as a kid on a long trip, in the back seat, quietly ignored, getting used to being ignored.

"How long have you been doing drugs?" asks Jess.

"I guess it's been over a year."

"So what did you do before that?"

Her big brown doe eyes look into mine and she looks so sweet and genuinely curious I do a double take and smile.

I tell her about university, about discovering E, and her eyes hold on mine, unflinching. Earnest. I look down and back at her. I'm usually the one taking an interest in other people, not this way around. In my tall, glass tower, I soften.

And this is how it goes. These beautiful moments of being seen colour me out of the bleak grey. I promise myself moments like these are impossible without drugs, that moments like these make it worthwhile. And it's moments like these I cling to and play over again in my mind that are impossible without the mirror of the world, without drugs. And it's clinging to moments like these that keeps me stuck in them. Seeking them. Whereas I will realize, eventually, we can't hold on to anything. We can't hold on to thoughts or to feelings or to people. Everything is always flowing and when we let it, we're not just coloured; we are colour. We are the light that shines into the world, so long as we don't let our own darkness obstruct it.

I head downstairs to even more people in the house. I'd been in my room for an hour, maybe hours. It's still dark outside and the stove clock reads 3:22, but everyone's lively and wide awake. An uneasiness weaves through me, but I puff up my chest, push it away. This is my party. These are my friends. I round the corner to the kitchen to David—in the nook outlined by custom crown mouldings, adorned by family vacation photos—unabashedly smoking a cigarette. He ashes it onto a plate with a kick-in-his-step enthusiasm, thawing my freeze of disbelief.

"What the hell are you doing?"

He looks up at me, his green eyes earnest, then at his cigarette, then back up at me, then back at his cigarette. "Oh my God," he says, getting up, holding his smoke like he's carefully taking a spider outside, opening the screen door to the backyard. I follow him out there, where others are also gathered.

"David! I've been kicking smokers out of the house all night!"

David, who had met my relatives from California in that very kitchen. David, who had posed with a hand on my shoulder for grad pics in front of my mom's SLR camera. David, who had made a fruit pizza with me, then ran away down the alley because we were stoned and my mom came home earlier than expected.

He shakes his head and we both crumble into laughter, then into a long, hard hug.

The crowd waxes and wanes and daylight pokes its head out, then intensifies. Somebody, maybe fifteen-year-old Jess, finds brownie mix and makes a huge batch. Somebody else cooks bacon. I'm still high and not hungry. That closing-in-on-myself feeling intensifies when Kevin and Twyla show up, followed by the mumbling drug dealer Junior. Kevin offers me crystal meth with a purple tinge.

"I helped make it," he says. "I need a pipe, though. Can I look in your garage for something to use?" There he finds a halogen tube and a torch to melt it down. It tastes off and sort of gross, but its familiar alertness kicks in. I lose track of Kevin and Twyla. Had I paid attention, I would have wondered why they were in the garage so long. Had I not been high, when I finally went in there again, I would have seen Kevin's surveying of the shelves, the tools, for what it was.

The sun goes down and back up and down and I'm turned around and an echo of myself. There's no David, no Danny, no Delia, no Grey. No Kevin, no Twyla. Junior wears his sunglasses and sits in my mom's spot on the couch where she cross-stitches and marks up cooking magazines and he offers giant lines of cocaine on the coffee table to anybody who listens or pretends to listen to his molasses mumblings, almost more painful than coming down. I'm scratchy inside and cold and tired and I feel sick and just want everybody to leave. But an echo cannot assert itself. An echo just reverberates.

But then Junior lights a cigarette.

"You can't smoke in here. You need to leave."

He ignores me and ashes onto the coffee table.

"What the fuck are you doing? This is my parents' house! There's absolutely no smoking inside!"

He coughs and leans back, facing away from me, his eyes protected under reflective lenses, if they even need protecting.

He takes another drag and exhales up, in the space between him and me. I'm full-on towering above him, hands on my hips, and he just sits calmly, looking straight ahead, puffing, and ashing, his cigarette. I could have grabbed his wrist, kicked him, pushed him—my anger violent.

Instead I turn and go into the bathroom, bawl into the mute of a towel. I bawl for the hollow space in me that feels like it'll never be filled. For the strangers wedged inside my house. For screaming in front of people who don't hear. I cry because my parents worked hard for this house, because they work hard to keep it clean and beautiful and now this sociopathic oaf who I keep around solely because he sometimes gives me drugs is ruining everything. I cry because I let this all happen.

The bathroom door handle then turns and Jess, the stranger from the Kootenays, slinks in and shuts it behind her. It's the same bathroom I sat beside Blossom in when everything felt so warm and easy.

"He's a fucking asshole," she says.

I can't stop my tears or sobbing and she hugs me.

"I just don't know what I'm doing. This is my parents' house and they're good to me and I'm just so fucked up. I hate this so much and I don't understand how he can just sit there and not move."

My words are snotty and I'm a mess and she just hugs me hard and stays cheerful. "You know what? Fuck him. You're amazing to have all these people, but if you want to be alone, we'll all leave now. I'll make everybody leave." She puts her arms on my shoulders and looks at me. It's exactly what I need at the exact moment I need it—somebody to take the reins of my life and lead. "Okay?"

I wipe my face and nod. "Okay."

And, somehow, fifteen-year-old Jess rallies up the slumped, drug-addled group and ushers them out of the house. Gives me a hug and leaves me alone where I lock the door and curl up in fetal position in my bed holding myself, imagining this fifteen-year-old holding me and stroking my hair and telling me everything is going to be all right.

32

It's a grey day inside and out and the broken blood vessel that turned the white of my eye red hasn't cleared and I'm late for my shift at Value Village, again. I step through the front doors steamy, wearing my deep purple velvet coat that doesn't quite zip up, and speed walk down the centre aisle underneath the halogens. My fingers are cold and I'm covered in a sprinkling of rain. As I pass the manager's office through the double doors at the end of the main aisle, I hear my name. She nods me into the chair across the desk from her. I sit down, heavy and stripped of resistance. I'm tired—exhausted—and have no fight in me. No defence. My eye is red and my hair is dirty and my coat doesn't fit right. I have nothing to hide behind.

"We're going to have to let you go," she tells me.

"Okay." I pause without raising my eyes from her wood-panelled desk. "Starting now?"

"Starting now."

I don't ask why. Maybe Raj said something. Or maybe my missed shifts and red eye are a liability. Maybe somebody saw me exchange money for a baggie at the till. All I know is that, in a way, it holds the searing relief of the blistering first layer of a chemical peel gone.

⌒

Then, summer. Summer like I'm walking through a tunnel adorned with Polaroid pictures, each hanging off a string. Each a stand-alone glimpse of a moment, tied to nothing.

⌒

It's a warm summer night—T-shirt weather—and I'm at a park adjacent to English Bay, watching the fireworks, the brilliant display of flashing colour and music on the ocean. The Celebration of Light. Around me, Grey, David, Elise and hundreds of thousands of others have their necks craned, chins up, eyes reflecting the multicoloured explosion synced to Annie Lennox's "No More 'I Love You's.'" Me, neck craned down, chin tucked in. Between my crossed legs on the grass, the *Oh Holy Fools* CD case, its cover bright and colourful—a carnival. Lines of faces frame the action on green summer grass. But of those faces—dozens of them—none are smiling. None of them. They're immersed in this world of colour, and they're not happy. Underneath the sky of fireworks, I'm crushing a small collection of crystals with my driver's licence and social insurance card. I push the powder into a line. In the sky, a shaken bottle of sparkling champagne, a popped cork, an explosion of colour, awe. Nobody notices me lean down. Nobody notices me snort the line with a five-dollar bill. Nobody notices me brush the remnants with my knuckles off the CD case and put it back into my purse. Annie Lennox sings about demons in her room, about desire, about despair.

⌒

A different summer evening, Alice's friend picks me up from the SkyTrain. I sit silent in the back seat as the two of them chat and giggle our way into Vancouver. I look out the window and squint my eyes at the scenes blurring by and condemn myself for not being more free-spirited. More talkative. More open. And this shrinks Little Me inside further. Weakens her and makes her frail. I don't use all the power and love in me to hold her. I don't honour her and give her the acceptance and understanding she needs. I beat her up. And that makes me even quieter.

We end up at the Cambie, on the patio, and I wear sunglasses and smile and laugh at all the right moments until my cheeks hurt from the forced movement.

"You're so quiet. Why don't you talk?"

Alice's friend looks at me. I hate this question.

"I don't know. I talk."

I awkwardly play with my hands under the table, shrink more, look away until somebody else picks up the conversation.

At the end of the night, Alice gives me a hug, not a kiss, and I hand her the CD I made the sleepless night before. The cover, a detailed pencil drawing of love and drugs and mushrooms and skulls, took me twelve hours. Songs like "Enjoy the Silence," Duran Duran's "Come Undone" and the Rolling Stones' "Wild Horses" tell her how I feel. Tell her I understand romance and baby, I want it.

On the SkyTrain, I'm once again a hot stranger and can breathe deeper. No one can see me for who I am—inept and awkward—on a five-, ten-, twenty-five-minute train ride. I look "cool," so that's what I am.

Alice breaks it off the next day, telling me, "I listened to that CD. I know what you want from me. And I can't give it to you."

Somewhere amid the bruising and the tears, I feel relief.

33

Kind of like running downhill, there's momentum. And there are brakes. The brakes, you control. The momentum, you don't. And there are things about the momentum that feel primal. That feel exactly how you think things should feel. So you brake less and less. And the momentum builds.

In August, I get a job at Zellers department store in Langley. On my first day, I walk past three girls at three tills in my black skull hoodie. I'd safety-pinned a rainbow stripe down its centre to scream "I'm gay!" at anyone who wondered. At anyone who'd know what that meant. I make friends right away. Christina is bubbly and naive and loves Lindsay Lohan and the colour pink. Giulia is a wry butch with Italian features and demeanour, who prides herself on exceptional-smelling cologne.

I always have a baggie of crystal meth in my pocket now. I take breaks and crush up lines on toilet paper dispensers and nobody's ever the wiser.

"Wow, that's a really, really beautiful colour."

I'm commenting on a lavender shower scrubbie to a woman with a dark crop of hair and burgundy lipstick and a hit-the-town jacket. A woman who would have otherwise intimidated me into silence. But with crystal meth coursing through my bloodstream, I'm fearless. I mean what I say. I take up space.

"Right, yeah. I love it too." She smiles, intelligent and sophisticated.

I hold her gaze, look deep into her eyes. "What a thrill to scrub with such elegance." I'm half teasing and telling her this with my eyes. She laughs and averts her eyes from me, just for a moment.

"You're really something," she says and returns my deep stare and something inside me flickers.

The next day, my manager Marla pulls me aside and says the owner of another store in the mall called her up and told Marla she was so impressed with me, she wanted to scoop me up to come work for her. She said going through my till was the best retail experience she's ever had.

"And I told her, 'Hands off!' You're ours." Marla is sixty and gruff with a scratchy voice and a twinkle in her eye. "Keep it up, kiddo."

There are other days, though. Cold-from-the-inside days. Days when, during breaks from the lineup, I run to the bathroom and throw up. Days when I jumble my words and struggle to stay upright. Days when any sound rising above the hum of the department store zings my nervous system, like a bad freeze at the dentist. Days I don't want to associate with anybody. When every customer through my till feels like the heaviest of burdens. Days when I'm tired in a way only drugs can make me.

⌒

The Buddhists say something like: We all have everything we need as little seeds inside us. The joy seed, the grief seed, the compassion seed, the fear seed. All these seeds, in the fertile soil of ourselves, all the time. And we can choose. We can choose when to bring the supportive ones up. That's what they say.

⌒

My parents go away, apprehensively, for the second time this summer and I invite over my new friends from Zellers. I snort crystal meth in the downstairs bathroom and look at myself in the mirror. Gaunt and hot, just how I want to be—knowing full well my opinion of myself will wane with my high. I step into the living room where Christina and Giulia lounge about, unaware that I'm high. We're drinking wine and port I took from the garage. I put on Bright Eyes—song after song that turns me inside out for them to see.

"I just love Bright Eyes," Giulia says, and I can tell she means it how I mean it. Christina squishes into me and swishes her wine and laughs. I've latched on to Giulia, though, longing for what hurts deep inside me to connect with what hurts deep inside her. I kiss Christina but watch Giulia looking at the ground, moving her head to "Waste of Paint," Conor Oberst singing about loneliness, about shame, but also about perfect love and the soul.

Days blend and I let the house fill up again while my parents are away—but this time, only with close friends. It's 8:00 p.m. and, being the end of August, dim. We're sitting in the backyard in a circle of chairs, smoking pot and cigarettes. Christina, wearing pink and white, exits the screen door to the house and approaches my chair. Touches my shoulder. I stiffen and ignore her.

"I'm going to work now. Hopefully I can get off early."

I don't move. She lingers just outside my wall, hesitating, waiting, confused.

"Okay, hopefully I'll see you later," she tries again, waiting for the same warmth I'd given her when we were alone. I don't. "Okay, then." Her cheeriness takes a nosedive and I let her walk away unseen and unheard.

And yet, earlier that week, I enveloped her in warmth. In all-night conversation and cuddles and laughter and sex on English Bay Beach. We went to

Denny's and she ate and I crushed up a line on the toilet roll dispenser in the bathroom. In the early morning daylight, she drove us from Vancouver to her home in Aldergrove, deep in the Fraser Valley where the depths and mystery of the ocean and the tall trees that line it morph into sprawling, hilly country-side—matter-of-fact farmland. I was high and she must have been exhausted. When we finally made it into her bedroom in full-blown daylight, we took off all our clothes and I went down on her. And then I held her, wide awake, as she quickly fell asleep.

⌒

Grey, unlike David, always says yes to getting high. It's a summer night warm enough for just T-shirts, and we each take long stinging lines of crystal meth and hop onto a SkyTrain downtown, each toting a brown bag with Colt 45. We drink and talk and talk and talk and get off at Granville, walking fast through the corridor of the train, up stairs and past plumes of homeless people spread out in corners and against walls. The air is heavy and tinged with fast-food grease. A man holding a well-used cardboard sign with "Anything helps. God bless" neatly penned in black marker meets my eyes. He looks tired. Deeply tired. I'm wide awake. The flashing hand above the crosswalk and the street lights and car headlights and the neon signs along Granville stand out, clear like my mind, clean and uncomplicated.

"Art gallery?" I ask.

It's a night without plans. All possibility. And we feel it, we both do, I know it.

"Fuck yeah, buddy!" Grey's laughing and sloppy and leans against me. Like a big brother. Like a sidekick.

The steps of the Vancouver Art Gallery are a hub and tonight's no differ-ent. Some are homeless, some are looking for a good time. Some sip out of bot-tles in brown bags and some tote their sleeping bags. We join the ragtag group and sit underneath one of the stone lions. A girl around our age wearing a tight shirt that sparkles, even in the shadows of the night, turns and passes me a joint.

"I've been sitting here for five hours," she says in quick, spurty dialogue. She chews her bottom lip, her jaw moving in and out like an involuntary twitch. Her words flow rapidly: "Super good crowd."

I take the joint and inhale, using my thumb and forefinger to avoid press-ing it to my lips. When I turn to exhale, away from the lion, toward the crowd, I see a grubby-looking man holding a guitar. My high-induced confidence pushes me up from the concrete, cool beneath my palms, and I approach him, noticing, as I do, that each string is double: a twelve-string guitar. He turns slightly as I get closer, stealing glances at me through the corners of his eyes.

"Wanna play?" he asks before I can ask him. "The strings are the same—if you can play a six-string, you can play this."

He raises the guitar and I take it, sitting beside him, starting off imperceptibly. The guitar feels natural in my hands, the sound unlike anything I've played.

I start Matchbox Twenty's "Push" and by the time I open my mouth to sing, I'm unabashedly at full volume. The smattering of people below are moving to, mouthing the lyrics. Grey looks up and smiles. I get louder. I've never sounded better playing guitar. Right here on these dirty steps is happiness. I'm the sun in a little solar system, essential. The girl in the sparkly shirt dances.

And yet, I attribute it. Here, on these steps, high and singing songs I love, I'm essential. Without crystal meth, though, I'm a star that died long ago. But people still think I'm here, thanks to the speed of light and the distance of the stars. Maybe that's how I fly under the radar for so long; people still think I'm here.

"Disarm": I'm not on the steps at all—I'm inside the song. *The killer in me is the killer in you... send this smile over to you.* Billy Corgan, his yearning, my yearning, his words for places so deep and buried inside me, the twelve-string guitar, the sun, this community, my high, my disinhibition, my voice, my voice, my voice, my voice. *Send this smile over to you.*

I finish and open my eyes, my body humming. A dapper-looking man in a baby-blue suede suit, blond slick of hair, is in front of me with a huge smile. "That was fucking amazing! Who the hell are you?"

His face has the telltale crystal meth shine and he looks like he could implode and leave a cloud of sparkles.

"I don't know." I shrug. "I'm Erin. From Surrey."

Grey is facing the luminescent water of the fountain across the grounds, obscured by a black curtain of hair.

"This is Grey." I yank at his arm and he turns to shake the new guy's hand.

"Hey, man, how's it going?"

"Fuck, you guys, good. I'm Dean from Port Hardy. All the way at the top of Vancouver Island." He folds both Grey and me into his energy. "I fucking love music. I just haven't been around it for so long. This feels so good. So good!" He yells "so good," causing a blip in the murmur on the steps. "Sorry, guys," he says to everybody and laughs at himself, and he and Grey scheme a plan, me so pumped full of the love of music, I'd probably say "Yes, yes, fuck yes" to anything.

The plan: we go back to my parents' house with its plethora of instruments from whistles to rainmakers to the piano to guitars. They're still on vacation. It's what we need to do, like breathing.

"Ambience. We can create multi-levelled music with ambience," says Dean, and I'm smitten, not by him but by the idea. Of sharing music, of making something beautiful, of life—real, red-blooded living. So we ride the SkyTrain back to Surrey. Wait at Surrey Central for the 501, which doesn't come for an hour. We get off at 160th and walk thirty-five minutes. By the time we get there, we're out of drugs and something's shifted. There's no ambience. There's barely even a band. And Dean is looking worse for wear. The morning light pouring through the living room blinds reveals a raggedy quality to his blue suede suit; a greasiness to his hair, now dishevelled; a beady sneakiness in his eyes.

In me, a growing desire for sleep and solitude. Dean is still talking a big game. "I know a buddy at the Vogue and we can get in there and do a show and another buddy plays bass. Fuck, we just have to start booking shows and it'll come together. It'll totally fucking come together. The Railway Club, aw, man."

I'm sitting on the piano bench, my right hand on the keys, half facing it, half facing them, grey clouds accumulating inside me, the bridge from my brain to my mouth shoddy and breaking down. I'd tinkered a few notes on the piano and Dean played a few shitty chords and Grey played the whirly whistle up and down and laughed and did it again and that was it. I don't know if Dean even has a place to go and I have to start my Zellers shift in six hours.

"Oh, fuck," says Scheming Dean, "let me go through your till. I'll pick up a ton of shit and you just ring some of it in. I'll split it fifty-fifty." He glances at Grey, who already has his eyes, more serious than usual, on him. "Or 33.3, 33.3, 33.4." He giggles but is no longer cute. No longer dapper.

I'm instantly bothered and tired and a laser red slices through the clouds inside. I surprise myself by saying no. "No way. No fucking way. I can't lose my job."

"I won't say I know you, promise. If it doesn't work, that's on me."

"Dean, if I don't ring stuff in and you get caught, they'll know. Can't do it. I just can't lose this job."

"Fine, I won't say another word."

They both leave, but I'm unable to sleep in time and spend the entirety of my shift a bag of bones, cold and on high alert. I finally ease my guard as the clock ticks closer to the end of my day. Then I see him. He rounds the corner where the magazine stand is adjacent to my till, pushing a cart mounained with stuff, by now looking like a homeless crystal meth addict. As promised, he looks at me, but only by glance, then heads slowly toward the door. His cart is barely nudging the outside air when two loss-prevention officers grab his arms, manhandle him into handcuffs and cart him away. He must have stuck to his word about not implicating me, though, because I never hear anything about it or see the guy again.

That night, exhausted and still with the house to myself, I smoke a joint out my window and tuck myself into bed. That's when I notice my carpet. Wedged in the green fibres, it appears, are chunks of crystal meth. I pick at it but can't get hold of anything. I pick some more, unable to comprehend how I see it so vividly but can't feel it. I get out of bed and onto my hands and knees and scour the carpet, all across the room, picking and looking, picking and looking, for possibly hours, before I give up and fall asleep and dream disturbing dreams of bugs in my hair and finger-sized holes in my head.

34

It's getting cold again and I'm tumbling, the moments of beauty and lightness fewer and fewer and my world growing dark and confusing—the light mere streaks that catch my gaze before disappearing from my field of vision. This is the point where I'm not sure what holds me. This is the point I wonder whether the invisible grasp of these drugs is stronger than I thought it was. I tumble and it feels like I hit a bottom. And then I tumble some more.

If it feels exhausting, that's because it is.

I'm on the SkyTrain, shivering shoulders curved into my hoodie and high on crystal meth, my hip bones protruding in just the way I like them to. There's a difference between high day one and high day four. There's a coldness to day four, a fleetingness, a reaching for something always out of grasp. It's dark outside and I'm staring at my reflection—a flashing impermanence I observe without a flicker of emotion. That's the thing about crystal meth. It lets me intellectualize on my feelings without feeling my feelings. That's its superpower. That's now my superpower.

I'm heading downtown by SkyTrain to meet Alice. We pushed restart on our relationship after our summer breakup and are now strictly friends, which works well for us both. She started dating Jazz, a thirty-six-year-old punk cowboy who deals cocaine out of a dive bar in the Downtown Eastside. He's a quick-witted dick with tight leather pants and a cowboy hat who goes everywhere with a little Pomeranian tucked under his shoulder and says things to Alice like "Wanna go fuck?" and she shrugs and nods and they disappear for twenty minutes and now it doesn't bother me whatsoever. Friends.

Though I'm engulfed in my crystal meth habit, I find myself, with Alice, crouched in corners of underground parkades unfolding keno tickets from Jazz and using twenty-dollar bills to snort long lines of good coke, hanging out in dive bars, elbows on sticky long tables where strangers come and go, meeting in bathroom stalls throughout the night to stay high. I always head back to Surrey and Alice always stays in Vancouver with Jazz.

I get off the SkyTrain at Metrotown to take a line and use the bathroom in the Bay. As pale as I know I look and as hollow as I feel, I don't actually *care*, which is liberating. Normally, I'm inundated by the screaming body language all around me. How the clean-cut early-twenties dude on the SkyTrain peers up and down a nearby girl's long exposed legs out of the corner of his eyes; how a business woman with a Louis Vuitton purse and I've-got-this heels plays with her fingers and crouches forward, less confident than all her props exude. Every person tells a story and I'm a speed-reader, taking on emotions and insecurities and awkwardness, feeling as transparent as those I observe. Feeling tiny. Crystal meth grows me to normal size and makes that all go away. I crush up a line on the toilet paper dispenser. I've learned to love its wasabi sting. Wide awake. My ears and head feel warm and this makes the sorrowful exhaustion underlying everything go away. I could throw up. And I could talk to anybody.

Back on the windy SkyTrain platform, cold piercing through me, I reach for my baggie and find nothing. My bus pass and ID. A pack with four cigarettes. The train approaches, slowing in the tunnel, "Expo Line" flashing red on the sign above, those on the platform standing up straighter, picking shopping bags off the ground. I have to go back. I have no money and I have no options. And not having more crystal isn't one of them. I battle away the panic and put my arms on the shoulders of logic, which speaks through me: *We have to backtrack.*

Under the illuminating halogens of the department store, void of even a shadow to hide my shame, I trace my steps heel to toe, heel to toe, and about halfway between the bathroom and the entranceway, there, right in the middle of the aisle for anyone to see, is my baggie.

Alice is nearly as pissy as Jazz when I finally get off the SkyTrain at Stadium.

"Dude, where the fuck were you? It's fucking freezing."

"Long story. I got held up." I elbow her gently, which is usually enough to make her lighten up, and this time is no exception. "Sorry."

The night turns out like it always does. Jazz and his Pomeranian. Long tables of drinkers, lukewarm beer, sticky elbows, laughter, students, pinball, bathroom runs, toilet paper dispensers, long lines of cocaine, my hands around my baggie in my pocket.

The bar clears out and quiets down and the bartender locks the door and dims the lights. Because of Jazz, we're the in crowd along with a dozen others—some in groups, some alone. I've been nursing the same beer for hours; it's now as warm as my palm, its glass covered in my fingerprints, a ghost once here. The music is cranked so loud people can't talk, but nobody's trying to anyway. The bartender wipes the counter with a white cloth, raises his eyebrows to me about my beer and I shake my head, take a little sip—piss-warm lager. Alice is off with

Jazz somewhere. I need to get going.

Then, the familiar violin on "Bitter Sweet Symphony" slips into the bar like an old friend we all somehow know. And the stirring is palpable. The lyrics hit and slumped eyelids turn alert, craned necks push up. I look around, a wave of sentimentality hitting me as I, like every single person in the bar, open my mouth to sing along to the tune from 1997 that we all know, we all feel.

Beckoned to life at this dead-end bar on this dead-end evening in our dead-end lives, we all look around, pulled out of our individual little worlds by this song, by each other, by the lyrics we all so clearly feel in the lonely depths of ourselves. We smile at each other. We see each other. All our pain, all our reasons we're in this Downtown Eastside bar after closing. We're here, together, and we understand—we really, beautifully understand, if never in any other moment, if not one of us knows a goddamn thing—we really understand. We're not alone. We swear we can change our moulds. We swear.

⌒

I exit the warm bar to the cool night. Feel for the baggie in my pocket. Just one line left. My high is waning and it's freezing as I cross the wet street toward Stadium SkyTrain station. The light from orange street lamps slides in my vision. Closed signs streak. My footsteps are loud. A car, blocks away, swishes sound. The last train leaves Waterfront Station at 1:20 a.m. I have just a few minutes. I need sleep. I pass the clear line from where the Downtown Eastside meets Gastown. Where down-and-out meets yuppie ritz. Just a line, just a block. Excess and lack. You could almost jump back and forth between the two.

I round the corner to Stadium Station. To the metal gate pulled across the entrance. The sight reverberates through me like the booming laugh of a villain. My thoughts scramble to understand. I'm late, but not that late. I left the bar at 1:12. I've been out here for only a few minutes. This is impossible. I have time.

And then I realize. It's Sunday. The last train left Waterfront Station at 12:20 a.m. *Fuck.* I grasp at my baggie, at my last line. Do I call Alice and third-wheel on her couch? Taking up too much space in an already tiny apartment? I imagine picking up the pay phone and telling her my predicament. Imagine the pauses that would follow. How her voice would drop an octave. How she, cornered, might reluctantly tell me to come over.

Freezing in front of the metal gate, bellowing "no," I am a paper flower, and there's a dark storm on the horizon—ash grey and dungeon red, it's coming for me. I can't withstand anything less than friendly, so I cross off that option and wander toward Granville.

If Stadium is a sleeping giant, Granville has one tired eye at half-mast.

I'm cold from the inside of my bones and I'm coming down so I feel just rattled. But I refuse to take my last hit. It would make me want to talk, but there's no one to talk to. It would make me want to do something, but there's nothing to do. Nothing to do but shuffle up and down Granville. There's a certain kind of sadness like a thick and fuzzy blanket just out of reach. Somehow a comfort in its anticipation.

I have a quarter in my pocket so when I see a pay phone I slide it in, punch Giulia's number. The wry butch from Zellers picks up, groggy and helpful, trying to find solutions.

"But why don't you just call Alice?"

"I just… can't."

My tears fatten in their ducts.

"Are you okay?"

"I gotta go."

"Erin."

"I gotta go."

I barely get my words out without a waver and hang up, my palm lingering around the warm plastic of the phone. Every exhale feels heavy. I need to move. Moving seems to slow the crinkling of my insides, even just a bit. I walk, slowly down Granville, then up Granville on the opposite side of the street. Homeless-looking people are clumped in corners. A man rattles his cart down the middle of the street. I'm lonely from my depths. Steam rises from a grate as I pass it, illuminated against the night, and a weightlessness overtakes me, a soft urge to just lean into it and evaporate.

I turn down Nelson, which is even quieter. As I cross a side street, a man—portly and finely dressed with a horseshoe of white hair—is crossing the same street from the opposite direction. He's looking at me, head-on, and for the first time all night I feel seen. I smile at him, want him to slow down, to talk to me, to be my friendly uncle with a scarlet face after too much holiday Shiraz. But he doesn't slow down. He averts his eyes. He mumbles.

"You working?"

It's like he reaches inside me, finds the only remaining glimmer and snuffs it out.

☾

"I want out of this," like a quick slash across my mind. Not there, then—swish—there. Then not there again. To get out, though, would mean turning from the promise of warmth, of comfort, of safety and backing away into the cold unknown.

35

I'm in the smoking room at Zellers, on my fifteen, staring at the ceiling, at the circles of yellow and strings of dust, and feeling like a crumpled paper bag. The smoking room is tiny—I could lie across it either way—with a rectangular table and an ashtray in the centre. Then, a jangle of the door, the handle turns. It opens. A woman I've never seen before, nearly my age, wearing the red Zellers golf shirt, bustles in, closing the door and looking at me and smiling and reaching in her purse and laughing all in one inexplicable motion. She sits down across from me. Her eyes are polar-ice blue, her curls tight. She smiles and little top-cheek dimples appear. A space between her front teeth. She lights a cigarette and takes a long drag, exhaling upward, looking at me square on. I shift in my chair, my mind spotlighting over small-talk topics but drawing a blank.

"Are you coming down off crystal?" she asks me, still smiling, those eyes of hers staring straight into mine, no curtain of inhibition.

It makes me feel seen. Her name is Lenni.

⌒

Christina leaves Zellers and gets another girlfriend and I hardly hear from her again. Wistful thoughts float across my mind. Her glancing at me with a smile. My hand on her leg in her car, cruising the freeway. Knowing looks between us, between our tills. Her naked torso on mine. The thoughts sweet, but stripped of real feeling, so I push them away. Focus on a conquest that tangles me in rope and keeps me uncomfortable. Because, somehow, this feels easier than opening in the way I would have to open to really let somebody else in.

Giulia now has a skinny, punk-rock, Polish girlfriend who she's crazy about. And this magnetizes my desire to make Giulia want me instead, while knowing that if she took a sharp turn to take me up on it, I would run in the opposite direction as fast as I possibly could.

It's what feels comfortable, familiar, stimulating—this whirring state of chaos and colour. It's what I think I need. What I'll think I need for a long, long time. I'm not ready to sit with my stillness. I'm not ready to feel what's there. I'm not ready to love what's there like *I'm* everything I need.

In Giulia's Langley basement where she lives with the lady from customer service, I channel my rainbow of emotions into something that makes sense. A conquest. An easy line from A to B. Where I want something and I try to get it. It's sensical, compared with the peaks and dips that live within me, heightened by the peaks and dips manufactured by crystal meth and cocaine. A conquest. Something simple.

Giulia tells me I shouldn't do drugs and I use this as my ticket. I have a flap of Jazz's coke left over from the night before and a sizable baggie of crystal meth tucked safely away. We're in her room and it's neat and tidy and without knick-knacks. The carpet is beige and plush on my bare feet; the bed, in the centre of the room, a floral print that'd be easy to pay no attention to. The walls are wallpapered but otherwise blank. We could be in a hotel. There's a vanity with a CD player on it. We're listening to a burned CD with songs I recently downloaded.

"Give it to me."

Giulia knows only about the coke. Her palm's outstretched and I can barely hear her over the music.

"Give you what?"

I slink backward toward the bed, ready to give up the flap completely if she wraps her arms around me and holds and loves.

"You know what."

She's walking toward me with her straight-backed authoritarian gait. I can smell her cologne. I slip the flap into my jeans pocket. The room is bright.

"I'm not giving you anything." I make sure my words sound like an invitation.

She comes closer and grabs my wrist. My other wrist. I look into her eyes—deeply into her eyes, and she into mine, and for a moment, we see each other. There is lust and there is tenderness. There is uncertainty and desire. Overtop of it all, a sheen on a lake, there is pretense. And there is music. Dashboard Confessional's "Vindicated" plays out of the CD player's cheap speakers and it's sexy and it's wanting and it's conflicted, lips and fingertips.

Giulia's mouth is small and round and determined. We wrestle for hours, until all my senses are in overdrive. Until all those feelings, those peaks and valleys, those swirling emotions, those tangles, those knots, are focussed and flowing. Sensical.

In the end, Giulia flushes my leftover cocaine down the toilet, wholly unaware that the whole thing is a guise.

I leave Giulia's late and get off the bus in the belly of Fraser Heights and rap on Grey's door; he's expecting me. The warm fuzziness has turned scratchy and the days I've been awake feel apparent. I need more.

I need more.

We smoke crystal in a pipe and jam out to Radiohead's "Creep," me playing Grey's electric guitar, him on bass. His mom works nights so we don't have to be that quiet and we play it over and over, me singing, him bobbing his head, his shampooed black hair swaying, a couple of late-night creeps.

At 3:00 a.m. I need to go home. I'm feeling like a bad picture on a TV, bzzz in, bzzz out, a flicker away from being irretrievably gone. My bike has been leaning against Grey's concrete carport for days. It's an eight-minute ride home. The suburban streets are quiet and all the houses are dark. I ride in the middle of the street, feeling sick and struck by loud silence. I look at Ava's house as I ride by. Also dark. It's November and although I can feel its air chilling my hands and face and uncovered neck, the cold doesn't matter, in the same way splashing wouldn't bother someone already soaking wet. I'm cold from the inside of my bones and it feels like I've been like this forever. As I ride, the sidewalks liven with people. Hints of people. Mirages that disappear when I get too close. Strangers or friends, I can't tell.

Last time I saw Knight, he looked at me sneeringly and pointed to the forest behind the tennis courts. "We have a noose strung up in there for you," he had told me with Junior at his side. Junior had fronted me $225 of E to sell, and I took it all myself, sharing caps with Christina and Alice. I'd been taking side streets and paths ever since to avoid a confrontation just like that.

A block from my house, I see Knight leaning against a lamppost wearing a cowboy hat. I slow and approach apprehensively, but just when I'm close enough for him to grab me, he disappears. Another mirage.

I take the pills I got from Kevin's mom a while back, clonazepam or something—she said to take five for sleep—and they kick in around 4:00 a.m., dreams of teeth falling out and holes in my head waiting for me, enveloping me into their holding cell. Keeping me there the rest of the night and through the next morning, then late into the afternoon, when I wake up gasping for air. Like I'm not drowning, not today. Wrestling with some force that needs me alive while everything I'm doing says I shouldn't be. The first part wins and I suck breath into my lungs, hard at first, then easier.

Hard, then easier.

I lie there, staring at the stars on the ceiling that I can't actually see but know are there. We'd sponge-painted stars on my ceiling—my mom and I, silver and gold—sometime around when Comet Hale-Bopp slowly crossed the sky for all our eyes to see. Sometime around when school was clamour and home was clamour but I got a new theme to my room. I chose space.

The house is quiet. My limbs are floppy, like they've all fallen asleep and won't wake up. But my head feels fine. And possibly clearer than it's been in a while. I manage to get to my window, where the cool air feels good and I can pop out the screen to smoke an introspective cigarette. I'd been wasting so much time on the superficial and transient pursuit of getting high. Like it really does something for me. Like not-high me isn't worthy. Like she can't be herself. I take slow drags and stare at the black asphalt outside my window, an oval lit orange by the street light. Is this high I'm chasing itself a mirage? Do I keep getting closer and closer and closer and closer, yet never grasp what I'm actually looking for? What *am* I even looking for?

"I exist as I am, that is enough."

The words, Walt Whitman's, but I have to say them out loud.

The words I'd first read as a child. Attached to the string on my tea bag, on a thumbnail-sized rectangle, I'd read them with the burn of squinting eyes. "Cinnamon heart tea," we called it—my mom and dad and Bobby. I don't recall its real name. I found those words and I pasted them into the inside lid of my jewellery box. Sweetness on my tongue, yearning in my heart already. "I exist as I am, that is enough."

I need that foundation in place. I need that foundation in place now. I lean my hand on my windowsill and my chin atop my hand. I know I have to stop. I know it. I know it like I knew it with Ava the second I saw her—that gut feeling, that connection. I know it like I know nothing else, really. Which makes me pay attention.

One of These Mornings

```
love
/lәv/
noun
```
an intense feeling of deep affection.

36

Yanking crystal meth out of my life—and yank it out I do—opens up space. And that space feels cold and gaping. Exhausted and fuzzy. So I breathe pot smoke into it. And all the hard liquor I can get my hands on. See, one thing can replace another as a talented magician pulls a fast one on his audience.

But still, there's suddenly more room. And I start noticing beauty. How trees reflect in shimmers in a puddle. How the crescent moon seems to follow me when I turn my head and watch it. How I put a pen in my hand to paper and feel a force coursing through me, communicating almost as if I've stepped aside. I feel alive. And I feel exhausted and anxious—the inevitable comedown. But I'm also sleeping again and my mind feels more spacious, the poison that's been nestled in there seeping out slowly.

But I'm like a magnet, seeking that perfect snap of connection. Feeling like completion comes to me, not from me. And right now, what's close to me is Lenni from Zellers with her polar-blue eyes and tiny cheek dimples. And I use all my energy, all my focus, to attract her.

I find her, often, on the same 501 bus to Zellers. I step on at the corner of 104th and the freeway and see her, immediately, at the back of the bus. I see her where she isn't, as well. In strangers' gaits and strangers' looks and in the simmering hope and love that gets my insides all sloshy. On the bus, I walk down the aisle past the indifferent and bored and unaware and feign surprise when I finally let my eyes meet hers. I sit down beside her, my body in overdrive, feeling like there's an opaque sheet between me and the entirety of the universe. That's what it feels like. That's why I grasp so hard; it feels like everything.

It's been weeks of this. Weeks of fleeting conversations in Zellers's aisles. Weeks of me picking up my cashier phone and dialling a floor person for a price check. Me, my cells somersaulting when she rounds the corner toward my till. Me, my stomach fluttering when she's going down the stairs and I'm going up, our eyes locked as we pass, her cheek dimples appearing *for me*.

Then, on the bus: "Want to help me decorate the tree tonight?"

It's dark when we're both off shift and we stop at the liquor store across from Willowbrook Mall and pick up a holiday pack of five flavoured mickeys of Bacardi rum. We giggle on the bus together. And coursing so close I could lay my hand on it, the universe. Number 365, Imperial Pines Apartments. Her key in the door. Two cats. A Christmas tree, small. Too small for four hands. A scratchy couch. An ashtray on the coffee table. Tangy Bacardi, straight from the bottle, lemon flavour. Raspberry. Blueberry. My world hums and brightens. I hum and brighten.

And then I wake up naked in her bed alone. Morning lines the brown square curtain. I push myself up and out of her bed, not bothering to get dressed. She's in the living room, smoking on the couch. My head's pounding.

She turns to me, her icy blue eyes expressionless, her face matter-of-fact. A half smile.

"What happened last night?"

She holds my gaze, taking a drag and blowing the smoke up before answering. I don't try to cover myself up. I think I know the answer.

"We had sex," she says.

It's what all the flirting, the looks, the butterflies, the tingles, the excitement had been craning toward—the tension of a slingshot, slowly pulled back. Leading to this exact moment. And I remember nothing.

And now, for me, there's no turning back. But still, it's one of those rare times in life when I get the exact thing I want. When the magnet finds its match and clicks into completion.

Like a game show: Will she get everything she wants? Finally?

The romantic in me whirs to life, donning a top hat and carrying a rose gently between her teeth. We fall in love in this swirling Disney way, in twirls and sparkles of the magic of the universe. Lenni tells me she hates flowers because they die, so I visit my dad at the warehouse he works at and hand-pick a bunch of feathers and wrap them beautifully in silver with a bow and present them to Lenni in a swooping demonstration of romanticism and she giggles and scrunches up her nose and I love her and I'm happy and I gush to the world.

"Finally, I feel like my head's clear. It's like I feel like I've been stumbling around for years in this dark valley," I tell Delia. We're on her front porch, snow falling, snow covering everything, everything a dark and pale orange.

My thoughts move through my mind like jellyfish, pulsing and pausing. Hanging where they are effortlessly. I take a drag of my cigarette, noticing bare branches against the grey sky in the backyard. In just a few months they'll be lush with new leaves—a reminder. Delia turns to me. "And?"

I smile, feeling high on introspection and the burrow of love I'm visiting from. "So I've been in this valley, this dark valley, taking all these drugs to feel—no, to simulate—the sun beating down on me, because that's everything

I'm missing. And I wanted. And it works and I think I feel it. It feels so real. But then it disappears and I'm in the same dark valley all over again, looking for something. But then I hear this voice. I hear this voice that's coming from somewhere new. And I realize. That voice? It's not in the valley with me. And I realize—I don't have to be down here."

"Let me guess. Lenni's voice?" Delia's response is flat and unimpressed.

"The voice of love," I laugh, knowing this annoys her. "But seriously, yeah. So now I realize I don't have to wander around searching. I can climb out." My eyes meet hers and I feel them shining. "I can climb up."

"And she lived happily after."

I hold my stare. There's a tinge of genuine oomph in her voice. "Yeah. Exactly."

Of course, it's just a trick of the light. More me being seduced by the light I see rather than the light I feel inside. Because I can barely feel it, let alone see it—the warmth of the light inside.

Delia doesn't say much else, but I can tell she's touched by my sentimentality because, a week later, she makes me a CD.

"It's about love over drugs," she says, pushing a silver, unlabelled disk in a paper sleeve into my hand. And it's perfectly curated. "This Place Is a Prison" by the Postal Service. "The Drugs Don't Work" by the Verve. "Change" by Blind Melon. And punchy love songs like Ben Lee's "Don't Leave" and the Postal Service's "Such Great Heights."

It's the ideal soundtrack to everything I'm feeling, but everything I'm feeling is cut from the same cloth as everything I'm trying to escape. This insight crystallizes just days later, on another drunken night in Lenni's living room.

She turns to me, eyes ablaze for something, and I can tell it's not me.

"Do you want to try heroin?"

37

The first two times I try heroin, I don't like it. It cocoons me, which is opposite to why I started using drugs in the first place. It slumps me in on myself and I blur from consciousness to mini-dreams triggered by shapes behind my eyelids. Like curtains opening onto new realities.

"It's called nodding off," says Lenni beside me on the couch, pupils nearly engulfed by irises, lids at half-mast.

Heroin's expensive—towering over crystal meth in price. But buying it isn't like hemming and hawing over Egyptian cotton sheets; if you need it, you will buy it, cost notwithstanding. It's a habit my Zellers paycheques don't quite cover.

I move in with Lenni almost immediately by just not going home anymore. The couple of times I do, they're targeted missions, peeling a few blank cheques off their book when my mom's in the kitchen and my dad's watching TV. Back at home, I write the name of a Zellers co-worker on the cheque, forge her signature on the back, then slip it into the bank machine for cash back, thinking this'll keep my parents off my scent. And it works, for a bit.

Imperial Pines Apartments, where we live on the third floor of Building A, looking out onto the courtyard rather than the street, is one of about ten or eleven apartment complexes lining 150th Street in Guildford, breaking only for Guildford Mall. It's not uncommon to enter the front lobby—often smelling like fried food and old attic—to a musty panhandler with a hand outstretched from a rail-thin wrist.

"No, sorry." I avert my eyes and wait for the elevator, pretending I'm alone in the lobby. And it's not uncommon to step over a person slumped into sleep or heroin in the side stairwell on my way to Zellers in the morning. Our neighbour uses crack and has a missing tooth and listens to "Eye of the Tiger" on full blast every day, popcorn walls trembling. Jenni has three cats and lives adjacent to us in the courtyard. Half obscured by her sunshade on the balcony, she sits at her plastic table all day, chain-smoking, gossiping to anyone who comes outside about neighbours I don't know. I shudder at stories of bedbugs and silverfish, always down the hall from our one-bedroom apartment, or around the corner, or down a level.

And that's how life goes, isn't it? One thing leads to another leads to an-other leads to another and you're saying no to panhandlers in the lobby of your apartment without air conditioning on a knee-sweating, sweltering summer day. One thing leads to another.

As it goes, a series of losses—self-inflicted losses—fuels my burgeoning heroin addiction. On one hand, things are idyllic. Lenni and I are wholly, abso-lutely, blissfully in love. That finally-found-you magic. At Zellers, when I'm not chained to my till, we peruse the chips and chocolate aisle and pick out snacks for later, thanks to the cheques I get from my parents and our HBC credit cards, which soon plunge us both into debt.

"It feels like free money," I grin at her above the DVDs in Electronics on a short break.

⌒

It's love I want, really. Even drugs are more conduit than destination. To be seen. To be heard. To be loved. And maybe that's simply an intrinsic part of being human. Like in Plato's *Symposium*—those ancient Greeks getting drunk and arguing about love—this idea that we were all these big, round double creatures with four legs, four eyes. Like, two women, two men, a man and a woman. How one day Zeus cranks back his arm and splits us all in half with a lightning bolt. And here we are now yearning and longing and searching for our other half forevermore. Love. Like we're lacking half of who we are until we find it. That's the fairy tale, isn't it? I feel it in my maddening depths. I hate that I feel it in my maddening depths.

⌒

"Do you want to do a smudge? Let's do a smudge," Lenni says in her snappy, start-stop voice. She unlinks her fingers from mine only to unlock our apart-ment door. Inside, I place the plastic bag with groceries from London Drugs on the counter. Black cat Lucy squeaks at me from her perch on the stove. Kit-tencat, driven solely by food, rounds the other entrance to the kitchen, plants her front legs and meows at us both, looking back and forth between our faces.

"What's a smudge?"

Lenni smiles. "You'll see. It's a cleanse."

I wrap my arms around her and kiss the back of her left ear and then her right. "I'm in."

We sit facing one another cross-legged, our knees touching. She slides a box from under a shelf and pulls out a dried, fragrant plant wrapped in a bun-dle. With a lighter from the box, she lights it and wafts it in a circle around her head like a conductor who intrinsically knows each beat. Sage. It's aromatic and powerful and I gaze into her eyes in disbelief that someone so smart, so spiritual, so unique, is in love with me. Lenni seems to hear my words, my feelings, although unspoken. There's a wisp of smoke hanging in the air between us like another entity.

"I love you," she says. "I'm gonna call you Punkin."

I soar off a cliff in a triumphant release—arms open and outstretched, sun warming my face.

I beam out my response: "And I love you, my lady."

"Hey. You want to pick up?"

I nod automatically, my uneasiness the tiniest of slivers, nearly imperceptible underneath my swirling desire for her, for the drug that now warms me up and makes my entire being feel more compatible with my surroundings than I'd ever felt.

I pick up the phone and call this dealer, Picasso. He can meet in thirty for once; he'll call me when he's parked at the edge of the parking lot, where one tree grows out of a triangle of soil. An hour later, the phone rings.

I pull open the passenger door of his silver hatchback and push an empty McDonald's cup off the seat. He's smoking and wearing sunglasses at night. "Two for thirty-five dollars," I say and hand him three wrinkled bills. Right now it doesn't hurt. Right now it's excitement, not desperation. Right now it's fun and adventure, not need. I don't need this. I don't need this, yet. He hands me two points and I rush back upstairs to Lenni, to warmth, to happiness. She has the rolled-up bus transfers and two pieces of tinfoil ready. I put a breath of heroin on my tinfoil, hold the lighter underneath it and breathe in its tangy aroma. My body warms and my world slows and I slump into total relaxation like I'm at a luxury spa in a tropical country. I lean back on the couch, its scratchiness inconsequential, my brain quiet, my body weightless. I light a cigarette and close my eyes and I'm a kid again at the Canada Games Pool in New West. It's hot and my bare feet are padding the concrete from the change room to my lesson, happy, my suit colourful. The water is warm like the air and I'm treading water and laughing. Heroin's like that. Little dreams. Little realities of the past or the future or the present just alive behind your eyelids, a dream—a pleasant, easy dream. I wake up to a tower of ash, perfectly preserved atop my cigarette butt—impressive in its dangerous implications.

When we run out of money, I call my parents again and can tell from the way my mom picks up the phone that something's off.

"Did you take our chequebook, Erin?"

I'd gotten greedy and when they didn't notice cheques disappearing, one evening when they were focussed on the television, I slipped the whole book into my pocket. On the phone, my mom pulls from certain to firm to insistent to angry.

"What are you doing with yourself?"

I listen for a moment, then hang up and we don't talk for three months.

⌒

Lenni fails to pass her three-month probation at Zellers and gets a job working at a vacuum telemarketing company. I'm oscillating between a growing physical discomfort and relief and using heroin nearly every day—all my money going toward it, even above the cheap cans of soup from London Drugs.

So when I'm hungry, I'm really hungry.

On one of those evening Zellers shifts with so few shoppers the tinny music is audible and the racks get super organized because we have nothing much to do, a woman with a heavy Punjabi accent comes through my till, handing me a gift card for payment. Her hair's frazzled and she looks distracted, so after swiping her gift card I place it on my till and hand her back an empty one another customer had left earlier.

"You've got $18.16 left." I smile, bracing for blowback that never comes. Her eyes dart across mine and she's gone, stuffing her receipt and the card into her purse. Simple. Smart.

After my shift, I buy three giant bags of chips and licorice with the card and waltz back into work the next morning to zero repercussions, like it didn't even happen. So I do it again—indiscriminately.

The next woman who comes through my till with a gift card stands straight-backed and assertive and has small gold hoop earrings and sleek black gloves and a curated tuft of hair and she looks into my eyes and speaks in that unwavering tone that can only mean I-know-my-shit.

I hand her back an empty card. "You have $72.43 left."

She nods and carries briskly on her way and I breathe a sigh of relief.

But that same week, Marla gently asks me to join her in Bev's office. Bev is the big boss, which can mean only one thing. They confront me and I have no recourse other than to admit it. I sit there, staring at a speck of black on Bev's blue, organized desk and nod, the shame and embarrassment of it curling my shoulders inward.

"You know, we didn't think you would actually admit this, so thank you, Erin, for that."

Bev is both soft and stern. I'd used my HBC rewards card with my haul from the second lady's gift card. The proof was easy with a few taps of a keyboard.

Marla looks pained—her beloved dog having just nipped an unsuspecting jogger. And Bev speaks the words I know are on the way: "We have to let you go."

I wait at the bus stop in the biting winter air, a grey version of myself I barely recognize. I distract myself with thoughts of warmth, of Lenni, of heroin. Then, the halogen-lit bus and a ten-minute walk home stripped of its gusto, my thoughts loud and mean.

⌒

In these moments I'm as one with my thoughts as I'm bound by gravity. So when they're destructive or going tough places, I escape. I escape into the mirage of warmth, of love, of getting high. No way do I recognize the long journey of observation, of picking apart, of challenging my own thoughts, of applying compassion and curiosity. These tools—as far as I know—don't exist.

⌒

By the time I get home, Lenni has already picked up and the apartment's clean and lit solely by candlelight—that warm, romantic glow that eclipses everything. With my jacket, I shrug off yet another failed attempt at a job, another broken relationship with my parents. I take off my shoes and leave the confusing scramble of the world to shrivel outside in the cold. Here, in the warmth, I have everything I could possibly need. Lenni hands me a rolled-up bus transfer.

"I got fired," I tell her. Lenni's smiling and her eyes are at half-mast. I take the transfer, the lighter, the tinfoil, the small pile of sand-brown powder that removes the remaining splinters of what hurts outside—outside this warm place of total comfort, this womb.

I inhale and hold it in as long as possible. Breathing out, my body relaxes and the confusion, the darkness, the scramble, is smoothed into nothingness by the all-encompassing, feel-good pleasure. My mind settles into the moment and we sit on the couch, heads back, conversation pointless, close our eyes and I'm gone. When we wake up, we have sex on the living room floor. It's after 3:00 a.m. and everything's quiet and the curtains are still pulled to their sides and all the windows in the courtyard are dark. Lenni is lying there, absent-mindedly scratching at her face, and a layer of skin is coming off. We're both naked. I rest my chin in the middle of her chest.

"Let's go outside."

"Outside where?" Her face scrunches, her two cute little indents.

"Outside onto the balcony."

She flashes her eyes at me, looks away, then back at me. Laughs. "Really? We're naked, Punkin!"

I smile. "Exactly." I pull her up by the hand and she follows. Outside we giggle quietly and I stand tall and straight-backed and light a cigarette for its long, introspective drags, surveying the darkened windows for hints of movement that don't unveil themselves.

Lenni is antsy and goes back inside before I do. I lean on the railing, noticing the cold beneath my bare feet and the chill in the air and a feeling of peace, hidden in the darkness of shadow, of vulnerability without being seen. I know we won't have to worry about our heroin supply for at least the next couple of days. And I wonder, *Is this good enough? Is this happy?* And then the worries clang in my mind, like coldness seeped in: No job. No parents. Heroin addiction. Physical heroin addiction; there's an aching in my legs when too much time elapses between fixes and I feel itchy and sweaty and agitated and I sneeze a lot and waiting for Picasso isn't just annoying now, it's physically painful.

Now, walking away would mean mild physical discomfort. Soon it'll mean physical agony. A scratchy, unbearable second after unbearable second stretching, me hoping this second is the one that includes the "I'm here" phone call. I see it coming, feel it coming. But it's like those emotions we just zip up and slump away into a barely used closet, where they quietly take up space.

This night, this morning, these questions are inconsequential. And like a sunset, like lights going out in the theatre, like looking into a kaleidoscope, the bigger picture goes dark, those uncomfortable questions of "What does it all mean?" drop from sight, leaving only me, Lenni and heroin.

38

I go see Twyla in New West where she's living in a recovery home, not long after we veer in opposite directions. We meet at a Starbucks just off the SkyTrain, and for the first time in a long time, her eyes don't dart but relax on me in familiarity with a kind of familial love that's there—perpetually there—despite layers of hurt and complication.

Her cheeks are freckled and there again and I hug her hard, the daggers of betrayal bygones.

She tells me she's thirty days clean. She still talks like a waterfall.

"Yeah, I'm feeling a lot better. I was so fucked." She shakes her head and we take a table outside, each lighting a cigarette. I'm not high and not feeling great, but it's bearable. "It's crazy. I mean, I was living in a shed. I was pretty close to whoring myself for drugs." A picture, in my mind, of us going to a Whalley dealer's house in the early morning hours. How she disappeared into his room while I waited in the common area. "I was trying to see Kevin for a bit. That's why I only have thirty days."

I examine her face. "You... used again?"

"Just pot, but still. The program says you can't use anything. That you'll never get better until you don't do any of it."

Her words are a bell that rings true, but its sound is drowned out by a rainstorm of words I don't understand: *Relapse. Trigger.* "The program?"

"NA. Narcotics Anonymous." She looks at me, assessing what I choose not to talk about. "You should come sometime. Bring Lenni."

"When is it?"

Twyla laughs a genuine laugh that holds the beauty and rarity of a sunrise witnessed by someone prone to sleeping in. "It's always. There are literally meetings all the time. Like every morning, every evening, every noon hour, every city. Right now we go twice a day."

"I'm sure we could... find the time for it."

We both laugh, dabbing out our cigarettes and pushing back our chairs at the same time. As we hug goodbye, Twyla pulls a sealed envelope from her purse and hands it to me.

I soon learn, sitting in a mothbally basement church meeting with metal-framed chairs and yellow-stained-fingered participants, that being in the program involves admitting to yourself and others what you did wrong.

At home I open the envelope to Twyla mourning the rubble of our friendship. To her saying "Sorry" but not naming what for. But I know what she's saying sorry for: my dad's tools that I didn't know were gone until he came home, that she and Kevin always denied taking, but I knew. I know it, and she knows I know and she knows we won't, can't, go back to what we were but I know and she knows that that's okay. It's a clean slate, but we've veered and that's okay.

⌒

By summer, I get a hostess job at Ricky's All Day Grill in Fleetwood, a short bus ride away. Lenni gets a job as a maid at the Sandman Hotel in Langley. The sweltering heat of July livens the apartment's courtyard, a three-storey U shape, forcing open sliding glass doors, glimpses of lives—Jenni with the three cats gossiping about her friends on the land line, its stretched cord pulled from inside; a baby crying; a man yelling at someone; murmured conversations, some hurried, some lazy like a slow river.

I'm sweating behind my knees and sitting on the balcony, my eyes barely above the railing. I can't stand being inside where three fans are blowing around hot air. My body needs to stretch, to pull, but doing so brings no relief. I tap my foot on the floor and shift my weight around uncomfortably, trying to let Hole's *Live Through This* album take me from my discomfort.

A key in the door's lock like a sigh of relief.

And then, crack. Crack, like a nuclear bomb, like a lightning storm that lights up a black sky, like a magnificent humming that swoops you from the earth in a cacophony of light and colour—and then drops you before you can figure out what it's all about.

Lenni brings it in with laid-off tradesman Bob—a could-have been, a never-was—from the first floor with a moustache and demeanour that reminds me of my dad.

Bob opens his hand and a toothpaste-white pebble rolls down his palm and clinks onto the coffee table. I look at Lenni. "Paid for?"

She nods. "We got a deal, though. We just have to give Bob one hoot."

I inhale from the Brillo-stuffed pipe we picked up with a fake flower in it, from the corner convenience store. I inhale without apprehension, without fear, without curiosity. A motion. A new motion. In seconds I'm leaning on the wall of orgasm, of divinity, the pleasure receptors in my brain wasted and screaming. "Fuck yeah, baby!"

And then I start eating through my life like Pac-Man. I tote the guitar and amp I'd bought with income from being an extra down the elevator and out the front door and into the passenger seat of Picasso's car. "Can I get sixty bucks for this?"

Picasso quickly shakes his head, a punch to my gut, his bagged eyes refusing to meet mine. "I need cash, not shit. I'll give you twenty."

My anger simmers into a boil, but I'm at his mercy; I can't say no, so I don't.

Outside, a hot and dry summer that swallows me up. From gentle, new, green leaves, from blossoms, from bone-chilling drizzle, from snow, light and heavy.

Along the way, as the world changes around me and I cling white-knuckled to my immediate reality, I lose friends. I put them down gently, like bouquets on graves, and keep walking. Or, they scream out of my life. Delia comes around near her birthday with Grey, looking to get high.

By this time, I don't care about ritual, nor see any perk. I'm using heroin to escape and prevent dope sickness and I'm a fiend for crack.

I downplay my searing pull of need to Delia and Grey, who sit against the living room wall, legs pretzelled overtop each other, the energy of sports fans about to catch a playoff game. I try to keep it together.

"Honestly, crack is so good. If you want a rush…" I give her a pointed look, a you-don't-know-what-you're-missing look, all my powers of persuasion locked on their target. Inside, a sharp muddle alleviated by only one thing.

"Twenty," Delia says. "That's all I'll spend on crack."

Scraping on my insides, a tightness in my throat. "Honestly, twenty won't do anything. There are four of us. How much do you have?"

"Erin, twenty is all I'll do."

One hoot—one electric, magnetic, big bang of a hoot and its utter rush of white light, of euphoria, of three minutes—then I'm puking up blood in the bathroom. Leaning over the toilet, cool on my cheek, I don't know where this is coming from, but it's between me and the one thing that I need: more.

More.

I know what happens next only because—eventually—Delia tells me about it.

I emerge from the bathroom wild-eyed, all my human instincts gripping to one thing: more.

"How much more do you have?"

"Erin, I'm not spending any more money on crack."

"But how much more do you have?"

And then I'm on her, snarling like an animal, reaching for her pockets, reaching for the more in the only way I can. More. More. More. Grey is there and pulls me off, my face wet, fists in a tantrum, Lenni horrified and off to the side, a monster of my making, her making, a being lost to everything but the pursuit of more. A being lost. I end up face down on the carpet, sobbing. Grey steps over me. Delia steps over me. She stops taking my phone calls.

Some scream out of my life.

⌒

And then, David. David, who could always take it or leave it. David, who tried heroin for the first time with us. A hot summer day in the apartment, me just home, two cats splayed out, not moving an ear at my presence. I put on Jane's Addiction loud enough to quash "Eye of the Tiger" on repeat through the walls. I sing along to "Jane Says," particularly loud the part about not being sure what love is, but knowing when someone desires her. My insides crinkly, my outsides sweaty, I'm okay because I have forty dollars folded in my pocket. It's one of my two settings these days: okay; not okay. A red light blinking on the answering machine, a familiar voice.

This is not that call. It's not that call.

"Hi, Erin, it's Linda, David's mom. I'm just calling because David said you were going to pay me for the Tool tickets I put on my credit card. That's $180 for you and your girlfriend. Thanks, Erin, give me a ring when you can."

I consider her message—we'd paid for those tickets ages ago. At least I thought we had when I handed David a bunch of twenties. I'm staring down at the answering machine, at the dirt accumulating in the white lines of its speaker, when I hear a key in the door. Lenni enters in her usual bustle, carrying too many bags sagging from their handles. She's light and happy—I can feel it. We have money right now; we're okay. She comes around the corner, her face shiny with sweat. She sees me.

"What's up, Punkin?"

I tell her about David and the money. "It's not like him at all. He's usually super honest and trustworthy."

Lenni gives me a pointed look, her blue eyes saying, *Oh, you're so cute to think he wouldn't rip you off for drugs.* I nod, absorbing what I really do know.

"Fuck."

⌒

By the time a waning summer stops sputtering out warm days, David had broken up with two new boyfriends—laying down new lives and new habits, new families and new apartments, collecting mannerisms like little tattoos.

Sometimes I wonder if we're each the product of everyone we've ever met, ever loved, ever shared our bodies with. I wonder if we're all made up of pieces of each other. Some contribute in the most minuscule way, a toenail; some are as vast and as essential as our guts.

David ends up in a studio apartment—a box off Cardero and Davie downtown. I visit him on a day that screams Vancouver autumn, its sideways downpour forcing man-hand-sized red and orange maple leaves off their branches to slick the sidewalk. I stand freezing under the awning of his plump and concrete-grey apartment building and wait for the scratchy intercom to buzz. Once I'm up the elevator and through his door, we hug, hard. He's boiling a kettle for green tea. Pink Floyd's *The Wall* is on the TV in the background, its flashing drawing me in as David clinks around the kitchen.

The lyrics to "Nobody Home" grab me, my guts bulging between the fingers of its grasp—the shit on TV, on being a keen observer. The sliding glass door fogs up, muting the grey outside. David's skinny, really skinny. His ribs poked me in our embrace. I'm skinny too because food is less important than heroin and Lenni and I are broke. I'm scraping scraps off plates into my apron at Ricky's, tracking the dishwasher kid's eyes to make sure he doesn't notice. I eat ravenously in the broom-closet bathroom.

David and I used to be pudgy, both of us. Were those better days, in high school under the facade or weird truth of being young and in love? I was at least two people then, if not more. David was at least two people too. All those things we—well, I—would never talk about.

I sure wish I had.

We went to his grandma's family picnic one year, me silently crushing on his pretty older cousin and her big brown eyes. The grass green and shimmery white from the hot sun, David and I win a three-legged race, collapsing on each other in laughter. The men of the family, tanned muscles and shovels, dig a rectangular hole in the ground, and in it, the women bake a salmon. David's parents are gay and nobody knows but them, and us. David and I are gay, and nobody knows but us. We eat the perogies David had bragged about for weeks, for months, every time we bought a bag of frozen perogies and bacon from Giant Foods and cooked it all up in a greasy mess that we stuffed ourselves with until another bite would make us puke. It was a different kind of excess. "My grandma makes the best perogies at the family picnic," he'd say over the snap of bacon grease. At the party, just as full, David presents the also-famous money cake, made by his grandma, full of coins like nickels and quarters and other useless pocket change. He pushes me to eat more, to stuff myself, feigning sadness that his "poor little grandma" went through all this effort. We're in the bathroom.

Beige tiles and potpourri. I know he's fucking with me but I play along and take a bite, my insides bursting, his eyes on me, big and green and playful. Another bite. I groan in mock and real discomfort, until I clear my plate. He pats me on the back, kisses me on the cheek and plops his cake into the toilet, his mad cackle blending with the swirling water of his flush.

Were those the good days? Or were those just good moments?

Pink Floyd lyrics, yanking at me from the TV: wild eyes, urges to fly, nowhere to go. David comes around the corner, hands me a mug by its handle. I settle into the loveseat and he settles in beside me, his hand around my shoulder, a new kind of love.

"So I got a job at Blenz on Robson."

"No way, David! That's so freaking awesome."

In my mind, the aroma of freshly ground beans, warm yellow lighting, Java Hut, handing the goth girl a free coffee, her shy, smiling eyes.

We normally don't make small talk. He scratches the back of his head, his pale and rail-thin arm like an alarm. He has bags under his eyes. I wonder how I look to him. I'd gotten high a few hours ago and still feel stable. I put my hand on his leg. Gently, "How are you doing?"

"You know, okay." It's weird of him to sputter. "I actually got another job too."

"No surprise there. What does this place cost?"

It's tiny, smaller than my living room.

"Nine hundred twenty-five bucks."

"Location, location," I say and smile. He's a three-minute walk from English Bay and in the heart of the gay district—cafés and clubs and rainbow banners proudly on lampposts. "So what's your other job?"

He hangs his head, a dying flower, its weight too heavy to bear. "I'm a masseur."

I laugh, automatically. He raises his eyes toward me, guilty-like.

He tells me that they're gay massages. That it's easy, that you just give a happy ending if they want it. They always want it. Jon, his ex, his stiff and repressed ex with the apartment overlooking Coal Harbour, knew a guy who knew a guy. And he's making bank, David—a hundred bucks every time, plus tips.

"They love me." His voice emerges singsongy from its cocoon of awkward.

"Of course they love you." I take a deep breath.

"Anyway," he says, "I'm good with it. Oh, and I have a dealer down here now."

On the TV, the song "Comfortably Numb"—the pinprick, the screaming.

David's leaves to meet his dealer and is back within minutes, drops on his T-shirt, wet arms and wilted hair. But on his face, a big smile. That's kind of the thing about David. When he's down, he retreats into candlelight and unanswered phones and notebooks. Kind of like me. But otherwise, he's happy-go-lucky, affectionate and ever-laughing. Also kind of like me.

David and I, we were both at least two people.

He pulls a flat tin from under the couch. Before opening it, he looks at me, his hand still on its lid.

"What, David? This is starting to feel like Jerry Springer confessions or some shit."

"I just want to warn you that I'm going to shoot it."

My body zings cold. "What?"

"I just wanted to know what it felt like. And let's just say there's no going back."

I feel sick, a two-hand wringing of my guts. "You just wanted to know what it felt like so you started sticking a needle in your arm?"

My words are saturated with contempt, which I'm stuck in like goo, and I fumble with my thoughts and fumble with my words until David hands me a square of tinfoil, carefully, with a hit on top of it and a lighter and a rolled-up transfer and I light the lighter and breathe in the tang, hold, exhale, and I'm ironed out, smoothed by heroin, and nothing else really matters anymore.

⌒

It doesn't go anywhere. It just waits in the shadows. (Breathe. I could just breathe.)

⌒

Later that evening, though, I wrinkle again, staring at the popcorn ceiling from bed, beside Lenni.

"Like, he could literally die. He could take too much or have a bad batch and could literally die instantly." Tears pour out of my eyes. Lenni's elsewhere, also staring at the ceiling. I wipe my face with the heels of my hands, suddenly the loneliest person in the world. "What are you thinking?"

Lenni doesn't move, her eyes still focussed on the ceiling, light years away from me. She's quiet, at first. Then, "I'm thinking… I wonder what it feels like. Shooting up."

A gut punch, I'm down. I move closer to her, as close as I can get. She doesn't move, her eyes cold and on the ceiling, me wriggling inside. The tears come again and I move from her side, a space, irreparable, between us. She doesn't flinch.

Could we possibly, within the vast universes of our selves, find thumbs to suck and bumper pads and highs and all the love we seek from others? This, I don't know.

The loneliest person in the world.

39

Nodding off on heroin is sort of like conscious dreaming. A speck of light visible when you close your eyes becomes the corner of a scene, rapidly expanding onto a new world. This new world is often mundane—a scene at work that didn't exactly happen, or at home, or on the bus, or with people you love or with people you barely know. You watch with interest, removed from the real world where your body's slumped into where it is, almost like you're dead. But euphoria drums through your bloodstream. The simplicity, the presence, the yammering of the mind muted, the body light. But, the cost. The cost eclipses everything. The cost is your life like an hourglass, sand sifting away to nothing, disintegrating without pause, falling to the ground like ice crystals in the excruciating cold, glinting for a breath, gone forever.

And where I once found glints of beauty, there's now only darkness, only desperation. There's only Lenni rifling through guests' belongings at the Sandman. There's me, aware of the camera above the till at Ricky's, palming money into my hand, slipping it into my apron. There's our phone, cut off. There's paying rent late again, and again and again, somehow always able to scrape together the $565 needed to keep our apartment. There's opening a new bank account at BMO with an overdraft and exhausting it immediately. There's cashing fake cheques at Money Mart where their "no holds" policy is covered by high fees.

Our fridge is all condiments and Friskies. Lenni and I circle the mall most days to collect cigarette butts so we can roll our own. Even the ones with a pin of white before the orange filter can be pressed and emptied for a few strings of tobacco. We're resourceful, but there's a ceiling to minor bank fraud and scavenging.

During one of those warm blips in October where my arms sweat under the heavy humidity of my brown fleece, when my skin is crawling and I'm on the bench outside the mall waiting for Picasso to show up, I meet Do-Good. He's on the bench beside me, dark and Kenyan and wearing a tacky tourist shirt snug enough to reveal his gangly frame. I'd have completely ignored him had he not turned to me with a big white smile, accent thick, gold chain around his neck.

"Alo gur, what you do?"

I can't tell whether he's twenty-three or thirty-nine. I expect him to hit on me, I expect to shoot him down, I expect Picasso to pull up, I expect to inhale away this godawful feeling.

But he surprises me.

"Yoo meet up?"

I assess him. His sunglasses are oval and mirrored and I avert my eyes from my reflection, pale, scrunched, pained. Does he know what he's asking? Is he a cop? He moves his hand toward his pocket and flashes a surprisingly large wad of bills at me. Like salve. I risk it: "Yeah, why?"

"Yoo get rock?"

"I can. I'm getting down. How much do you want?"

He hands me five twenties. I only have one. My brain works fast.

"Don't you want some down too then? It's better to end with that so you're not feigning."

I have no idea what he understands and what he doesn't.

"Yo okay gur. You got place?"

"Place?"

He nods his chin toward the line of apartments on 150th Street, across from the mall. All those bills carry a lot of weight. There are two of us, one of him. I size him up one final time and nod.

"Yeah, my girlfriend's there waiting for me. Our dude friends will probably show up too. But yeah, you can come."

How it goes is about how I expect it to go. I slip our twenty back into my pocket. Do-Good has no idea. Lenni's what-the-fuck is placated by the mittful of crack and heroin. We get high on the couch, the three of us, first on crack, then heroin. Do-Good seems simple, and harmless. Crack can yank the crazy out of anyone, but he just yammers in his increasingly indecipherable accent. He's a bouncer at a Whalley nightclub, he says. He's killing it in tips, he says. We plow through the drugs, Lenni and I both taking more, Do-Good oblivious. Climbing the rungs back to uncomfortable reality, Do-Good pulls more cash out of his pocket—$280 on the shit-coloured coffee table, a decipherable statement: "We have sex."

"Uh, what?" says Lenni, her eyes ice, darting to the money, to me, to him.

He's smiling around the question, his head back against the couch, a cockiness I hadn't yet seen, or noticed, like, *I know you will do exactly what I ask.* We look at each other. I scrunch my face at her. I don't want to have sex with him. I don't want him to leave with all that money. I don't want him to leave with all that money more than I don't want to have sex with him.

"We have sex," he repeats, not budging, not shifting his air of cockiness.

"Uh, no," says Lenni, and he puts his hand on the bills, pulls them back into his pocket, squirms. He must want it as bad as we need it. I shoot Lenni a look.

"Bedroom?" he presses.

"You can't touch." Lenni negotiates with him. "You can look but you can't touch. We pick up first, though."

We all take our clothes off. Crack makes it better. He doesn't touch. He can't even get it up. I pant on top of Lenni, put on a show, his mouth open, white teeth, red tongue, black lips, limp dick against his leg. He moves toward us a few times but I push him away as easily as an obedient dog. This is okay. We hide extra heroin and breathe it in after he pushes the door shut behind him. We get his phone number. We want his phone number, just in case, but we tell ourselves we're not going to use it. We do. Again and again and again and again we use it, until he stops taking our calls.

◠

There'd always been glints of beauty here. There's no more beauty here.

◠

It's late, after midnight. Lenni and I are both dope sick and broke.

"What about Johnny? Would he front?" Lenni asks me, our resources depleted.

Last time I went over to Building B, it was the middle of the night. Johnny is needle thin and has wounds all over his face and track marks down the veins in his arms. I buzzed him not knowing what I was walking into. I'd heard stories about dealers on my floor having girls in there for days. The thug dealers, though, the coke and crystal ones. How one girl ran out naked from Diego's apartment. Those are never their real names. Spiked hair and full cigarettes and gold chains. She escaped; from what, I don't know. I don't want to know. But it settles in me anyway, an uneasiness around my guts. An it-could-happen-to-anyone.

That last time at Johnny's, I lingered between him and the unlocked door and handed him my twenty. He disappeared around the corner, for a long time. It was quiet. I kept my hand on the door handle. He returned and leaned over a scale on the counter, his body an upside-down L, and he nodded off, still, like he was embalmed like that. I cleared my throat and he woke up and finished what he was doing and I took my drugs and got out of there, speed walking through the hallways, heart pumping: *You. Shouldn't. Be. Here. You. Shouldn't. Be. Here. Get. Out. Get out. Get out.*

"Nah, not Johnny. He couldn't afford to front."

"What about DJ and Les?"

We go upstairs. Les, a seventy-year-old dumpster diver, has been known to share. "I only need a bit, girls," he's said to us before. The lights are on, and DJ lets us in to the smoky apartment. No risk of sex kidnapping here. Derek's at the table in a red jersey, smoking a cigarette. He's tough and tall and freckled. I knew him around Fraser Heights, before. Or of him. We tough-guy nod at each other. Lenni and I have four dollars. Derek has fifteen.

"I think I could scrounge up a dollar for a couple nice girls," says Les, scratchy voice, toothless smile. I have the edge of a dealer on call. Derek doesn't. Not tonight. Lenni and I just need one hit and we'll be fine, able to sleep.

Picasso says he'll be an hour. Says he'll try to get there sooner. At 3:00 a.m., I cross the deserted mall parking lot to the bench. It's cold and it's dark. I could throw up. My skin is crawling like a nauseated line dance, sticky floors, exhaustion, up and down the entirety of my body. Lights move up the street, a car, hope, the dance freezes like time has a pause button, and, no. The car hums past. Every second is searing. Every second is stretched. The sky turns from black to deep blue. I stare at a crack on the asphalt in front of me, stuffed with tall grass, albino and limp. Every hour is searing. Every hour is stretched. The sky, now pink.

Then, near the field, a figure. A figure that materializes into Derek. I can see the rage in his gait before I see his tight face, angry eyes. I'd been palming the money over and over; I slip it into my pocket, white-knuckle the bench, brace for impact.

"This is fucking ridiculous, give me back my money."

I try reason and softness: "Look, Derek, he said he'd be here. He'll be here."

"No. It's been over two hours. I don't need this bullshit."

He lifts his arms and looks around. He's wearing only a wifebeater now. His arms like two-by-fours.

"He'll be here. Seriously any minute now."

"Give me my money, Erin. I'm not fucking around."

"Look, you got me to call my guy. I called him. He's never not showed up. He'll be here soon and we'll all be happy."

I need this. I need this more than anything.

"Bitch, I'm not going to ask you again."

The storm. He grabs me by the hoodie and I'm off the bench, my white knuckles futile in defence. I swing around him in a semicircle and am on the ground, protecting my head with one hand, the money in the other. *Something in me wants to live. Something in me wants to live.* I curl into fetal position. Where it all began. Before need. Before life. Before the loudness of the world. Before turning to the external. Before the space. Before the gaping hole inside of me. Before filling, filling, filling. He kicks me, hard, in the stomach. One hand on my head. One hand on the money. He kicks me again. I take in a loud and desperate breath, my lungs screaming for air. Air. I need air more than anything. I breathe and breathe and breathe and breathe and look up at his face, tight and wild. He cranks his arm back, his fist aimed at my face. It'll knock me out, I know. "Okay!" I scream it. "Okay!" I release the money.

"Fuck you for making me do this," he mumbles and picks it up and he's gone.

The asphalt is cold. Cold against my cheek and I'm sobbing into it. Sobbing into it like I'm a baby, fresh born, the pain of the world like a sucking black hole in my centre. And then, the sound of footsteps.

A woman, bundled up. I force myself up. She's looking at me with blue, concerned eyes. "Are you okay? Are you okay?"

I push myself up and I'm in her arms, sobbing. Sobbing into her scratchy jacket, the smell of mothballs, warmth. Sobbing for everything I've lost. Sobbing for everything I need. She holds me until I pull back. My teeth start chattering. She's holding a phone, open.

"I saw that all. The whole thing. Okay. I'm calling the cops." She pauses, asks gently, "Do you want that?"

I nod, slightly, again. I think I want that. I don't know what I want. She's pacing in little circles, shaking her head. The phone's to her ear. I linger at the corner of her, stuck as a feather waterlogged with mud and smeared on the inside of a dumpster. *I wanted to live.*

"Can they come to my apartment? Three three one."

Her eyes, her concern; I burst into tears again. She pulls me into another embrace.

In my ear: "It's okay. It's okay. You shouldn't be out here, girl. You really shouldn't." She holds me and I let myself blubber and sob. I think about my childhood fantasies of being left on a hill in the rain and being comforted by someone, a woman, a warm blanket, holding me, warming me, telling me that everything is going to be okay. Is this that moment? Is this what I really need? Is this what I really seek?

Heaviness and confusion weigh on me and I feel secondary to myself. Like I am, once again, Little Me, trapped deep inside. Drugs were the key. Do I need a new key?

I return to an empty apartment. Something gives in my brain, like a door welded shut suddenly jarring open. Cracks of light. Cracks of possibility. When Lenni comes through the door minutes later, she runs to me, more curious than concerned. Her sentences rapid fire. "Where were you? Are you okay? Derek said he left you lying in the parking lot. Is that true, Punkin? What happened?"

I look up at her, from my depths—a full body between us, a chasm.

"Did you get any down?"

"I did. I have some for you."

My body relaxes instantly. My skin's still crawling, but I relax into it.

"The cops are on their way."

"Do you want to get high first?"

"No."

I shove down the thermostat and round the corner, open the fridge. The Miracle Whip rattles out of the door onto the ground. I kick it and leave it in the corner, close the fridge, drop to the ground against it, press at the sticking-up linoleum, sharp on my thumb, sharp on my fingers. I grab the skin of my thigh and twist. Of my stomach. Nothing hurts more than I already do. I cover my face—palms hard against my eye sockets, a black curtain over everything. Lucy curls around my legs.

"Fuck it, Lucy."

My heart's going. First step, police. The knock comes seconds, hours, minutes later. I'm ready for them to take me somewhere, maybe. Maybe that's something I'm ready for. I get up, take a deep, longing breath, focus on the crack of light between the bottom of the door and the floor. I put my hand on the doorknob, cold metal. Steady myself. From the uncertainty of the future. From the agony of now.

I open the door.

The cold front hits right away. Two officers. Looking at me like I'm a caricature. A call. A code. A job. A mark. A junkie.

The female officer pulls on black gloves and it feels deliberate. Like they knew what they'd find when they got the call. Her voice is glacial. "There was an incident in front of Guildford Mall?"

I look down at their shiny black boots, side by side. A shrivelled-up carcass, I am. I backpedal, downplay everything. Okay, but they have to look around anyway. When they leave, I linger in the doorway until they push open the stairwell door, far at the end of the hall. Without turning around, without changing their minds, without coming back for me.

I collapse against the wall by the door, hollow and exhausted. I sob into my bent arm until Lenni towers above me with a square of tinfoil and a lighter and rolled-up bus transfer. I take it. I inhale away the discomfort in my brain, in my body. Eventually, I sleep.

But still, something's changed. A pin of light, in the corner of my world.

A Good Start

passion
/ˈpaSH(ə)n/
noun
strong and barely controllable emotion.

40

Sometimes, change is walking through a door, shutting it behind you and suddenly everything is different. But change can also be as subtle as growing taller, growing greyer, growing bigger. The way, peppered with epiphanies and revelations and backwards steps and progress. And the only way to really see that change has, indeed, happened is by looking at yourself today. And looking at yourself before. Through a photo, through a journal entry, through a reaction, through a choice.

I remember. I remember who I was before my wanting became needing became so sucking and huge it turned me inside out. I remember my thoughts were once grand, supposing of human nature, curious about big concepts like time and space and love. I remember being sentimental and wistful. I remember playing guitar like a slow dance with my soul. Drawing like the big answers were there. Writing, like it's a dear friend, there in the absence of everything and everyone else.

I remember. Or, maybe, I predict.

But still, that speck of light. The idea that even though my body feels like a ghost town, who I was isn't really gone. That maybe Little Me is still in there. But didn't I dislike her? Didn't I think she was too shy, too awkward, too aware of her arms, too empty? Was I wrong, then? Am I wrong now?

These days I'm just trying not to starve or feel dope sick. "I don't really care about music," Lenni had said casually one evening and I realized I had let go of the string that held my love for music. I look at her now and wonder if I ever loved her at all. If I ever loved music at all. My brain is a messy logjam of thoughts. Without drugs—before things got this narrow—would I have learned to play guitar? Would I have wondered about the world? Would I have loved deeply? Would I have become so philosophical?

Yet—do I actually have the ability to dabble in a way that lets me preserve the beauty? If I took drugs away, would I just go back to Little Me draped deeply inside, unable to express anything, wanting more than anything to express everything? I feared I would. I feared *that* would be the cost. But now, that cost feels more bearable than this chain around my neck. This world limited to my line of vision and need for heroin. This *stuck* in a womb, well past my time.

And so, a tiny speck of hope. A tiny speck of hope based solely on the thought that the life that pushed me to drugs in the first place is a better life than the one I'm living now. A bleak revelation it is, but it's something to hold on to, and I do.

᎐

Here's the realization. Here's the eventual realization. Nobody's meant to stay in the womb forever. To be in the womb and to be in the world are as inextricably connected as life is to death. To be in the womb is to be in the world, for those of us lucky enough to be born. To be in the world is to inevitably die. In seconds, minutes, hours, days. Years, decades.

So, those of us lucky enough to be born into the world and to stick around long enough to seek that warm place of total comfort—well, maybe we should be a bit more patient with ourselves, with each other. Look around and re-member that it's only the world—vast, full-of-possibility life—that can offer us the discomfort that reminds us we're alive. That being here is a privilege and being here holds no guarantees other than: on a Monday, Tuesday, Wednesday, Thursday, Friday, Saturday or Sunday; in January, February, March, April, May, June, July, August, September, October, November or December, we won't be here any longer.

᎐

The day Lenni and I resolve to stop using heroin, I'm at the pay phone in the mall, punching in my parents' number, confessing. I tell my mom everything. I tell her that I'm done, getting clean, stopping. It's around 2:00 p.m., and inside, hands rub against sandpaper, increasingly rough. There's apprehension in my mom's voice when she thanks me for telling her, invites me to an afternoon bar-becue on Sunday. I hadn't seen them in months, at least. Three hours later I'm at Ricky's, concealing a twenty-dollar bill under my palm. By the time I turn my key into our apartment after work, sandpaper's rubbing ferociously up and down my veins, inside and out, around all my organs and the inside of my skin. I'm sweating and could puke and can't handle another second. Lenni's on the couch and I press into the space between her and the phone, the couch scratchy and aggravating and me a scream suppressed and I put my hand on the phone before I see that her pupils are pin dots and her voice slow: "Hi, Punkin."

By the time I show up at my parents' house on Sunday afternoon, I'm as high as I can be. The driveway's empty, so I round the side of the house, through the gate where my dad is working in the garden. I wave, from a distance, and sit on top of the picnic table, my feet on the bench, light a cigarette. My dad puts down the weed whacker and pulls off his ear protectors, approaches, happy, and—hesitates. I've never been on heroin around my parents and hadn't thought twice about it, until now. His entire face makes a defeated sigh; he looks like he could cry. It stabs me. I jump in, act casual. "Where's mom?"

His voice comes out diminished. "She's just picking up a few things from Greenfield's. She'll be back soon." And then, somewhere between gently and suspiciously, "How are you doing?"

"Oh, I'm good. You know." I concentrate on holding up my eyelids. "Work was super busy, but I'm glad to be off now."

He accepts this level of conversation.

"Everybody loves their brunch."

We both plant smiles on our faces and mimic the sound of laughter.

41

Lenni and I tell Les upstairs that we're finally getting clean.

"Good for you girls," he says, his scratchy voice, his skin and bone, his faded tattoos, and he really means it. This tugs at me. "You'll still come visit," he says, looking up from his kitchen table, blue cigarette smoke twirling past his face to the yellowed ceiling, dumpster treasure covering the table no meal's ever served upon.

"Yeah, Les, we will."

The summer is beating down on us when Lenni and I take the bus, its seat sticky under my bare legs, to Park City Methadone Clinic in Whalley. We'd heard about methadone—a synthetic, long-lasting opioid that prevents physical heroin withdrawal—from Dragon with schizophrenia downstairs, who'd sold us his once or twice. The reception area is crowded with people at various stages of down-and-out. The faces of the ladies behind the desk are tight—hardened by being the wall between clean and not clean, sick and not sick.

Are there stories of hope here? Are there stories of change? It doesn't look like it. It looks like surrender, but the exhausted version.

A lady behind the desk looks past me, speaking in staccato. "Name? Two pieces of ID?" She pushes a paper toward my fingers and their increasingly hard grip on the mottled plastic. "Fill this out."

Dr. B. meets with us individually, recommending methadone withdrawal programs where we inch up to a daily dose that keeps us feeling good for twenty-four hours, hang there for a moment, then taper into a detox, eventually. "We could plan to get you into a facility at that time. But for now, let's look at getting you off heroin."

The *how* is simple, at least in the shoddy little room in the shoddy little clinic where—I imagine, now—funding doesn't seamlessly funnel. Come in, do a pee test, if you're positive for heroin, you get a warning. Too many positives and you're out. Come in, do a pee test, if you're negative for heroin, you get your scrip and a pat on the back.

Lenni and I begin our daily trips to London Drugs at the mall, where we drink our methadone mixed with the children's drink Tang in front of a pharmacist.

And, simply, the crawling skin, the sweating agony, rumbles to a stop. And, not so simply, I don't—stop. Not heroin. Not fully. Not right away. Even though my life is grey. Grey in the morning, grey looking at the person who I thought was the love of my life, grey at work, grey in the evenings. I feel like a zombie. But a zombie cursed with remembering how much I used to feel. How passionate I used to be.

And I'm not the only one who remembers. At Zellers, before Lenni's piercing and distant eyes saw past my layers, there had been another girl—a pretty, chubby, tattooed, black-haired punk rocker with glowing emerald eyes. She came through my till one evening, our eyes on each other's like a silent language swirling between us, whispering "her." It made her turn around, scrawl her number on a piece of paper. It made me pick up the phone at the end of my shift and dial. It made us meet that very night, at the Starbucks in Chapters across the street. I tell her everything, words waterfalling out of me, admission after admission, all wrapped in a rationalizing "I'm clean now." Which I was, for a while. We had our first kiss—a fire first kiss—and she burned me CDs and she fucked me in her hot tub, splashing while her parents watched the 11:00 p.m. news just inside see-through curtains. She played guitar like a rock star, even had an album of her own, and introduced me to pretty song after pretty song and she looked me deeply in the eyes and would greet me cheery in the mornings with coffee and she'd cook complex vegan dishes; service with a smile. She bought me an electric keyboard for ninety dollars and I promised I'd pay her back, meaning it, my love for music abuzz. But then, Lenni. Then, that morning I woke up naked and in love and stripped of the previous night's memories. And then, heroin. I told myself, "Blake is too cheery in the morning." It all felt too easy. But really, I was flooded with the colourful uncertainty of a love that wasn't sure about me. Which felt more titillating, familiar, aligned. A match to my internal blueprint of love where I was never quite sure how the person glimpsing into my eyes actually felt. So I pushed a quarter into the pay phone at the mall and told Blake "Sorry, so sorry," then bowed out of her life and into the shadows of the world. And, soon, I toted that keyboard downstairs and into Picasso's car—"Please, just one"—and then days passed and then months.

And now, years.

Through the rectangular portal of MSN Messenger on a monitor too heavy to carry alone, Blake pops up online. In me, not an attraction, but a whir of connection. I miss something about her, or who I was when I was around her, or something I can't quite name. Me, a whisper of the personality she met, a waif with dial-up internet, a pin dot of hope, a frustration of a memory of who I used to be. But I open up.

I open up, I open up, I open up.

"It's harder than I thought," I type. "I thought it was all physical, but it's not."

"You're too smart and passionate to let that shit run your life," she types back.

She saw. She remembers.

The speck of hope in me expands. As does our friendship.

⌒

The year stretches on and Lenni and I ping-pong between holding on and picking up. We go stints without, strategically gobbling up the wanting hours of our days watching TV shows on DVD from Blockbuster, eating grocery store crostinis and tater tots ravenously, the greasy oomph filling up the kitchen, flooding our senses. A craving, a satisfaction. And when my mind screams *heroin*, which it does all the time, I put a TV in front of it, which helps, a bit. We watch every series we can get our hands on until our Blockbuster trips become frustrating meanders of *we already watched that, we've already seen that, that was a shitty movie, I don't know what to get*, and on. We still pick up, but less—the methadone keeping the physical symptoms in check. But we still call Picasso every couple of days, one of us giving in and the other crumpling along.

And, somehow, my mind—an ever-swirling pool of colour and desire— starts lusting after other things. It lusts after freedom from Lenni, from the mundane everyday, from domestic routine. It lusts after a co-worker, fantasies of going down on her in one of the long backroom booths at Ricky's, daylight still pouring through the skylight, restaurant risky with customers. It lusts after building a big, beautiful life with a funny and beautiful acquaintance.

My mind reaching, no longer for heroin, but for love, warmth, connection. Always just outside of reality, always unattainable. Maybe, though, I'm reaching for *more*. The version of more that isn't addicted, but rather wants a better life. The distinction, though, like a faint dotted line.

Although painful in their unattainable nature, these fantasies inject a shake of possibility in me that I haven't felt in a long, long time.

Yet still, the craving for the warm and fuzzy peace of heroin remains magnetic. Because while I'm a suave Don Juan in the easy fantasies of my mind, I'm a clunky awkward robot in reality. At work I approach tables of strangers with my stomach in knots and a waver on even simple phrases like "Are you ready to order?" I walk through the mall toward London Drugs hyper-aware of how my arms hang off my shoulders, mean internal voices disguised as my own interpreting strangers' neutral looks as angry, their glances as judgmental.

I'm somehow both exposed and invisible.

It's like that scared, shy, timid little mouse from high school has been dormant this whole time but she's back—and more timid.

But still, somehow, the thought that I might be better off as a scared, shy, timid little mouse with richness of thought and big imagination, than as a junkie only looking for her next fix, stays with me. And grows with each grey day. It grows even when the blandless outside and the blandness inside are barely discernible. It grows until one day the ping-pong ball drops off the table, bounces a few times on the floor and then settles into a dusty corner. And I stop.

I stop.

It's not a revelation, but a culmination a long time coming. Not picking up takes everything in me, but—somehow and suddenly—I have enough strength to not pick up. It's the only thing I have strength for—not cheeriness, not confidence, not happiness, not peace. Just to not pick up. To put my hand on the phone, and then take it away. To sit on my couch like a ticking time bomb and let it tick down to zero, to brace for an explosion, to note that there is no explosion. To breathe. To wait. To wait it out. To hold on.

I'm reading *A Million Little Pieces* by James Frey, a book about a man who gets clean. He's eventually embroiled in controversy because he calls inspired fiction "memoir" and lies to Oprah's face. I watch the whole thing, the pacifier of daytime television, fuzzy picture, rabbit ears. But controversy aside, he's on to something and I feel it. *Hold on* are the words he uses to get and stay clean—at least that's how he depicts it in his book. I use them like an emergency lung transplant. *Hold on, hold on, hold on.* Especially those first few days like a guttural, gasping breath. When the urge to use clangs loudly in my head as I toil around the apartment, cleaning, reading, playing guitar, hiding under the comforter on our bed, restless and a hint of a human, knowing heroin would be so easy to get: *hold on.* Knowing heroin would fix this. Knowing just as strongly, though, that fix is temporary, ever fleeting. Because right there, wedged into my internal chaos, that speck of hope has grown, no longer possible to ignore. To the addict in me, it's a stain. To Little Me, curled into fetal position deep inside myself, it's salvation. So I hold on. I hold on and on and on and on, literally through seconds at first, then minutes, a day, then days. I'm not dope sick, but I'm raw. And through that rawness I hold on, and the rawness stays and I let it. I'm a hemophiliac cut, and yet, still, I hold on.

42

Lenni takes a bit longer, but soon she stops using too—like she can feel that my resistance, this time, is final. We start ever so slowly reducing our methadone intake and we fold into ourselves and we fold into each other, slumped on either side of the couch, soothed by fuzzy television and rented DVDs. Me, clinging to the promise that the numbing pattern of TV, eat, work, TV, eat, sleep, repeat, is better than how things were. I'm not sad, I'm not happy, I'm just existing and it's all very bland. I feel internal tugs of excitement, but they're all wrapped in impossibility: sex with people I shouldn't have sex with, new apartments we can't afford. We start spending all our money eating out at White Spot and Red Robin and the Pantry—floppy whirs of excitement that end before they begin and leave me full and fat and wanting.

But I hold on. And know well enough what those whirs of excitement can turn into if I get bland and stir-crazy enough. So we sign up for free drug counsellors at Surrey Addictions, out of a glass office tower beside Gateway SkyTrain station. Within days, I'm sitting in a tiny, beige and generic office without a window or personalization, fiddling with my fingers, quietly assessing the woman who is supposed to be assessing me. Her eyes are flat and she runs through what feels like a checklist.

"So what would you say is most wrong right now?"

My stomach is floaty and apprehensive and I look at my dirty runners, trying to give words to the feeling that's been with me forever. A feeling of lack, of needing to be filled. A feeling I don't really know how to temper sustainably. One that I distract myself from by hyper-fixating on a love, or overeating or doing drugs.

Everything you ever did was intense, my mom'll tell me, years later.

I study the counsellor's face, which is impenetrable. But not in that been-around-the-block, bullshit-tipping-point-reached way. More like this-is-my-job-but-not-my-life.

"I don't know. It's something that I can't really name or explain," I tell her, defeated.

"Okay, so that means you're really okay, then."

It's a statement, not a question, and although what I mean is "No, I am absolutely not okay," the timid little mouse just nods and says, "I guess so."

It's my first and last appointment. And that space inside me is screaming. And I'm determined to not go back to tinfoil and agony. And diner food and *Judge Judy* are making me want to crawl out of my skin. I need something. I'm done fucking up.

⌒

David's cheeks are filling in again and he's smiling more, attending Narcotics Anonymous compulsively, so on a Tuesday evening I ball up my apprehensions, chuck them into a dismal corner and, with Lenni, meet him at St. Paul's Hospital in Vancouver. I haven't touched heroin or any other drug aside from cigarettes and methadone for over a month.

The tendrils of cool ocean extend up Davie Street, round the corner at Nelson and move me to shiver. We march inside, take seats in rows, in hard chairs, a smattering of hands around red Tim Hortons cups, the smell of stale cigarette smoke on clothing. A few lit halogen tubes pattern the ceiling, casting shadows. The group chants a bunch of things in unison—"Keep coming back, it works"—and I shift uncomfortably and glance at Lenni, who rolls her eyes. They use the word *trigger* over and over. Like if triggered, using is inevitable. They say they're powerless over their addictions. Powerless. I squirm—it feels like the easy way out. I have to believe I have power over my addiction. Without that, what do I have?

A man shuffles to the podium in a worn sports cap, lanky arms, grey face, grey stubble, massive, weary bags under his eyes.

"Downtown Langley was a trigger for me," he tells the crowd. "When I finally went back there, I was right back in it. I got my girlfriend pregnant and she lost the baby." Tears well up in his eyes and it makes him look more alive. The crowd stares, silently. Some nod. Some nod hard. "I can't go back there, I know that now. That's all I have to say."

"Thanks, Wayne," they all chant.

David glances at me and I give him a "That's it?" look. The man is obviously desperate, has no resolution and—everybody just thanks him? David smacks my leg with the back side of his hand and continues staring ahead. Lenni rolls her eyes again and half shakes her head.

After the meeting, David, Lenni and I and about thirty others crowd outside the door and light cigarettes. *The unofficial NA trademark*, I think. David, his shoulders pressed against mine in the tight space, is laughing with a pair of clean-cut guys behind him. I touch his forearm and he turns.

"I just don't understand," I say. "That Langley guy was obviously helpless, literally doesn't know what to do, and people just thank him! Thank him for what? I just don't understand."

"They're thanking him for sharing, Erin."

"And this triggers thing. I mean isn't it dangerous to just walk around with triggers everywhere? You need to get over your triggers, not avoid them!"

There's a fire in my gut, which feels nice. Which I've missed, I'm realizing.

"Well," he says, his brow furrowing, "you're powerless over your addiction."

"But are you really? Or is that just what they repeat until you think it's true? If they chant it over and over it'll become truth, won't it? But what if it's a trap? What if everybody's just hooked up to NA now rather than the needle?"

David hunches his shoulders as if I shoved him.

"I'm sorry, David, I didn't mean… it's just that I refuse to believe that I'm powerless. There has to be accountability or you're fucking doomed! And with NA you can just relapse and relapse and you're welcomed back with open arms. I just don't buy it! There has to be a deterrent! Consequences!" I quiet my voice. "Or mistakes will happen. People could die."

I don't mean him. I couldn't have meant him.

David, equally soft-spoken: "It works for a lot of people."

I take a deep breath and my mind flashes to the last time I saw Twyla, at the New West coffee shop, smiling and relaxed. She's now been clean over a year and has a good, kind, long-term boyfriend, also from the program.

"I can't disagree with that."

Just then, a tall guy in a tight neon T-shirt with a '90s boy-band swoop drapes his arm around David's shoulder. David pushes his chest up and shoulders back and wraps an easy arm around tall guy's waist.

"This is Adam," he tells Lenni and me. Lenni's peering into the crowd, blowing smoke toward the concrete ceiling.

We shake hands.

His words take effeminate leaps: "Awesome! Great to see you out! Are you in the program?"

"No, I'm not really in the program. I'm doing it myself."

"By yourself, sweetie?" He looks at me with unmistakable pity, the leaps slowing, then stopping, then crouching. And then, as if he didn't hear me right: "So you're not in the program? How long have you been clean?"

Now I puff out my chest, my inner strength, once a nearly obscured pin dot, incubated into something bigger. "Just over a month."

He's suddenly quiet and nods and nods. "Okay, well, good for you. Good for you!" This is what he says, but his words are so saturated in pity, he may as well have said, "You poor, sad, disillusioned addict. Only the program works. You're so fucked, sweetie."

I shake my head, jump my eyebrows, reflect back his snark: "Right."

Yet the truth of it is that I still need something. I know I can get and stay clean, because I know it's not about the drugs—not really. But what's it really about? I've soothed myself with so many things throughout my lifetime. Does it go back to sucking my thumb? Is there something underneath all that soothing that needs looking at? That needs love? Or is this just a by-product of how we're all hurtled from the warm provider of the womb into an ever-loud, ever-tempting world where we're left ever searching for fulfillment? Maybe it's all about finding the least chaotic option.

⌒

The fire of indignation from my NA experience downgrades from blaze to smoulder as I search for something other than pacifying television and heavy comfort food. So, along with Giulia and Lenni, I go to the gym.

My parents started running in the '80s by fluke. My mom's mom mailed them jogging suits from her home in California—one grey, one teal. They put them on and started walking toward the corner store. Within a block they felt silly, like they should be running because they're wearing jogging suits. So they ran to the corner store. And then they ran back home, where—sweaty and humming with that filled-up kind of feeling, that magic zest, that delicious side dish to exertion—running stuck. Simple, silly things can change the trajectory of a life. Of lives.

At the gym, while Giulia and Lenni awkwardly hop from exercise bike to Stairmaster to rowing machine, I gravitate to the treadmill. It's in a corner of the gym's upper semicircle that looks down onto the mirrors in front of the weights section. So I see myself, from a distance, pale and putting on weight. And I see muscles in muscle shirts pumping iron in front of mirrors down below. I've never been on a treadmill, but I press start and it moves. I'm flooded with uncertainty, nervousness, but there's something else driving me, so I press the up arrow until it's fast enough for a jog. And it feels jarring to my muscles—all of them—but it also feels like an awakening. I decide, while moving, to go for thirty minutes. One foot in front of the other, exactly how things are right now. Seconds stretch, just like they do while I'm dope sick and waiting for a dealer. But, in me, a whir of excitement. There's something different here—like an empowerment from the inside. I'm jogging slowly, but I won't stop—not for thirty minutes. In the mirror, from a distance, I look determined—almost like someone else, exactly like myself. The red seconds tick up, listening to music loud.

Eminem shouts "Lose Yourself" in my ears, which I know how to do. My core aches, my thighs burn and my brain shouts *I can't do this* but I've heard that before and keep going. I need those red numbers to get to 30:00 without stopping. There's something there, I somehow feel, though I don't know what. Persistence has smashed out of its inner compartment—the stubborn he-man within, more real and alive than any of my resistance. More than anything, I have to get to 30:00. I can't stop. I can't give up. I won't. And I don't—29:59 turns over to 30:00 and I press the speed button down, walking, then sauntering, and then I step off the machine to an oddly familiar feeling. I'm wobbly-legged, but also—and it bubbles up like a triumphant sea unicorn spiralling up from the dark depths of the ocean—elated. An ocean geyser of elation. And wrapped in a sweaty, tired, stubborn, accomplished mess, I feel high. And it occurs to me just how similar running is to heroin, but flipped. Like the hard part, the comedown, comes first. Then you're filled, flying, satisfied. With effort, one can replace the other. I feel it like I feel gravity—as fact. And running sticks.

43

I'm down from seventy milligrams of methadone per day to just ten when, one afternoon, I forget to take it. Because my dose is so low, I have to take it precisely every twenty-four hours around 3:00 p.m. or the dope sickness comes on hard. Even still, my skin starts to crawl around noon every day, but knowing I have a date to sip it away keeps it manageable. I'd gone for a thirty-minute run just after noon, so when the time comes to take my dose, I'm still basking in its sweet residual ease. Nearly late for work and also distracted by my rumbling stomach, I grab my shades and apron and I speed walk to the bus stop a block away. The bus is pulling up just as I arrive out of breath and discombobulated. I get on and settle into the blue plastic seat, the diesel smell, and the bus circles the mall, then turns onto 152nd toward Fleetwood. I look out the window at Cash Converters, Mac's, some shoddy-looking apartments. Suddenly feeling off, I backtrack in my mind and remember: not opening the fridge, not taking my methadone. I'll be late for my shift with a single misstep. Lenni's already at work. A survey of friends in my mind is a city on fire with burned bridges, save for Giulia, who's also at work deep in Langley. I haven't discussed a detox facility with the methadone doctor since that first appointment months ago, and haven't been back to Surrey Addictions.

Each hour at Ricky's gets worse; I'm sweating and losing strength from inside my bones. My skin is crawling in alien lumps of discomfort, teasing my nervous system meanly. One of my favourite regular senior customers is celebrating her eightieth birthday with her four best senior-citizen friends. White, meandering ringlet curls, stylish clothing always—today, leopard print—she'll often step through the double glass doors wearing her sunglasses, do a hero stance and pull her shades down so we see her eyes, playfully scanning the room. Normally, she lights me up with her presence. Normally, I'm thrilled to see her. Today I feel like I'm lugging word after sentence from my mouth and footstep after arm movement from my body. It's her birthday and I can barely smile at her, barely look into her eyes. I take their order and when the cook rings the food's-up bell, I pile their plates onto one of the big trays I've carried hundreds of times. I climb the two stairs to the section they're in, and somehow my arm loses all strength and I drop the tray. Spaghetti slides from its plate onto the turquoise-brown carpet. A bowl of "extra hollandaise" for the steak Neptune slumps beside it, rubbery shrimp bouncing to a stop on the carpet. I freeze, feeling more exposed than when Constable Kekoa looked me in the eyes and said, "It's you." And then, as I do, I run.

I turn from the five surprised faces with a sharpness up my core and tears pushing at my eyes. I round the bar where the hostess is filling up Tabasco bottles, where my manager, stirred by the commotion, looks confused, concerned, says, "Erin?" Past the warm kitchen and the happy Punjabi banter, past the dishwasher turned away and soapy fumes and the schedule on the wall promising me shifts and income and the shelves stocked with rubber gloves and maple syrup and, already sobbing inaudibly, get myself into the reprieve of the bathroom and close the door and slump down against it, my body's resistance to its deep sadness a flooded moat. I'm crying out of embarrassment and I'm crying out of shame and I'm crying because I don't know whether I can ever really be happy. I'm crying for the years I was a slave to drugs and for the friends I've lost and for love—the only thing I ever really believed in—feeling like a total ruse. If I have no drugs and love isn't real, who the fuck am I? What's the fucking point? I cry for all this and for all the uncertainty and I cry because I'm sweating and my skin is crawling worse than it has since I stopped using heroin and I cry because I've gotten myself so hooked up on drugs I have to endure physical trauma to be set free. But then, set free to what? Where?

I'm on the dirty floor with my head hung between my elbows and my legs, sobbing, snotting silently, liquid pouring, dropping, falling from my eyes, my nose, my mouth.

There's a light knock on the door. "Erin?"

It's my manager Robyn, and her voice is soft. "Are you okay, hon?"

Hon, a trigger point since Soela, now caresses my everything with gentle care. I wipe my face with my shirt and stand up and look into the mirror. I look as awful as I feel, the whites of my eyes red, my cheeks pink. She knocks again, still gentle, and I wipe my face again and I open the door.

"Hon, it's okay. Shit happens and the kitchen's fixing it. We're all good. They don't even care. Just get yourself together and carry on, it's all good." Her dark eyes look hard into mine, then her face softens like an exhale. "Maybe two trays?" I laugh, in spite of myself. "Yeah, two trays."

Upon successful delivery of their supper, they goad me, kindly.

"There's She Who Throws Food!"

Laughter.

"What, you thought the carpet was hungrier than us?"

More laughter.

I know it's friendly, I know it's light, and though I'm known for goofing around with customers, their words cut into me and I can only muster "Yeah, yeah" without breaking even the hint of a smile or looking into any of their eyes. The birthday girl looks disappointed and it overwhelms me with sadness.

When I get home I feel worse still, but it's happening—it's inevitable—so I pour the rest of my methadone down the sink.

"Fuck it," I tell Lenni, who looks at me in horror, who's not ready herself, who just two mornings ago was a crying heap on the kitchen floor because she wanted to make me pancakes but couldn't figure out the recipe. For whom I couldn't muster any tenderness, whom I know I'm leaving, even if I don't know it consciously. "I have to do this eventually. It may as well be now."

I call my parents and tell them. My dad offers to pick me up and take me to a walk-in for something that could help. We drive around and around Surrey but all the clinics are closed. He buys me Gravol for my nausea. That night I lie in bed and toss and turn, feeling growing pains in my legs, my entire skin crawling. Lenni snores beside me and I sweat and twist the sheets and eventually move to the couch, its material aggravating against my skin. I happen to be off for the next three days—a relief, knowing I can't sleep. I stare at the popcorn ceiling, tinged yellow like a heavy smoker's finger, my heart beating in my chest. A rolling discomfort pushes me up to stand on one leg, which somehow helps until it doesn't and then I'm pacing and wide awake. The threads of the carpet tightly rolled in on themselves are bumpy and irritating on my feet. Beside the sliding door, the multicoloured sheets I draped in triangles one candlelit evening are now dirty and limp. I resist screaming in frustration, instead pushing, forcing it inward, down, down into the depths of my being—a lifelong inclination to muffle myself.

I cover the floor with a sheet and lie on my stomach and with one knee push my leg into a triangle and, somehow, manage a sporadic sleep. The next day I smoke cigarette after cigarette and heave myself into clothes, out the door, out the apartment and around the block. Being on the move helps. My mind glides across the idea of heroin—how one inhale could fix everything—then glides over knowing that would mean enduring this all over again. I'm past the point of no return. I get home and watch episode after episode of *Curb Your Enthusiasm*, settling into a restless push-and-pull loop between distraction and hyper-awareness of my body's discomfort. Gravol does nothing, nothing I do does anything and I just hold on and hold on. On the fourth day, I go back to work for a four-hour shift, feeling like a snail that's lost its shell. I get through on the bare minimum, then back home to writhing around. Lenni watches TV beside me, but every time she tries to put a hand on my leg I push it away. "Sorry, I just can't."

After the fifth day, the physical effects slip down a notch, but the psychological ones move up. I feel more exposed than I ever have—like Little Me's a curled-up animal in a shitty zoo with only fake plastic palms to hide behind.

In a way, I'm reborn. But it's like everything ahead of me is a blur and everything behind is too destructive to turn to, despite the temptation in its familiarity. I worry about running—that maybe methadone was the only reason I'm actually able to run. I worry I'll never shake this exposed feeling. I worry that when I leave Lenni I'll never find love again. I worry that love is an illusion.

⌒

What if, what if? What if everything works out perfectly?

⌒

My legs are still aching two weeks after the tray-dropping night at Ricky's, but I put on my running shoes and plug in headphones and exit the apartment, waiting until it's dark outside because I'm still feeling exposed. Between then and now, I've regained my appetite and I stuff that feeling down with food, television and chain-smoking. But despite my full stomach and smoky lungs, I put on my headphones and start moving in the cool air. Sidewalks quiet, apartment building after apartment building with more windows lit warm yellow than darkened, Pearl Jam's "I Am Mine" in my ears, thoughts on my side: thirty minutes; I can do this, I can do this, I can do this. And by the time I start down 108th with its traffic and its strip malls, Fabricland and Mac's and Robin's Donuts, my stomach breaks into a giddy dance and I laugh with the delight of a happy surprise.

Despite everything, my body knows exactly what to do. Despite everything, I still have running.

And thus continues my life, for several months, similar to how it was when I was on methadone: smoke, eat, watch TV, work, smoke, eat, watch TV.

But running helps the glimmers expand and I'm feeling music again—whirs of non-drug-induced connection. I go out for a run and love—like want to hug with joy—the cool air on my cheek from under the humidity of my grey Zero hoodie. I go out for a run and love the glow of the street lights and the pattern of light they project so silently, so reliably. I go out for a run and love the shoe print immortalized in sidewalk concrete and wonder where that shoe is now, buried deep in a landfill or on a shelf at Value Village or still on the foot of the one who left the print.

It's like running gives me awe and wonder back, as though the world has parted for me and I eagerly step through.

And—awe and wonder can only come from being in the world, can't they? The awe of a string plucked on a guitar. The wonder of a cat lightly snoring, its tail moving in micro-fits, dreaming about... what? The awe and wonder of consciousness itself—this gift we all share. All of this can only come from being in the world, not perpetually safe in a womb that lacks longing, yes, but also awe, also wonder.

But still—what about when I don't run? All of that is gone like a TV screen shutting off, a horizontal white line and then nothing and I'm enveloped in grey fog, blah.

So, more running.

On April 15, 2007, I run my first race, crossing the finish line of the Vancouver Sun Run in fifty-eight minutes, thirty-seven seconds. There's a picture of me, in non-running clothes, shoulders back, smile on my face, hungry belly peering out the bottom of my shirt, sunglasses that look like they belong more on a dial-a-dealer's face than mine, crossing the finish line. The thrill of it gives me a bumbling hug and I feel capable of anything. Of blending in with forty thousand sporty runners who eat bananas for breakfast and go to bed at 9:00 p.m. An inner pride blooms like a rare and beautiful flower and it leaves me with the alluring question of: What next? And the whisper of an answer: Anything.

More isn't always destructive.

I'm still stifled in the apartment, in my relationship, and though Lenni limped along after me in detoxing off methadone, she's still stuck in front of the television, the line between her using and not using tenuous. And I feel myself again and again unwilling to extend her a hand. Guilt pecks at me, as does sadness for the love we shared—her blue-eyed knowing, "Punkin," the we're-in-this-togetherness. But it's time for me to leave. It's a feeling I can't shake.

In April, shortly after the Sun Run, I tell her. And in May I leave, moving into a small ground-level basement suite overlooking a gully that I rent from one of the cooks at Ricky's. It's a whoosh of relief and a taste of a new kind of freedom. Of fresh, clean, clear air. Of possibility.

After the Storm

habit
/ˈhabət/
noun
**a settled or regular tendency or practice,
especially one that is hard to give up.**

44

Tapering off methadone at first, I'm awash in grey. Lighter grey for good moods, like a seagull feather; darker grey for bad ones, like a storm cloud. But all grey. As time goes on and I settle into my new basement suite with its hardwood floor and La-Z-Boy chair and computer and new old bookshelf that I lovingly decorate with faded concert tickets and photos, those good moods and bad moods stretch further apart. Some days, energy exudes from my chest and I feel part of everything, moving down the street, through the world, through the universe, meant to be here, happy. And some days, I'm curled on the living room hardwood in fetal position listening to lilting and melancholy Azure Ray, rain beating on the house, the attempted romanticism of candles, feeling meek and crumpled. But better these ups and downs than bleak grey, I figure. I'd been stuffing down all sorts of emotions for too long, but by the time I'm in my own suite and the air starts warming and I haven't had a drink or considered using drugs for months, I begin stacking my life. It's not intentional, really, but life—real life, where I am right now—is like a Jenga stack. You lose pieces and gain pieces and although one horrible event could make the whole thing clatter down, a foundation of equally meaningful pieces means it's more apt to stay upright. You're more apt to stay upright. For years, all my pieces were the same: drugs, getting high. But now, there's variety. There's friendship. There's guitar. There's music. There are dreams. There's work. There's running. And all these pieces stack into a life.

Later, much later, I go for a hike in the snow, in the cold, alone and present up the trail, what normally clouds my mind dissipated, my boots crunching through the frozen top layer of snow—crunch-boosh, crunch-boosh, crunch-boosh, its pattern rhythmic; in the wind, corners of crackly leaves against corners of crackly leaves. And then, atop a tall, leafless, nearly boughless tree, a raven. A triplet of sound from its beak—a calling. And what I hear is: Be-here-now. Be-here-now. Be-here-now. An instruction.

After the Vancouver Sun Run, I train for and run my first half-marathon. My parents pick me up the morning of the race in their Mazda in the foggy dark, hand me a Starbucks dark roast, hug me from the front seats. Our relationship wordlessly mended itself after I moved out of Imperial Pines. It's a downpour at the start line at the University of British Columbia. In me, a fluttering excitement, a nervousness, a pride. As we start running, my dad pulls ahead of me and I pull ahead of my mom and it's just me and the other runners bouncing toward Stanley Park, fog-hugged ocean to my left. Placebo's version of "Running Up That Hill" plays loud in my ears on the fast down, deep bass pounding. I turn my head toward a view of the ocean between tall, rain-slicked trees and splash into a puddle, soaking both my feet. I laugh, unexpectedly loud, and look around, alive with presence, in awe of life as it is, pouring rain, soaked feet, burning lungs, glee. All the other runners are in their own worlds. Uninhibited, my laughter reverberates through my cells, delight washing through my being, warming my body, rushing through my veins.

So, like friendship, guitar, music, dreaming, work, running, there's laughter. There's laughter like an old friend I didn't realize I missed like a lost limb.

⌒

Although things are steady—steadier than they've possibly ever been for me—I start a direct course toward my Achilles heel, forgetting the havoc the promise of love can wreak on my life.

It creeps back into my life as a whisper. First, I just want to have sex. With anyone. Alice and I reconnect and go out for a couple of lunches and adventures, shifting our relationship into a true friendship, so when our decision to have sex comes up over quesadillas on a sunny oceanside patio in White Rock, it's like a business transaction. She comes over one afternoon and we put in the *Party Monster* DVD and sit in the tight rocker, our hands all over each other, rain pouring outside, until she gets up and pulls me by my hand into the bedroom. Our sex is fun and easy, but maybe too easy because it doesn't rev me like I want sex to rev me. For better or worse. So I join dating websites—Superdyke and Plenty of Fish—but can't feel the zing of attraction through faces on screens and struggle to type back to people, however hot they appear. Besides, I don't know what I'm looking for other than to be magnetized.

But I do date, a bit. A tall sporty lesbian who wears polo shirts, a summer romance, an immaculately clean car, a snorty pug, my interest waning with the season and hers growing until I break it off.

See, love that doesn't feel like I'm being stuffed into the trunk of my own life doesn't feel real.

I meet Kye at some gay event, hot and cocky and strutting across a stage in drag. She holds back just enough to keep me curious and we have sex twice, me a slow lover, her hurrying it along. Then she stops calling.

This floods me with something a bit like sadness, an emptiness. An emptiness that whispers *Look at me* but, louder, screams *Fill me*.

And longing is suddenly back, all scratchy and uncomfortable with its stretching seconds. And I'm writing sappy poetry and feeling like the earth is crumbling beneath me. I sit with it and sit with it and run and pour myself into my journal and pour myself onto my friends. But when all these avenues still leave me with this brutal emptiness, I do the only thing I'm certain can help the searing. I drive to the liquor store.

I drive to the liquor store and park in a slot right out front, my headlights reflecting in the glass storefront for a blink before I take my keys out of the ignition, noting the bottles stacked on shelves on the other side of the glass. So easy. It's so easy. It's been months, nearly a year, since I've had anything other than cigarettes.

In my stomach, a clenched fist. In my brain, a small voice of reason: This won't work for long. In my brain, a booming voice of need: Feel better, feel better. In my brain, a voice of rationalization: Just get beer. Beer's not vodka, not Fireball, not sambuca, not gin.

Hand on car door handle, push open, light rain, thick fog, gentle mist. Eight steps, metal door handle, indifferent glance from employee, easy nod like I'm here for my after-work beer, my happy hour. So easy. The cooler, thin black handle, sticky *shhht* pulls it open, cool air on my face. Fist in stomach tighter, my body on autopilot. Easy. A six-pack of Sleeman Honey Brown. On the counter, twenty dollars cash, change, no bag, no receipt, thanks. Drive home, park car, round side of the house, key in sliding glass door, beer on counter, drawer opened, bottle opener. Cardboard up, hand in, bottle grabbed, cold condensation on palm. Beer cracked. Big fizzy amber sip. Big fizzy amber sip. Big fizzy amber sip.

It's that easy to come undone.

45

A few months before leaving Lenni, I meet David at Starbucks in Fleetwood, near both Ricky's and his mom's, where he's holed up. His parents had banded together to form David Watch, chaperoning him constantly while waiting for a detox bed. It's his dad's turn to chaperone and he gives me a nod before sitting several tables away from us and picking up a newspaper. David hugs me with warmth, but his face looks grey and his limbs gangly.

"You look tired, David. How long do you think you'll have to wait?"

He shakes his head and speaks with the defeatedness of a dried-up champion. "I don't know. I don't even know if I actually want to go. But, you know." He glances at his dad, who may or may not have been listening.

"So what are you doing in the meantime?" I feel myself slipping into a parental role of lecturing and disapproval, from which I can't seem to evict myself. Because suddenly, my problems seem small. Who cares whether or not I should leave Lenni? Who cares about the meaning of it all? David is barely hanging on, it seems, and I have no idea how to help him. I feel socked in the stomach; I don't know what to do.

"Well," he starts slowly, carefully, "my mom is making sure I get clean syringes." He perceives my contorting face but forages on: "And heroin."

I haven't yet considered the value in harm reduction. In keeping a person who will use drugs regardless safe and supervised. The thought of him shooting up terrifies me. I can't and I don't temper my voice. "Can't you just smoke it or snort it while you wait?"

For a nanosecond, amusement raises the corners of his lips and shines out his eyes, but before I yell at it to Fuck Right Off, he looks away. Mumbles, "It's hard to go back, Erin."

Now I notice the pinholes on his arms. Now I'm the defeated champ. "David, you could die."

"I know, I know."

"Seriously, you're going to detox so you obviously don't want to keep doing this. Can't you just still get high but just not shoot up?"

He nods like he hears me, but we both know that doesn't matter. The line crowds our table and baristas bustle about, smell of freshly ground coffee twirling with symphonic music. It's the world I want to be part of, and I want him to be part of it too—rather than syringes and basements and parental supervision. David's dad signals that it's time, and I hug David, hard, with tears in my eyes. There are tears in his eyes too, I notice.

By the time I move out of Lenni's, David had left for and returned from detox. Giulia tells me that he's over at Lenni's all the time, calling up dealers and nodding off on the couch.

Helplessness is watching somebody you love slowly drown from behind a Plexiglas wall. You pound on it with your fist and, sure, they may glance in your direction, but they don't come toward you. Your fist feels bruised and you can't look away, but it's gutting you.

Just days later, my desire for connection welling in me, I call up Aubry, who's about to move to Vancouver Island to finish her social work schooling. She works with Giulia part-time at Zellers, and I'd always been drawn to her sass and intelligence and beauty, though so far we've been more acquaintances than friends.

I pick her up and we drive to the ocean—Crescent Beach, where the tide is out so far it melds with the horizon, and seagulls float in the wind. We're both bundled up and sit side by side against driftwood, the smell of salty air and seaweed in my throat. My heart feels unguarded and vulnerable, but in a sweet, not scary, way.

I tell her about David and Lenni, about my confusion around always needing something. That I always need a big run or a big plan or a big person to feel okay. I'm feeling like a black nonsensical squiggle on a white sheet of paper, feeling my speech getting frantic. I take a deep breath.

"It's exhausting," I tell her and light a cigarette.

Aubry's green eyes are illuminated by the brightness of the bay. She just listens, sometimes looking at me, sometimes gazing out at the horizon. The ocean air is crisp and the tips of my ears are cold. When I speak again, it's slowly.

"I know I'm doing it, but I just don't know what to do. I know I have to hold on, but I don't know what to hold on to. I know I need something, and that it can't be drugs, but I don't know what that something is. Aside from running. But I can't run every day. I'm tired."

Aubry, still looking outward, finally speaks. "You know," she says thoughtfully, deliberately, "I like coming to places like this to confess."

We both stare straight ahead, and in me I feel the enduring power of the ocean, the clouds, the overwhelming number of minuscule grains of sand, how the pull of the tides smooths them. I glance at Aubry. Her green eyes are so intense and wistful it's like I asked a question, though I hadn't.

"I like coming to places like this to confess," she repeats. "Because there's room for it."

Every time I'm on a beach, I remember this.

When the rain starts to pitter-patter, we go to my place and watch *A Home at the End of the World* beside each other on my floor, then I drive her home in the dark of the late evening. Before saying goodbye, we cling to each other in my car like it's the most natural thing in the world. She wraps her hand around the back of my neck. We're still holding each other in an embrace without explanation, without pretense, when she speaks again.

"Whatever you decide to do, you'll excel at it." Her words and her hand on my neck feel like everything I need. "You are smart. You are strong."

I nod and we both loosen our grip and she gets out of the car. My eyes trail her to her townhouse. She waves goodbye when she reaches the front door and closes it behind her and then she moves to Vancouver Island and I never see her again.

46

By the time Scarlet walks into my life, I have both the taste of love and the taste of alcohol on my tongue again. I'm pulled into her orbit the moment I meet her. Cooler nights are luring in summer and I'm drunk at a queer youth party house tucked into a neighbourhood a few blocks from Costco. It's the weekend and weekends are okay for drinking, I tell myself. I swing open the front door from inside, and there Scarlet is in a crowd on the deck—tall and standing surprisingly upright for being at a drinking party, dark wavy hair looping around one side of her neck and down her chest. Her eyes are deep blue, deeply intelligent. She's dreamy and oozes sexuality; my body picks up on it when I draw near her, circled by gay boys. She takes a drag of her cigarette and blows it toward the pot light above before speaking.

"*The Secret* really works, it's crazy. It's power of attraction. The way you think."

I'd read the bestselling sensation—or, rather, got twenty pages in before my eyes hurt from rolling them so much. But her deep and lilting voice makes me almost agree with her.

I speak before the gay boys have a chance to respond.

"*The Secret* is a total marketing scheme," I say, my booze-fuelled confidence fully online.

We spar back and forth about the book, energy and eye contact building between us until the gay boys butt out their cigarettes and go inside and she admits, "It's not like it's great. But the ideas make sense." She smiles a cocky half smile and holds out her hand. "Scarlet."

I take her hand, shake it and linger, letting go more softly than I would with any other new friend. I look deeply into her eyes, my borrowed confidence wearing my skin. "Erin."

Within a week, we're drinking together regularly and I'm revved up sexually, but Kye still hasn't called me back, hasn't said no, hasn't officially stepped out of my life. And I've built up stories of possibility that keep tinkering in my mind, so ignoring it isn't possible. So around Scarlet, I pin down my sexual prowess—and I have to pin it down hard—although it doesn't stop us from getting our bodies close and feeling the electric sexual energy surge between us.

It's like I have one foot on shore and the other's on a boat that's slowly pulling away. I'm not ready to jump to either side—not yet—so my legs strain and pull as I squint into the distance to see if Kye is coming for me.

On a Friday night, Scarlet and I mix Red Bull and Jäger with blue Powerade and drink it on the SkyTrain between Gateway in Surrey and Stadium in downtown Vancouver. I'm drunk and alert before we arrive at Lick Club, a lesbian hole-in-the-wall bar. It's stuffed with women, some sitting around the bar on tall stools but most packed onto the sticky dance floor with its bassy *MMM-chic-MMM-chic-MMM-chic*, sweeping multicoloured lights, sweaty dirty dancing.

And Scarlet can *dance*. On the dance floor I'm sweating and swooning at how her body ripples perfectly to the music and how she easy-smiles through it and when I sit on a couch for a breather she straddles me, daring me with those eyes, rubbing against me to the beat of the music. My resolve wears thin and I put a hand on each of her thighs, pushing with each finger, breath catching in my throat, her fingers around the back of my neck, nails scratching lightly against my spine—resistance and invitations. We spend the rest of the night dancing close, cheeks red, bodies on fire.

After the lights come on at Lick, we head to her friend's loft twenty-five storeys above downtown Vancouver. It's light by the time we try to go to bed, and her friend is out at the World or some other after-hours and Kye is on my mind again, but when Scarlet reaches for me we make out and our tongues are sliding together and the hum of our bodies is almost muted by their closeness and my hands are around her waist pulling her toward me, and then her fingers are on my belt and I want her to unzip my fly and reach behind my underwear—but Kye, so I grab, gently, her wrist.

"I'm sorry, I can't."

She sits up abruptly and scowls. Her voice is so flat, her question doesn't feel like a question. "What's going on."

"Look, I really, really like you, and I'm really, really attracted to you. It's just that I'm in this grey area with someone else. And it just wouldn't feel right right now."

"Okay, Erin, well, talk about mixed signals."

"Fuck, trust me, it's mixed signals in my head. I just want it to be right, okay? Trust me, I'm really fucking attracted to you."

I reach for her again and things get awkward and blocky and she gets up to pour a glass of water, adopting an air of aloofness. I sigh and stand up and pull open the sliding glass door to the patio. Outside, it's quiet—that in-between time when the late-night partiers have crashed and the early risers' alarms haven't yet sounded. The sky's a pale pink like a single drop of red food colouring mixed into a bathtub. A taxi drives by, small as a toy car. For a moment, I wonder how I got here again. I think about running—I'm training for a half-marathon in Victoria—and feel sick. I think about Scarlet in the sweaty room with disco lights and lesbians and feel uneasy. I don't know what I want. I don't know what to do. I think about Kye and feel unsure. It's so quiet, so cool. I clasp my hands around the railing and look down, wondering what would happen if I fell. Would I become a dramatic story for Scarlet to tell future lovers? What if I jumped? My bare arms sprout goosebumps and the cool air and my thoughts make me shiver. I turn around and pull the door open to go back inside.

47

One of the Jenga pieces in my life stack is growing increasingly bulging and weathered, so however carefully I incorporate the smooth and straight pieces, the stack just keeps tumbling. There's Scarlet and gin from the bottle and, like an unexpected side-swipe, cocaine. And then there's my reinvented friendships and running and music.

It's like my past has a grip on one hand and my future has a grip on the other and they're pulling me from either side, straining my arms, but I'm scared to let go of either. I'm scared to go with one or the other.

So I shift my weight—first leaning to one side, and then the other.

⌒

"I'll be at the finish line with a cigarette and a beer," Alice tells me in a perfect depiction of how life feels right now. We're in Victoria and wandering the downtown harbour past buskers and artisans, blue sky, cool air. Tomorrow I'm running the Royal Victoria Half-Marathon and we're staying in a tall downtown hotel with one bed. I laugh and for a second feel free, and then my mind nosedives with the thought of Scarlet.

I'd given in sexually shortly after my resistance that morning in Vancouver, and it sharply reversed our magnetic pull. We did it in a pool and in the shower and at my house and at her house but then suddenly it feels like I'm on the chase and she's on the run.

A night that began with her and me singing along at the top of our lungs to Metric's *Live It Out* CD in her car and gleefully making out during instrumentals ends with me at the O in downtown Vancouver with the 2:00 a.m. lights on, her nowhere to be found. I have her phone and wallet in my pocket. Eventually her phone rings with her ex-girlfriend's number. We'd run into her on the dance floor earlier and I tried to ignore how Scarlet looked at her. I go to her, at a tiny one-bedroom on Davie. She points out the couch with a slack face and retreats into the bedroom with little more than a glance at me. I'd yelled "How could you just leave me here?" when she finally called, me crouching and confused outside the O's locked doors.

"She needed somebody, I had to go, I couldn't find you," she'd told me coolly.

I'd yelled, "I've been here all night!"

I lie on the scratchy couch alone, biting back tears and exhaustion and turning over on the futon, angry with no outlet. After a fitful hour, I open the door to the conjoining room. Scarlet's lying on top of her ex, their arms around each other. They both just look at me. I'm taken aback by the dagger of what I'm looking at and the absurdity that led to me standing there uselessly in the doorway. I'm done. In my mind, I'm done. When I speak, it's cold and measured.

"I'm going home."

Scarlet's unfazed and her voice holds no hint of sympathy. "You'll leave my phone and wallet?"

Three days later she calls and I force myself to ignore it, although I can feel pieces of me wanting her to want me, to regret what happened, to be sorry, so sorry. And then I'm in Victoria with Alice.

The night before, we lay side by side and she wrapped her arms around me and pushed against me with her hips.

"I'm sorry," I said, truly meaning it. "It's just that things with Scarlet are so up in the air. If I did something with someone else, it just…" Her green eyes bore into mine. "It just wouldn't feel right."

"She's an asshole, Erin. Are you even 'together' together?"

"It just wouldn't feel right."

⌒

It's a beautiful day for the half-marathon, which follows the shoreline of the ocean. Sun-sparkly waves crash onto the beach and the breakwater as upbeat song after upbeat song plays through my headphones: "Don't Fear the Reaper," "Baba O'Riley," "Lose Yourself."

Maybe it's the other runners—strangers I'm inextricably connected to, as we sway like migrating birds from oceanside to heritage neighbourhoods with lush, loved gardens, by spectators clapping hands of all sizes. Maybe it's the lineups of volunteers pressing cups of water into my hand at the aid stations with admiration and kindness and pride in their eyes—inextricably part of it too. Maybe it's Alice, a true friend, waiting for me at the finish line. But a wholeness cuddles me and I'm okay. More than okay. Waves of ecstasy, naturally created ecstasy, roll in me and I'm without dread, without anxiety. With everything I need.

⌒

Whole. The provider and the one provided for. This is always the goal. But also, I will eventually realize, it's also always the reality. Even when it doesn't feel like it. Especially when it doesn't feel like it.

⌒

As I approach the finish line, earlier than I thought I would, Alice is standing out in pure black against the colourful spectators. Her face blooms into excited surprise and she jumps and starts cheering, lit up fully, lighting me up fully. I wave like I haven't seen her in years and something deep in me revs up and I sprint, fast, crossing the finish line feeling like I could shoot off into space in a glorious celebratory adventure.

Alice is running beside me, her platinum shag bobbing in and out from between spectators.

"That was fucking amazing! Erin! You were so fast!"

I hug her across the fence, laughing, a deep, real laugh, interrupted only by a volunteer touching my shoulder to hang a medal around my neck.

Pride blooms the most beautiful flower and the thought of Scarlet is but a tiny ant on the ground beneath it.

⌒

Back in Surrey, Blake is over and we're on the hardwood floor practising "Anyone Else but You" on guitar, rain pouring outside, mugs of tea steaming beside each of us, exchanging lead vocals, back and forth, singing "do-do-do-do do-do-do do-do-do-do" in unison, grinning into the music, the friendship, the connection—Is this happiness? This feels like happiness—when my phone rings. Scarlet. Music and friendship are humming in me and though I've ignored her calls for the full week I'd been back from Victoria, something makes me pick up the phone with a shrug. She wants to talk to me, please. Can I meet her at Starbucks, please. She understands what happened with her ex-girlfriend sucked, please.

I'd opened the door by answering the phone, and now I'm too curious, too wanting, it's too pulling to not walk through it.

"Are you sure?" Blake asks me in her sweet way, and I nod and become that friend behind the Plexiglas, a glance toward her pounding, nothing more.

At Starbucks the next day, Scarlet tells me everything I want to hear.

"The other morning I woke up, and I woke up," she tells me in what sounds like a rehearsed speech on the coffee shop patio, cigarette in hand, eyes on mine only sporadically.

"What do you mean?" I'm exhausted but curious. I want to scream at her to fuck off. I want to pull her in for a passionate embrace.

"I realize I've just been wasting time getting drunk, going back and forth with you. It's stupid. I want to do better. Go hiking and see cool things. That's really living!"

I nod. I feel the same way, really. Could this be a new beginning for us? I'm apprehensive, but hopeful. We drive straight from Starbucks to the Chief in Squamish and hike up it, both in jeans. We feel giddy and new. I feel giddy and new. Like a big eraser rubs away the past and the future, leaving us just meticulously outlined. Here, now. We get back to the car at nightfall exhausted and excited and renewed and head to her place with every intention to watch a movie, but when we arrive, her roommate pulls at Scarlet's arm and whispers something into her ear. I round the corner to a few acquaintances from the queer party house chatting upbeat and I join them on the plush grey couch, the happy sigh of a good, long day, the view from the top, the simplicity, the beauty. I tell them about the ladders and rope and the bold fat squirrel that ran across my backpack.

I notice a knock on the door somewhere within our conversation, I do, but it fails to alert me—the big eraser, perhaps.

Then, Scarlet and her roommate round the corner, looking at each other, giggling, feigning awkwardness but both clearly jazzed. Her roommate spits it out: "So, girls, we picked up some blow."

I look at Scarlet and Scarlet looks at the ground.

My body pangs, *Leave now!*

But my space inside, filled with love, with nature, with new beginnings, with hope, with desire—my space inside that is magnetized to Scarlet, no matter what, hoping for better, but accepting anything—can't leave. Just can't.

So I stay. I take the straw and breathe in a line, front tooth numb, and another and another and it wipes out that pang of resistance, or maybe it just pushes it down, but I stay all night until the cocaine's gone. And when blue lightens the sky around us, Scarlet and I get into a yelling match about something, probably *Why can't you love me like I need you to?* but disguised, and I storm home high and angry, 5:00 a.m.

I must have fallen into a fitful sleep because I wake up to banging on my sliding glass door. I put a pillow over my pounding head to ignore it, but a few minutes later the door slides open. Delia, who has my spare key, is suddenly in my room. Similar to my relationship with my parents, my choice to get clean also mended our friendship.

"Good morning, get up, get up." She picks up a sweatshirt from the floor and tosses it at my head. "Get dressed. You're coming with me. I have coffee."

Curiosity quashes my nausea and pounding head and I comply, stumbling out of my bedroom. She hands me a grande Starbucks from the table.

"Dark roast."

I smile at her. "Where are we going?"

"You're about to find out. Let's go, let's go."

We end up on the flats between Surrey and Langley where the landscape dips into a wide bed of farmland, making it one of the few places in Surrey one can indeed see for miles. She stops at a pullout.

"You may now have your morning cigarette."

I smile again, offering her my open pack.

We light cigarettes and lean against her car. The sky is a brilliant pink, dousing the farmlands golden. Clouds dot the sky and inextricably shine multicolour. Tears well up in my eyes and my hands and ears are cold, making me feel more alive than anything. I take deep, healing breaths between drags, feeling the much bigger picture of everything I'm undeniably part of. Feeling real. Feeling like maybe I don't have to do anything, be anyone but myself, whatever that means. Whenever. Without drinking, without drugs, without love, without running. Just this gift of presence in a beautiful world. Where everything truly is simple and beautiful.

Sometimes, perhaps, banging on Plexiglas works.

⌒

On one of my good days, David returns from his latest bout in treatment—this time, from a luxury centre in Ontario. His parents had desperately opened their wallets and funnelled money to the most expensive option they could find, hoping the bigger investment would equal success.

It's been months since I've seen him. Unsure which version of him I'll get, I pull up to Scott Road SkyTrain station nervous. When he bounds easily down the concrete stairs ahead of the train, looking calm and at ease, happiness twirls, tentatively, along my core, and I think his parents' plan may have worked. I get out of the car and we embrace and his stubble scratches my cheek.

"Oh my gosh, David, you look great!"

His cheeks have filled out completely, his face exuding the joviality I fell in love with when we were teenagers.

We get in the car and he hands me a leather bracelet with music notes and my name stamped into it. I put it around my wrist, a warm smile, waves of gratitude. He tosses a second bracelet, slightly larger, onto my lap and laughs.

I look at him wryly.

"I don't know your wrist size," he laughs and shrugs and pulls on his seat belt.

"Thanks, Chud." I hadn't used the pet name in years, but it spills out naturally. I'm warm with gratitude and relief.

We drive to the ocean.

There's room for it.

"This is the best I've ever felt," he says, as we walk along the sparse promenade in White Rock, breathing in the salty, cool air. He holds up his white T-shirt proudly with his pointer and thumb; I read it.

"Superdry," I say with a smile, looking into his eyes. He's here. He's really here. I put my arm around his shoulder. "I was so fucking worried about you, David."

"I know." He hangs his head, adding, "I'm back though now," like he read my mind. Like he knows I really know.

We stroll along the boardwalk and look at a blue heron still in the shallow water, the boats in the harbour, the starfish and barnacles on the wood that holds the boardwalk up from the bottom of the ocean. It's cold but we get ice cream and sit tightly beside each other. I have this feeling like we've made it. Like, against all odds, our boomerangs have returned home where life can, at long last, begin. A thought of Scarlet flits briefly across my mind, but I don't attach to it. Life is massive and life is vast and real love—not sex, not relationship, not attachment, not expectation—lasts forever.

It's a perfect day. One I'll never forget.

48

It's Sunday morning at Ricky's and I push through a crowd just to get through the front door.

"Thank God you're here. Table twenty-one needs their order, like now. Can you take them?" Sandy's face is flushed and she's yelling at the kitchen before I have a chance to reply. "These are supposed to be shredded hash on nineteen! Shredded!" She pushes her glasses back up her nose with her pointer and looks at me.

"Yep, no problem."

The senior couple at twenty-one are regulars, and though their coffee cups are empty and their menus are stacked strategically off the edge of the table, they're happy to see me. Waitressing is both a puzzle and a dance, and when I'm in a good mood, and allow room for the unknown, I'm adept. This is one of those days; I'm so on top of my game, I have time to help take down names at the front.

I recognize her right away, Greta Gaffry—the worst of the bullies from my first school all those years earlier. I'm sure she recognizes me too, but by the time we both realize, we're facing each other with but a metre of space between us. She's probably gained a hundred pounds, still has that pretty face that was so confusingly mean all those years ago. That face I grew afraid of and braced for impact from. The memories flood me like I'm trapped in a cube dramatically filling up with water.

I remember being at my locker once, seeing her coming from the corner of my eye, with a crowd around her. Before I'd ever sipped alcohol. Before I'd felt the stirrings of love. I remember pressing my locker shut with a measured breath out, knowing what was coming, then, having nowhere to look but directly at her, thinking that maybe she'd see I didn't want to fight.

"Little Boy," she'd said as a threat, and her crew closed in on me. I remember their muggy heat, how my heart picked up pace and how my ears rang, how I crossed my forearms over my math textbook and binder, how I tried to push through them. How Greta's stance stiffened, how I felt suffocated, how I tried to push through, how she spewed bitterly, "She just swung at me!" How she hit me, how someone else did, how I pushed past them, how she yelled "Little Boy, little freak," how I ran away, ran outside, how they chased me, how I got away, my feet squishing wet in the sucking ground.

I inhale a stressed, strained breath, standing there at Ricky's. But today is a good day. I'm on top of my game. I'm not a timid little mouse. I'm fit from all the running and I have a stylish haircut dyed black and red. My uniform is clean and I feel able.

I don't have to prove anything. My value is innate. I'm loved and lovable whether or not I'm fit, whether or not I feel able. My value is innate, my value is innate, my value is innate. This, a quiet knowing growing louder.

Everything slows. It's too late for me to turn away.

"Name?"

We both know I know her name. A tall man and a toddler hang behind her. This time, she's the meek one. "Greta?"

I bore my eyes into hers, our roles reversed, me not thinking about her, her day, her life, her mood, her feeling—her depth of feeling. Me, reclaiming what felt taken from me all those years ago.

"How many."

"Three?"

Her voice is so soft something inside me turns, almost.

My chest is tight and every word out of my mouth is curt. She steps outside with the rest of the waiting crowd, followed by the man and the toddler. I watch them get into a car at the top of the parking lot, watch the car drive away. *She knows*, I think. *She remembers.* I puff out my chest and feel satisfied, though I'm not sure why. I also feel exhausted, which softens me. She didn't exactly come across as the sharp dagger she felt like all those years ago. She just seems like your average human who maybe eats a little too much, who's just trying to raise a son. Wouldn't she want him to be kind? Maybe she's just like me, but trying to manage life with wine and brownies, just like I'm trying to manage it with gin and running. Maybe it was never actually about me. Maybe somebody in her life was bullying her—those hidden experiences we all have that make us move like marionettes, that make us feel in control of something, or worthy, or valuable. *My value is innate.* It can be easy to forget how multi-dimensional we all are. People make mistakes. I sure did. I think about sixteen-year-old me pushing another letter through a mail slot in the darkness of the night, full of hope and full of sadness. *I just wanted love. I just wanted to be seen.* I take a deep breath. I'm still feeling on, still feeling like today is a good day. I smile inside—a beautiful melancholy smile of deep knowing—and walk to the kitchen, a chapter of my life I hadn't realized was still open, closed.

49

A night followed by a night followed by a night of choking on water, gasping on air, slapping my palms against the surface. So many life preservers thrown at me so often, and finally I reach, push with all my might, palms against slick rubber, backwards in the water, choking more, heaving with the strength of my core, then, my cheek resting against the slick rubber, my head heavy and done, my body limp and submissive. This is where I'm at following a night after a night after a night of blurry chaos, of way-too-much. And with one ear I hear faint, beautiful music. I close my eyes and see friends and finish lines. This is why I go back to Surrey Addictions to get a drug counsellor for the second time, the Monday after Halloween weekend.

Thursday night, Friday night, Saturday night, I smear fake blood up and down my arms, my face, my legs. I wear dark, dramatic makeup and a tiny red slip and tell everybody who asks, "I'm dead sexy." Scarlet and I go to a youth drag performance and its after-party on Thursday and I get so drunk everything is moving, but still I get in my car and drive us home. We pull up in some quiet cul-de-sac on the way and yell at each other about something or nothing, though the memory is fuzzy both now and the following day. Slammed door, forgotten beef.

My hangover from Thursday subsides by early evening Friday, so Christina—another rekindled friendship—and I head to the Roxy downtown, but she's pass-out drunk by the time we're on the SkyTrain. The cross-armed bouncer shakes his head at us, Christina's eyes barely showing iris. "Nope."

Scarlet phones, as we'd planned to meet up later, and tells us to go to Tavin's house deep in Clayton Heights—another giant house in another giant suburban development where only the odd tree still stands, a token to what was.

My dad once explained that those tall lone trees, often preserved as curt nods to the pre-bulldozed landscape, are so much more susceptible to aggressive winds splitting them to the concrete below. The vulnerability of wide-openness.

Christina and I get to Tavin's, somehow, but no Scarlet—just Tavin, who we both meet for the first time, and Tavin's neighbour with the stubble and demeanour of a plumber. And cocaine, which now, or more like again, holds no second thought. We spend the night taking photos, playing dress-up. In costume, I look don't-give-a-fuck sexy, all fake-blood smears and sunglasses. All fake fur and fake confidence and fake love, making out with Tavin, who I'm not actually attracted to with her temple tattoo and white wifebeater. I tour the house abuzz and poke my head into Tavin's parents' room, them with reading glasses down their noses and kind, crinkled eyes—old hippies settled into sub-urban life—and sprawl across the base of their bed, their tan puffy comforter holding my shape. I can tell right away they like me, they see me behind the sunglasses, behind my fake-blood-stroked skin. They see me; I know they do.

Then back to the cocaine and fur and calamity and fake glitz and fake confidence. The neighbour leaves with the morning light and Christina goes to lie down in the living room. I reach for Tavin and she reaches for my belt and within seconds my pants are down and her fingers push inside me, swift and surprising—the quickness of her action—her fingers moving too fast, too soon, too uncomfortable. I'd flirted with her all evening, kissed her even, stuck our tongues together in photos. So it makes sense that this is happening. This—sex? I reach for Tavin's belt—that would make it make sense, get me on top where I'm more comfortable, more in control, but she pushes my wrist away and smirks like I'm ridiculous.

"I don't think so. That's never going to happen."

I recoil and lie back until Tavin stops and leaves the room. I lie there for a minute, not sure exactly what did or didn't just happen, then pull up my pants and go wake up Christina and get out of there.

The next morning I call Scarlet. "I thought you were coming over! What happened?"

She ignores my question. "Did you fuck Tavin, Erin?"

I pause. "I really wouldn't call it that."

"Fuck you, Erin! What the fuck!"

"Seriously Scarlet, it was weird—"

But she hangs up and doesn't return any of my calls that day. Push and pull.

Saturday night. Ash, a Ricky's co-worker, hosts a Halloween house party across the gully and around the corner from my house—a five-minute walk. I take enough Advil to make my headache go away and gulp gin from the bottle. I don't even try to take it easy; it's a slippery waterslide of falling apart, and I'm on it, limp.

"Are there any lesbians here?" I slur immediately upon arrival. Ash doesn't notice my state and points to a girl with a brown bob and stoic face, wearing a burlap hooded robe.

"She just went through a bad breakup."

I go to her immediately, assault her, I'm sure, with tangy gin breath.

"I hear you just went through a breakup? With a woman?"

I try to look at her like I care, but everything is moving. She squirms away from me and I persist until she says, firmly, "Leave me alone" and looks at Ash for help.

"Leave it, Erin," Ash tells me sternly.

I slump through the kitchen and onto the patio and sit beside Steph, one of the cooks at Ricky's, a year older than me. She has dark makeup around her eyes and is wearing fake tattoo sleeves.

I slur at her, "I tried to find a lesbian but it didn't work. Do you have a cigarette?"

White lights hang above us and the deck is crowded with costumed people chatting and bending back their white plastic chairs in drunken sprawls. I could throw up. I could cry. I rub hard at my temples. Everything spins.

"Sorry, you tried to find a lesbian?" Steph leans in to sift through my slurring.

"Yeah, but she just broke up. No dice."

I lean back in my chair. The lattice above my head blurs and I fixate on a single white light, blink deep purple, open my eyes, blink. I'm here, I'm not here.

"What about a bisexual?"

I look at her and although everything's moving, our eyes connect. "That's you?"

She nods, a smile, an invitation. I linger on her. What I really want is a cigarette. What I really want is the chase. The catch feels too easy.

"Well, we should do something," she says, handing me her lit cigarette.

I take a slow drag. Even half-hearted flirting feels like a chore, but I fake it. "Yeah, we should sometime."

"Sometime? What about now?"

I take another drag and look at her, blowing the smoke up, my body exhausted. We end up in the bathroom, messy drunk, not thinking about sound, her on the counter, using the towel rack to steady herself, me on my knees first, then standing, leaning over her. Then Ash, by now fully on to me, banging on the door.

"Erin, get the fuck out of there! Get out! Jesus!"

She bangs on the door again. We ignore her and finally emerge dishevelled, without tidying up the bathroom. Ash shakes her head and we walk by a long line of costumes looking at me like I'm scum of the earth. I swig more gin and, without thinking twice, brag to the other waitresses that I just fucked

Steph in the bathroom. So maybe I am the scum of the earth. Maybe I am.

I leave the party alone after midnight, following, without thought, the street lined with darkened houses. It's quiet and I'm ghostly, moving through the streets, the asphalt shiny black and intermittently covered by patterns of browned, fallen leaves. I walk and walk, one foot in front of the other, one street curling into the next, all windows darkened. Wind cools my face still caked with fake blood, cools the exposed parts of my legs between the bottom of my jacket and my boots. As I follow a path that takes me behind an elementary school, I realize I don't know where I am. I've never been on this path, never seen this school. And then it hits me—Ash's house was just five minutes from mine, but I've been walking for an hour, probably more. I emerge onto another street I don't recognize. I see no street signs. I wake into a mild panic. This is the suburbs, I think, attempting to comfort myself. If I just keep going I'll end up on a main street. So I keep moving, the cool air and confusion sobering me up. I'm turned around and can't tell which direction I'm heading in. All the streets, all the houses look the same. An aching in my legs is growing perceptible. My footsteps and occasional gusts of wind clattering bare branches are the only audible sounds. I round another corner to a trio of darkly clothed teenagers smoking in front of a house with light pouring out a ground-level window. I set my shoulders back and puff out my chest, projecting a don't-fuck-with-me confidence.

"Hey, what's the nearest major street to here?"

A shorter boy with curled-in shoulders looks at me through thick glasses, the streetlight's reflection blocking his eyes. "King George is like a block away," he says, motioning in the direction I'm already heading in. I follow his gaze, jarred. King George is at least five kilometres from my house. Which means I left the party and walked in the exact opposite direction than I should have. I fake smile at the teens, keep it cool, round a corner and lean against a lamppost. I could throw up, but focus hard on my throat muscles, push the feeling to stay in my stomach, take a few deep, necessary, calming breaths. I know where I am. I know how to get home. What the fuck am I doing? How did I get here again? It's like I'm the balloon on the end of an impossibly long string, starting to slump in on myself, a speck in the sky. What I really should be is the hand holding the string. How could I have let myself get so untethered again? Why?

I don't have the answers, I almost never do, so within days I'm sitting in front of my new drug counsellor. This one older, wiser, intuitive. I don't speak for long before she says, "I think there's some sensitivity there."

And she puts words to something I've always known. For as long as I remember, I've hidden my sensitivity behind endless disguises. Pretending to rifle through my tiny desk in elementary school to hide the tears flowing from my eyes. Pretending that I'm sleeping when I know Kegger was hit by a car and is dying in the living room. Pretending that it's okay with me that Scarlet was wrapped around her ex-girlfriend.

I can't pinpoint when or why I started putting my so-called negative emotions into a box, but I've been doing it for as long as I can remember, them slapping the walls of their confinement, stinging hands, loud, not liberated, ever, but toned down by the high of drugs, the high of love, the high of exercise.

It's like my counsellor reads my mind.

"It's a loss," she says about Scarlet. "It may look different than something like death, but you have to grieve it anyway. The tools you have right now are drinking and drugs. And it sounds like running, too, right?"

Her eyes are green and brown and surrounded by wrinkles and she looks at me like she sees me. I nod, and she continues. "But what if I told you pain is essential? To move through pain—and we are all capable of moving through pain—you have to let yourself feel it. It's the only way. You have to let yourself feel it and trust that it will help you grow."

I nod, slowly. I've done it before and there's no reason to believe things should be different now.

"It's also about recognizing your patterns, and then creating healthier patterns. And, well, you're here. So that says a lot."

I look into her knowing eyes and see myself sprinting across the finish lines. Playing guitar with Blake on rainy days. Giddy and Superdry with David. On the ferry with Alice, wind blowing our hair every which way. These things are healthy patterns; these things are freedom. I feel it like a lightness in my core.

"Yeah, that really makes sense."

⌒

This is the last time. My head is in a steel vise grip and I'm throwing up bile every forty-five minutes after getting home from a weekend trip to Victoria with Scarlet. It was an adventure until we stepped into a liquor store, then it's more of the usual. Me, getting cut off in a downtown gothic nightclub. Us in a late-night yelling match. Me sitting on a curb wavering toward traffic, a bus whooshing inches from my face, me as indifferent as a crumpled, sun-coloured burger wrapper littering the streets, tumbling with the wind. More of the usual. More of the same. By the time I get home the next day, it's mid-afternoon and as dismal outside as I feel inside, so I go to bed. This is the last time.

This is the last time.

The next morning, I'm not making empty promises to myself born from a shitty hangover. This time, everything I've been building—the steps forward, despite those backward—is culminating into this moment of transformation. It's how we learn, isn't it? The stops and starts. The getting closer, then falling back—each step forward a seat belt trying to click into place, metal shishing against metal again and again and again and again and again and again and again and again. Then, finally, a click. There's no big reason why this particular morning is different. It just is.

This is the last time.

Decades later, on a monitor, I'll see my womb. An empty space, indeed. But an empty space that I, and only I, am capable of providing for. I've always been the provider. I've always had everything I need.

Wrapping myself with my bright red down comforter and four pillows, I prop myself into a semi-seated position and feel a calm understanding cradle me. Rain pitter-patters on my window outside my cocoon. I'll emerge as something else. I'll emerge as both the one who needs and the one who provides. Equipped to deal with all my big feelings, my sensitivity—as precious parts of my passionate being, not pests in need of extermination. Suddenly, the space inside me feels *part* of me. As meant to be there as my eyes, my skin, my fingernails. Still, there's truth to "Some turn to Jesus, some turn to heroin," but there's also choice. Some things that fill my space make me bigger; others make me smaller. I know this now. Waves of understanding lull inside me, gently lapping at my corners, and I reach for the journal on my nightstand. Flipping through pages and pages of me agonizing about Scarlet, I put my pen to my mouth for a moment and lightly bite down in thought. And then I write:

THINGS THAT MAKE ME HAPPY

CROSSING FINISH LINES

BEING SOBER

BEING ASSERTIVE

LEARNING NEW THINGS

PLAYING GUITAR

It's a simple recipe and I have all the ingredients. And then I write:

I WILL NOT SACRIFICE MYSELF FOR A FUCK, A DRUG OR THE HEART OF ANY OTHER PERSON.

I smile into my pillow and flop over, as light as a raindrop, tracing the outline of blue around the edges of my blinds. Things are different this time. I know it.

Throughout the next year, I begin doing more of those things that make me happy, more of those things that make me bigger. More of those things that I actually have control over. After learning Scarlet was dating our mutual friend while still regularly having sex with me, I pick up the phone and tell her calmly, "I'm done." And I stick with it, finally. *Being Assertive.*

I test the waters with school, taking a psychology class at Douglas College and finishing with 98 percent and a feeling that maybe I can do this post-secondary thing after all. I apply to journalism school on the high from my near-perfect grade and get in to start that fall. *Learning New Things.*

I commit to running a full marathon in May 2008 and cross the finish line after 42.2 kilometres and four hours, thirty-five minutes. David's there to cheer me on, as are Christina and Delia, who's pregnant with her son. Crossing the finish line, I burst into tears and a volunteer wraps a plastic blanket around me, squeezing my shoulder. "What you just did was amazing," he yells near my ear, and I can tell he really means it. *Crossing Finish Lines.*

Throughout the year I learn what I already supposed: that I *do* have power over my addiction. That I have, inside me, everything I need to become and remain clean and sober. That drugs and alcohol don't actually do anything other than mask what must inevitably be felt, looked at, dealt with. And the things we feel, look at and deal with carry all the richness of life. *Being Sober.*

50

I awake at my casual girlfriend's house on a spring morning from an uncomfortable dream. It's March 21, 2009. In my dream, a giant house was burning, the wooden structure's beams and shape nearly obscured by monstrous orange flames and sparks standing out against a black night sky. David's there, and his dog Sammie who had died when we were in high school. As I move from asleep to awake, the discomfort of the dream burns off like a morning fog, but slowly.

The summer before, a very pregnant Delia and I head downtown and decide to surprise David with a visit. We buzz him from the front door of his building off Davie Street on Cardero, to no answer.

A blond woman with sunglasses approaches us. "Who are you trying to reach, girls?"

We tell her his full name, not expecting her to know him.

"David. Apartment 313? He's at the hospital. Nice kid."

A pang in my body.

"At the hospital?" I stare at the lopsided wrinkle beside her mouth, unsure how to process her words. Is he visiting the hospital? Did something happen? Is he in the hospital? Who is this lady?

"I'm the building manager," she says, her voice scratchy, reading our faces. "Yep. He's at the hospital. At St. Paul's. I think they took him there yesterday."

Delia and I share a glance, her face as apprehensive as mine, but she's good at taking the reins. "Do you know what happened?"

"I don't."

David's mom, Linda, is at the hospital when we arrive, a shadow of worry downturning her face.

"Erin. I was just about to call you." We hug. "How did you know to come here?"

I tell her about the building manager. "What happened?"

She shakes her head, looking more tired than I'd ever seen her, the bags under her eyes with a gravitational pull. "He overdosed. I guess he shot heroin and then started blacking out and then, thank God, had enough sense to call 911. But he passed out. The firefighters had to cut through the chain."

I shake my head, not knowing what to say. My body feels light, like I could disintegrate into the hospital air and get sucked into a vent and be pushed out onto the street into invisible fragments forever lost. I stand there, shoulders hunched slightly, staring at Linda's under-eye bags. Delia shifts, bringing me back.

"Can we see him?" she asks.

Linda nods. "Just be prepared, though. He's in an induced coma. He has a tube."

He looks so frail lying there with no shirt, his lips around a breathing apparatus. I kiss his forehead because I don't know what else to do, and can't help but let myself cry. Linda and Delia both rub my back. By the next day, though, he's awake, and the following day, he's discharged. He goes back into treatment, this time in Surrey, and, once again, immerses himself in NA. And it gets him better, for a while. But by early winter he's in the hospital again, this time by overdoing it on any drug he could get his hands on for a week. Relationship anxiety, I think, with his new boyfriend, who David cheated on pre-emptively. Not because that's what he wanted, but as a protective measure—I'll hurt you before you hurt me. Then he did a shitload of drugs. And yet, love shone out of his boyfriend's sparkling blue eyes. We could all see it. But a person can receive only as much love as they give themselves.

"He's asking for you; he'd like to see you," Linda tells me by phone. But I don't go. I can't bear it. After seeing him so frail, like a premature baby in an incubator, it's a sight I cannot handle.

By Christmas that year he is having good days and bad days and is on a waitlist for a treatment facility that will help him deal with the dual diagnosis he recently received—bipolar disorder and addiction.

The morning after that dream of the burning house, my girlfriend and I leave her place on foot toward De Dutch for breakfast. The sun warms the hair on my head and my face and the upbeat nature of spring evaporates the residual uneasiness of my dream. It feels good to be outside and walking, and the tips of my ears are cool, but it's warm enough that halfway there I take off my jacket and wrap it around my waist. I skip and I smile, thinking about my broccoli cheddar omelette.

I couldn't have known.

I'm halfway through my coffee and we're waiting for breakfast when my phone rings. David. The night before, I texted him on my way to my girl-friend's—two blocks from his mom's house—to see if he wanted to have a cigarette together. He texted back, "I can't, I'm about to meet Ryan. Sushi!" I wrote, "Have a great night!" He wrote, "You too."

I pick up my phone with a happy "Hellooooo?"

"Erin?"

It's not David.

"Yes?"

"Erin, it's Linda." She pauses. "Erin, I have some bad news."

Phone to my ear, I get up and exit the restaurant. My body instantly clenches. He's in the hospital again, I just know it. I push the receiver hard against my ear, bracing myself. My voice rises. "Yes?"

"Erin, David died last night."

I can't breathe and I can't believe her. My body is lead and I drop to the curb. All feeling whooshes out of me like a hard breath. My voice drops and softens into one meek, crackling question. "What?"

"We think it was a methadone overdose. We found some in the room. And him, this morning. I think it was an accident. He had made a burrito and was watching TV, Erin. Maybe he just took a swig." She pauses, her voice so official business. So serious and strong. "I'm sorry."

"I'm so sorry. I… okay." I'm crying and I can't stop, my body curling into a storm of pain and confusion, with waves crashing nonsensically every which way.

We hang up and I throw my phone into the asphalt as hard as I can and bury my head between my legs, sobbing. I stay like that until a restlessness pulls me up. An urge to run. An urge to smash the huge window where happy, ignorant motherfuckers who didn't just have their world shattered are eating breakfast. Rage like a night-grey electric storm. Fucking stupid breakfast. I hate it. I hate my omelette and I hate my waitress and I hate my girlfriend and I hate the sun and I hate the asphalt and I hate these cars and I hate the gas station and I hate the smell of gas and I hate the traffic and I hate the windows and I hate the trees in the middle of the boulevard and I hate the people waiting at the bus stop and I hate the bus and I hate the car dealership and I hate signs and I hate the blue sky and I hate time and I hate my skin and I hate my shoes and I hate my stupid pants and I hate I hate I hate I hate I hate I hate I hate I hate I hate I hate I hate myself. I hate myself for not visiting him in the hospital. I hate myself for ever doing heroin with him. I hate everything and I'm restless and I don't know what to do.

I don't know what to do, so I go back into the restaurant and I eat my tasteless meaningless stupid fucking omelette and tears roll down my cheeks.

I picture David's big green eyes smiling at me when he's being goofy, the way he hangs his head when he opens up, how he elbows me gently in the ribs to signal he knows exactly what I'm thinking. He's the person who knows me best in the entire world, and now he's suddenly gone; a massive piece of me now is suddenly gone. And I can barely wrap my head around what *gone* even means. The world is so goddamn big—he couldn't just be off it, a light gone out. It's too overwhelming, it makes no sense. And yet, the phone call was real. I'm awake. Wide fucking awake.

⌒

The last status he posted online before the morning he didn't wake up referred to a song by Muse: "Sing for Absolution."

"David sings for absolution."

⌒

My girlfriend stays with me around the clock for the first few days, and I attempt to go through the motions of life. I go to a birthday party, but the birthday girl's too happy so I leave.

On a photojournalism school trip, a man is singing and playing a sloweddown version of "Imagine" in an outdoor square. Pigeons flock up around him and brisk walkers barely slow and I feel nothing, and then I feel furious, and then I leave.

⌒

The problem is, there's nowhere to actually go that makes me feel even a minuscule bit better.

⌒

I keep hearing "Are you okay, Erin?" and I hate it. What the fuck do I say to something like that?

"I'm fine." F-i-n-e. "Fucked up Inside, Nice Exterior," as they say. I'm fine, I'm fine, I'm fine. F-I-N-E. FINE.

⌒

I can't write about it. For two years, I can't write about it. Anger, like a storm. Sadness comes with escape routes, and I take them. I chain-smoke. I walk for hours. I order two pizzas and eat them both, forcing the second one into my mouth despite being stuffed full. I remember what my counsellor said: I have to feel my feelings. But I have no idea where in this infinite blackness to even start.

⌒

And time ticks on.

⌒

Hey David, it's snowing. The sorrow of a phone call I can never make again.

⌒

Black, for a long time.

⌒

A disguised question from a co-worker: "Would you tell someone if you noticed they were gaining a lot of weight fast?"

⌒

Yelling matches with my girlfriend; fits of jealousy that whisper under all the screaming, "I'm going to lose you too and it's going to hurt."

⌒

Deep grey, for a long time.

⌒

Running, but half-hearted.

⌒

Journalism school, but half-hearted.

⌒

Endurance training, another full marathon. Getting H1N1 before race day, running the 42.2 kilometres anyway. If you glance at my race photo, you might think I look determined, but I know the real look: self-punishment. A body moving, a shadow of myself, joy locked deeply away, its key spit out somewhere near a broccoli cheddar omelette.

⌒

Fingers stained yellow with nicotine.

⌒

Grey, faint but perceptible lightening.

51

When finally my eyes rise above the bleak grey pain fogging in my life, I blink. I dream David and I meet in a golden-hour-kissed field, tall grass holding that deep yellow sunshine and his green eyes shining warm. He's wearing his Superdry shirt, and we embrace. Without exchanging words, we link arms and skip through the grass, the sun warm and all around us. This is love and that is forever—a love spanning our difficult years of high school, coming out to ourselves and to each other, then making our way separately and together in the world. We each could have been an infinite number of things, yet still, we each could have died. I wouldn't consider myself lucky or unlucky; this is just what happened. This is just how it is.

When I start to breathe again, there's other stuff there waiting for me. I'm still in journalism school. I'm still running. By the time I can once again take deep breaths, I realize I have weathered the worst tempest that has ever stormed through me. I lost the closest friend I'd ever had. But, I realize, I didn't lose myself because of it. I held on, and came out the other side. Forever changed, certainly, still in deep grief, but I can breathe again. I can look around.

To live is to feel—to let oneself feel—and finally, after all this time, I'm practising that. I feel the agony of losing my best friend. I feel the joy of watching another best friend, Delia, smile at her son as he runs through a puddle for the first time, unhinged with glee. I feel pride for receiving a scholarship for "exceptional promise as a journalist" and for getting accepted as an intern at the iconic *Georgia Straight* newspaper. I feel boredom and calm it with a bath. I feel nervous going to my journalism wrap-up party sober without being good at small talk. I feel apprehension when I'm accepted for a summer position at a newspaper in a small town a province over. I feel it all. I feel it all, and it's all underlined with acceptance. It's underlined with the fact that, yeah, I want to be warm and I want to be safe and I want to be provided for, but also this: I *am* the provider. Besides, wombs, like us, are not forever homes. Wombs, like us, have an eviction day. When we're ready—or more likely when we're not—it's on to the next thing. So I'd take the loud complexity of the world any day. Not its dampened version—not its quiet and small. So I feel it all. Whether it's nervous or happy or devastatingly sad, these are my feelings and I want them all. Every painful, joyful one of them.

⌒

With a slight tinge of exhaust from the lively street, spring is in the air and every breath I take as I walk from the SkyTrain station is fresh and warm. It's a year after David's death and I'm en route to my internship job in Kitsilano and just weeks from graduating journalism school. I haven't had a drink in a year and a half. On the SkyTrain ride from Surrey, I'd watched the pink and white cherry blossom trees blur by. They were in full bloom at the time of his death, which I talked about at his funeral—how the blossoms will be back every year, a wistful dreaminess of remembrance, of connectedness. A pang of sadness reverberates through my body and I see his face in my mind. His smiling eyes looking at me. His stubble against my cheek. This loss is a part of me now, forever. I ache for him, yet I also know that hole is forever filled with all these memories, all this love, as long as I keep breathing.

On his last Christmas, just months before he takes his last breath, I pick David up on a dim, late December day in the pouring rain. It's not long after his second stint in the hospital, and he's living with his mom again and doing better. Rain drips from his shortly cropped hair down his forehead and he wipes his brow with the inside of his elbow once he gets in the car, holding a plastic bag. His face shines with an easy smile and he looks relaxed. We hug tight, across the centre console, some of the rain transferring from him to me.

"Starbucks?"

He nods and we drive to that same Starbucks in Fleetwood where I accepted Scarlet back and where I begged him not to use needles. I pull into a spot right out front and my hand's on the door handle and my shoulders are up, bracing for the downpour, when he stops me.

"I have something for you."

I turn to him with a smile. "Really?"

He reaches into his bag and pulls out a present wrapped in snowman paper, about a foot long and thin enough that I can make a fist around it.

I pull off the wrapping paper to find an electric pepper grinder. I don't really ever use pepper. I look at David, smiling atop my slight disappointment and slight confusion at the random, odd present.

"Thanks David, this is really nice." I turn the grinder in my hands, trying to admire it.

"No, it's not." He bursts into laughter. "It's shit!"

I laugh too, but more uneasy like. He can't stop giggling, though, and it's contagious. We laugh and laugh, deep belly laughs and I don't even know why I'm laughing but it's a lightness, louder than the downpour outside.

"What's going on here?" I finally manage to ask.

He reaches into his pocket and pulls out a folded sheet of lined paper, slightly damp from the rain. The windows of the car are fogging up and the rain beats down relentlessly.

"This is 'Tartar Sauce.'"

He clears his throat and starts singing. I recognize the tune right away—"Mayonaise" by the Smashing Pumpkins. That song both he and I always so wistfully connected with, that I had recently told him I no longer relate to. "I don't *want* to be me, I am me!" I had said on a particularly good day. So he rewrote it. We sit there in my car, tears welling up in my eyes, tears welling up in his, as I listen to his beautiful voice sing the rewritten song a cappella.

Whatever fates rain down upon us, just listen up and you'll hear me, I'll always be there for you and I know you'll be there for me too.

"Tartar Sauce" takes centre stage in my mind on the SkyTrain that day as I watch the world blur by, the cherry-blossomed trees dotting everything. Reaching the *Georgia Straight* offices, I open the front door and climb the stairs with the expected knots in my stomach that come with any unfamiliar environment. I open my chest, my heart, and take a deep breath as I climb the stairs to the office, smiling at my temporary co-workers, and I head toward my desk, my chin held high and my melancholy taking up a space inside no bigger or smaller than it should.

Acknowledgements

Thanks to everyone who has believed in me and in this book from the beginning, and to those I've picked up along the way.

Thank you, Mom and Dad, for your love and support and suffering through your writer daughter baring it all.

Thank you to all my dear friends (I couldn't even begin to name everyone who has a place in my heart. Lucky, lucky me.). Thank you to my brother, family and communities including the spuds, Rene Unser and the P.A.C.E. crew and all my yoga peeps. Thank you, Leila Anna Naderi, Marley Chambers and Rebekka Augestine for your deep and endless love, friendship and support. Thank you, Shelley Wood, for all the talk-throughs, walks, runs, tacos, friendship and encouragement. Thank you, Katy Wilson, for you.

A deep thank you to Paul Lisicky—your early championing of this book truly changed everything. Thank you, Nikki Love and Scott Sealey for being early friend readers—your feedback and support carries me. To my writer colleagues and friends scattered throughout Canada and the States, including Charlie Stephens, Shelley Gaske, my Writing by Writers manuscript bootcamp crew and the newly rebooted Distillibus: thank you. To Zena Ryder and the CoW crew: thank you for being such a fertile ground for sharing, and for all your dedication to local writers. Thank you, Wine Country Writers' Festival for hosting the pitch session that led to this book's publication.

The utmost gratitude to the team at Caitlin Press including Vici Johnstone, Sarah Corsie and Malaika Aleba: thank you for your vision, thank you for your support.

Thank you, David, for being the brightest light and truest friend. You are so loved, through all of space and all of time.

Thank you to everyone who has found representations of themselves in these pages and have responded with grace, love, openness and understanding. I can't tell you what this means to me—you know who you are.

Thank you, reader, for joining me here.

Thank you, music; thank you, life; thank you, beauty; thank you, truth.

About the Author

Erin Steele is a writer, low-key philosopher and insatiably curious explorer of life. She writes *On Being Human* on Substack, is a 2022 Writing by Writers fellow and has been published in *Human Parts* by Medium. She currently lives in Kelowna, BC, Canada, where she studies all limbs of yoga, runs long distances on trails and nerds out on nature—particularly when the arrowleaf balsamroot explodes the hills yellow. *Sunrise over Half-Built Houses* is her first book.